BIBLICAL THEMES IN SCIENCE FICTION

BIBLE AND ITS RECEPTION

Robert Paul Seesengood, General Editor

Editorial Board:
Lisa Bowens
Stephen R. Burge
Siobhan Dowling Long
J. Cheryl Exum
Michael Rosenberg

Number 6

BIBLICAL THEMES IN SCIENCE FICTION

Edited by
Nicole L. Tilford and Kelly J. Murphy

SBL PRESS

Atlanta

Copyright © 2023 by SBL Press

All rights reserved. No part of this work may be reproduced or transmitted in any form or by any means, electronic or mechanical, including photocopying and recording, or by means of any information storage or retrieval system, except as may be expressly permitted by the 1976 Copyright Act or in writing from the publisher. Requests for permission should be addressed in writing to the Rights and Permissions Office, SBL Press, 825 Houston Mill Road, Atlanta, GA 30329 USA.

Library of Congress Control Number: 2023934289

Contents

Abbreviations vii

Introduction
　Nicole L. Tilford and Kelly J. Murphy 1

Adam, Eve, and Lilith
　Krista N. Dalton 15

The Tower of Babel
　Tom de Bruin 35

Noah's Ark
　Nicole L. Tilford 57

The Handmaid
　Rhonda Burnette-Bletsch 85

The Utopian City
　Steven J. Schweitzer 103

The Land
　Jackie Wyse-Rhodes 121

Babylon
　Jason A. Staples 145

Messiah/Christ
　Frank Bosman 167

Resurrection and Afterlife
    James F. McGrath 187

Apocalypse
    Kelly J. Murphy 207

Reading from the Twilight Zone: An Afterword
    Christine Wenderoth 239

Contributors..253

Index of Ancient Sources..255
Index of Modern Scholars..260
Index of Science Fiction Works 263

Abbreviations

A.J.	Josephus, *Antiquitates judaicae*
ABD	Freedman, David Noel, ed. *Anchor Bible Dictionary*. 6 vols. New York: Doubleday, 1992.
AJS Rev	*The Journal of the Association of Jewish Studies Review*
ASAP/Journal	*Association for the Study of the Arts of the Present*
b.	Babylonian Talmud
2 Bar.	2 Baruch
EJL	Early Judaism and Its Literature
EncJud	Skolnik, Fred, and Michael Berenbaum, eds. *Encyclopedia Judaica*. 2nd ed. 22 vols. Detroit: Macmillan Reference USA, 2007.
Eruv.	Eruvin
Gen. Rabl	Genesis Rabbah
Hag.	Hagigah
Hist.	Herodotus, *Historia*
Int	*Interpretation: A Journal of Bible and Theology*
JBR	*Journal of the Bible and Its Reception*
JCS	*Journal of Cuneiform Studies*
JHS	*Journal of Hebrew Scriptures*
JIBS	*Journal for Interdisciplinary Biblical Studies*
JJS	*Journal of Jewish Studies*
JLA	*Justice League of America*
JSOT	*Journal for the Study of the Old Testament*
Jub.	Jubilees
LHBOTS	The Library of Hebrew Bible/Old Testament Studies
Lit	*Lit: Literature Interpretation Theory*
NIB	Keck, Leander E., ed. *The New Interpreter's Bible*. 12 vols. Nashville: Abingdon, 1994–2004.

NIDB	Sakenfeld, Katharine Doob, ed. *The New Interpreter's Dictionary of the Bible*. 5 vols. Nashville: Abingdon, 2006–2009.
NIV	New International Version
NRSV	New Revised Standard Version
NTL	New Testament Library
Num. Rab.	Numbers Rabbah
PRSt	*Perspectives in Religious Studies*
RelSRev	*Religious Studies Review*
RM	Ra'ya Mehemna
Sanh.	Sanhedrin
SemeiaSt	Semeia Studies
Shabb.	Shabbat
SJOT	*Scandinavian Journal of the Old Testament*
Symp.	Plato, *Symposium*
WW	*Word and World*

Introduction

Nicole L. Tilford and Kelly J. Murphy

The Bible and science fiction. At first glance, the two seem to be opposites. One remembers the past; the other looks to the future. One is revered as sacred by people all around the world; the other is often indifferent or even hostile to religion. But which is which?

The Bible, of course, is a collection of texts written two thousand or more years ago. These texts record the relationship of a people with their God from creation, through destruction, and toward restoration. For Jews, the Bible (the Tanak) consists of twenty-four books, including legal codes, sayings of and stories about prophets and kings, and miscellaneous writings. Christian Bibles (the Old and New Testaments) include additional texts, notably stories about Jesus of Nazareth, whom Christians view as the Son of God and savior of the human race. It is misleading, in other words, to talk about "the Bible" as though it were a singular book. There is no *one* Bible; rather, there are *many* Bibles: Jewish Bibles, Orthodox Christian Bibles, Roman Catholic Bibles, Protestant Bibles, even variations within each major tradition. Yet, regardless of tradition, for the modern reader, the contents of these texts are fixed, they clearly take place in the past, and, for many, they count as sacred history.

Science fiction, however, is a more recent invention. Although elements of the genre can be traced back further (see Roberts 2005), science fiction as a recognizable category is largely the product of the late nineteenth–early twentieth century, a time of growing scientific optimism and religious skepticism. The name of the genre itself derives from pulp magazine publisher Hugo Gernsback (1926), who viewed "scientifiction" as a tool by which to teach the public about new scientific discoveries. Today, science fiction works vary widely, and there is an ever-expanding list of subgenres, each with its own unique characteristics. There are "hard" science fiction works that are grounded in "known scientific principles" (e.g., Cixin Liu's 2008 novel *The Three Body Problem*), and there are "soft" science fiction works where there might be "little awareness of science at all" (e.g., Walter M. Miller's 1960 novel *A Canticle for Leibowitz*).[1] There are cli-fi works that explore the effect of climate change on society (e.g., Margaret Atwood's *Oryx and Crake*) and space westerns that look for a brighter future among the wilderness of the stars (e.g., *Star Trek*). There are dystopian works that examine the breakdown of society and cyberpunks that contrast societal failure with technological achievement (e.g., *Altered Carbon*, 2002). There are even authors who are regularly cited as science fiction writers who reject the label. For example, Margaret Atwood, whose 1987 novel *The Handmaid's Tale* won that year's Arthur C. Clarke Award for Best Science Fiction, "prefers the term 'speculative fiction,' which she defines as stories set on Earth and employing elements that already exist in some form, like genetic engineering, as opposed to more wildly hypothetical science fiction ideas like time travel, faster-than-light drives, and transporters" ("Margaret Atwood on Science Fiction, Dystopias, and Intestinal Parasites," 2013).

Scholars often note how difficult it is to define science fiction. After all, as David Seed explains,

> it has previously been explained as a combination of romance, science, and prophecy (Hugo Gernsback), "realistic speculation about future events" (Robert Heinlein), and a genre based on an imagined alternative to the reader's environment (Darko Suvin). It has been called a form of fantastic literature and an historical literature. (2011, 1)

For these reasons, in his *Science Fiction: A Very Short Introduction*, Seed declines to offer one definition of the term, for "that way madness lies." With Seed and others, this volume does not attempt to offer a definitive definition of what science fiction is or what counts as science fiction, instead recognizing the diverse and ever-shifting identities of science fiction.[2] Regardless of precise definitions, we recognize that science fiction has been and continues to be a form of popular entertainment, amazing

---

1. For the distinction between these categories, see Wolfe 2005, 18, 21.
2. For readers interested in the debates about what constitutes science fiction, see Hubble and Mousoutzanis 2013; Latham 2014; and Seed 2011, as well as their extensive bibliographies.

the public with stories about fantastic worlds, alien peoples, and marvelous inventions. These stories are often set in the future, or at least an alternate present, and speculate about what might be.

Yet, one does not need to dig deep to see that the differences between biblical texts and science fiction are not as stark as they first appear. From the modern perspective, biblical texts relate events of the past, but from the perspective of those who first compiled and transmitted them, biblical texts also speculated about the future. Biblical prophets, for example, harshly criticized the religious practices of their day, spoke of a time to come when wickedness would be wiped away, and dreamed of a world in which the righteous would flourish. Biblical texts also contain alternate presents: stories such as the book of Jonah and the book of Judith (preserved in some Christian Bibles) are entertaining fictions designed to tell deeper religious truths.

Moreover, events in biblical texts are often as outlandish as science fiction narratives. People build towers that are so tall they reach the heavens. They construct vessels that save the last remaining life on earth. They die and come back to life. Historical biblical narratives speak of entering wondrous lands and meeting strange peoples, and apocalyptic visions use imagery that rivals even the most fantastic science fiction narrative. Today, biblical texts may seem comfortable and familiar, but when they were first transmitted, they were often as bizarre as tales of extraterrestrials and wormholes are to us.

Conversely, science fiction narratives are sometimes outlandish, but they are also often chillingly familiar. When heroes are not out gallivanting across the cosmos, they are next door, in the school yard or the ghetto, struggling against social injustices and moral inequalities that are all too recognizable. They consider past failings and suggest future solutions in the same way that biblical narratives use the past to dictate the future. In fact, many science fiction authors borrow their narratives directly from biblical texts, and even the most antireligious science fiction narratives explore the same themes as biblical narratives: trust, hubris, justice, peace.

Many people argue that science fiction asks something of its readers—or, perhaps, *does* something to them. Indeed, one of the most famous and oft-cited definitions of the genre is from theorist Darko Suvin (2016, 15), who calls science fiction the "literature of cognitive estrangement." According to this view, science fiction forces readers to question their suppositions about the world and reflect on reality in new, possibly transformative, ways. Harsh dystopian regimes, for example, compel readers to look closely at their own social interactions, while the compassion of extraterrestrials encourages audiences to reconsider what it means to be human. As science fiction and fantasy author Ursula Le Guin (1979, 19) argues, this "distancing, the pulling back from 'reality' in order to see it better, is perhaps the essential gesture" of science fiction. In this, science fiction is not too distant from biblical texts, many of which urge their readers to rethink what they know about reality: in biblical texts, punishment becomes a learning opportunity, exile builds kingdoms, and death transforms into new life. Biblical texts and science fiction works both deliver engaging, even if often terrifying, escapes from daily life. But they do so in such a way that provides an opportunity for their audiences to see things anew, from a slightly alternative space, and, perhaps, to see it better.

Furthermore, science fiction is not as antireligion as it is often characterized to be. In fact, many science fiction narratives privilege scientific thought and criticize religion as a backward mentality. Yet, alien worlds are filled with unique religious practices, and characters routinely search for and even find the divine. Some science fiction franchises are so popular that they have become cult-like in their own right. Fans gather each week at the same time and the same place to experience the next installment in their favorite series. They take yearly pilgrimages to conferences, where they dress in attire made special for the event and meet with select representatives (authors, actors, artists). They pay large sums for franchise merchandise, the rarest of which take on almost the status of relics. Official narratives—those produced by the franchise's creators or licensees—become canon, while fan fiction and unpopular narratives develop as apocrypha. Science fiction may be antireligious at times, but it sure looks like religion.

The Bible is not science fiction, and science fiction is not the Bible. But they are part of the same creative impulse: the human desire to dream, to consider worlds unseen, to speculate on what might be. Although unlikely allies, they work in tandem to push humanity toward a better state.

The Contents of This Volume

Designed to introduce undergraduates and the general public to the basic contours of the subject, this volume examines one piece of this relationship: the direct appearance of biblical themes and narratives in science fiction. In doing so, *Biblical Themes in Science Fiction* enters a number of long-standing conversations, including critical scholarship on religion and science fiction. Previous scholarly work on the intersections between the Bible and science fiction have approached the topic from a number of angles, often focusing on the ways in which broader religious concepts such as transcendence, morality, canon, and the sacred have impacted the development of the genre (McGrath 2011; Simkins 2016; Grigg 2018).[3] Others have surveyed how specific Christian themes such as divinity, creation, providence, the messiah, the apocalypse, and the church have influenced the entire genre (McGrath 2016; McKee 2007) or a particular corpus of science fiction, such as *Doctor Who* (Crome and McGrath 2013) or *Star Trek* (Neese 2016). Additionally, a 2021 issue of the *Journal for Interdisciplinary Biblical Studies* entitled "The Bible and Speculative Fiction" featured articles that explored the intersections of biblical texts, biblical interpretation, and science fiction from several angles. For example, Shayna Sheinfeld (2021) traces the religious tensions in *Battlestar Galactica* (2003–2009) with a particular focus on the character of Gaius Baltar and how he might be understood when read alongside the biblical figure of Abraham, particularly in early Jewish interpretation. Others, such as Frauke Uhlenbrauch's (2015, 2016) monograph and edited collection, focus on biblical texts and the way science fiction can be used to understand and interpret the Bible. For example, Uhlenbrauch (2015, 195) writes, "If we take into account the cognitive estrangement [science fiction] texts are supposed to evoke in their readers by juxtaposing a world in which one or more aspects are thoroughly unfamiliar, one notices that the contemporary Bible reader is in fact reading stories about an unfamiliar far away world."

In contrast, *Biblical Themes in Science Fiction* explores how biblical themes influence what we call science fiction. In other words, rather than using a contemporary category to look back at ancient genres, this volume traces how elements of the biblical materials appear in science fiction. How, for example, does the story of creation from the book of Genesis get picked up and used by science fiction authors? Or how do stories of spaceships fleeing doomed worlds draw on the biblical account of Noah

---

3. In a similar vein, scholars have also focused on other modern genres and their relationship to the biblical material. Readers who are interested in fantasy, a genre that at times overlaps with science fiction, are pointed to Aichele and Pippin 1992, 1997, and 1998. Garber 2021 is also a helpful exploration of the biblical theme of prophecy in popular fantasy and science fiction.

and the flood? Additionally, the goal of this volume is different from some of the previous work on the relationship between the Bible and science fiction. Much (though certainly not all) of the existing literature on the Bible and science fiction seeks to "deepen and encourage" the faith of its readers (Neese 2016, xxi), "help [readers] as they reflect on their own beliefs" (McGrath 2016, 4), or uncover how science fiction can be used as a "spiritual tool" to "forg[e] the faith of the future" (McKee 2007, xiv). In contrast, *Biblical Themes in Science Fiction* focuses on biblical narratives and themes more broadly, without presupposing a particular religious viewpoint.

In what follows, each contributor introduces a biblical theme and/or narrative, tracing it as it appears throughout twentieth- and twenty-first-century science fiction. The authors then focus on one example of science fiction—a novel, a film, a television show, or a video game—and how the biblical themes and/or narratives are invoked and, often, changed by the science fiction authors. The examples the writers of this volume turn to in their explorations represent the diversity inherent in science fiction, from hard science fiction to soft, from space operas to postapocalyptic tales. They are not exhaustive, nor are the themes they are chosen to represent. Rather, they are intended to illustrate key connections between biblical narratives and science fiction and provide a solid foundation for further exploration.

In "Adam, Eve, and Lilith," Krista N. Dalton reviews the creation accounts found in the book of Genesis, including their themes of gender difference, power structure, and the human quest for knowledge. Dalton then outlines how the rabbis understood Eve, who is named only in Gen 3, to be the second woman created; the first woman, unnamed in Gen 1 but whom the rabbis called Lilith, fled from Adam and became known as the mother of demons. Eve and Lilith became archetypal enemies: "great mother of humanity versus mother of demons, a chaste wife versus a willful temptress, bearer of life versus bringer of death." Science fiction writers, as Dalton explains, draw on the themes found in the creation stories as they explore the future of humanity. Adam and Eve, and sometimes Lilith, become paradigms for seeing humanity as separate from and perhaps better than the other creatures. Here Dalton focuses especially on Octavia Butler's Xenogenesis trilogy, later named *Lilith's Brood*, in which an African American woman named Lilith is the heroine of a story, chosen by an alien race to return to a destroyed Earth and begin humanity anew. Butler's work imagines a future that challenges the typical colonization narrative often found in the writings of white male science fiction writers, a future where Lilith—a marginalized woman—refuses to reinscribe the violence of the colonizer.

Tom de Bruin's "The Tower of Babel" explores the brief biblical narrative of Gen 11:1–9, a story about a time when humans all spoke the same language and tried to build a tower to heaven, only to be interrupted by the deity, who worried that this was "only the beginning of what they will do; nothing that they propose to do will now be impossible for them" (Gen 11:6 NRSVue). In response, God confused the humans so that they could no longer understand one another, scattering them across the world. In the biblical account, as de Bruin argues, "the story functions as an etilogy of linguistic and national diversity and as a warning against human arrogant audacity." The "curse of Babel," wherein God creates languages and nations, eradicates any possible human unity. Both literal tower building as a sign of human ambition and hubris as well as the curse of Babel appear widely throughout science fiction, often used as mechanisms through which authors critique their present, including human technological advancement. De Bruin concentrates in particular on Samuel R. Delaney's 1966 novel *Babel-17*. The novel explores how a new language—Babel-17—is created to be used as a weapon in an intergalactic war. The novel draws upon the biblical account to scrutinize the role of language in human behavior and relationships and the possibility of technological advancement gone wrong.

In "Noah's Ark," Nicole L. Tilford illustrates the long tradition of imagining what—and, especially, who—might be worth saving if the world were coming to an end. Embedded in the biblical book of Genesis is one of the world's oldest, and most famous, ark narratives, Gen 6–9. This narrative recounts the story of Noah and his family, who are saved by God from a divinely sent, world-destroying flood. Ark narratives such as Gen 6–9 force their audiences to consider what is most important to them and their social interactions. In the biblical text, the answer is Noah, who is saved because he alone in his generation provides a model for how humans should behave. For science fiction writers, the answer ranges from the young to the rich to the scientifically minded. Tilford traces three storylines from the British science fiction television show *Doctor Who*, each of which draws on the trope of the ark. She examines differing values these episodes place on human ingenuity and humanity's worth and how the changing answer to the question of who—or what—should be saved reflects the ever-changing contexts of the creators of the show.

Next, Rhonda Burnette-Bletsch's "The Handmaid" examines how the book of Genesis depicts tensions between wives and the women who often bore children for them, with a special focus on the story of Sarah and Hagar from Gen 16 and 21. She focuses particularly on how these narratives have been interpreted by marginalized women. As she writes, "in a patriarchal society such as ancient Israel, the bodies of women become mechanisms of inclusion and exclusion in the construction of community boundaries." Burnette-Bletsch then explores how this theme is utilized in some science fiction accounts, especially Margaret Atwood's 1983 *The Handmaid's Tale*. While the book—and the later television series of the same name—both cite the story of Rachel and Bilhah to justify the creation of handmaids who will bear children for women who are assumed to be barren, Burnette-Bletsch reveals how "the tumultuous relationship" between the central female characters of Atwood's creation is better understood as reflecting that of Sarah and Hagar. Moreover, Burnette-Bletsch exposes the way that "biblical interpretations of the powerful can be challenged by the theological intuition of the oppressed."

Steven J. Schweitzer's "The Utopian City" analyzes the ways in which science fiction draws on the idea of the utopian city, a construct that is found in both the Hebrew Bible and the New Testament, especially in texts that imagine a future and idealized Jerusalem (also known as Zion). As Schweitzer illustrates, utopian cities—biblical or otherwise—provide a means for authors to criticize what they understand to be the ills of the present while simultaneously offering hope for the future. Unlike the biblical tradition, however, science fiction writers often disrupt the concept of a utopian city, instead depicting such cities as "dystopia in disguise." Schweitzer traces *The Matrix* trilogy's use of Zion, depicted in the films as the only remaining human city in a world now ruled by machines. Ultimately the trilogy subverts the expected outcome. Unlike the biblical texts, where a final battle between good and evil ends with the righteous ensconced in the new Jerusalem/Zion and the unrighteous forever barred from the city, *The Matrix* rejects such a simplistic dualism: "utopias, according to the film, must be dynamic and open to change."

In the following chapter, "The Land," Jackie Wyse-Rhodes surveys how land has remained a category for reflection from the biblical texts forward, including in the genre of science fiction. Wyse-Rhodes begins by charting the various ways that the biblical texts picture land, from garden to wilderness to a lost possession in the face of exile. In both their deliberations on literal lands and the many ways that they invoke land metaphorically, the biblical authors use the idea of land to ponder the past, present, and future. When science fiction writers reflect on land, they often do so to ask important questions about human nature, including human tendencies such as arrogance or greed and the effects such propensities have had on the earth. To highlight how science fiction often draws on biblical themes around land—including idyllic gardens, disquieting wilderness brought about by human actions, and the future of humanity on earth—Wyse-Rhodes turns to Atwood's MaddAddam trilogy. While Atwood's novels focus on the negative impact that humanity has had, the world depicted in the MaddAddam trilogy also offers hope for the land, found in the idea of renovation—not just for the land but for humans, too.

In "Babylon," Jason A. Staples maps out the history of the ancient Near Eastern Babylonian Empire and the various ways it appears across the Hebrew Bible and New Testament, from the story of the tower of Babel to its appearances in the historical books, the prophets, and apocalypses. According to Staples, the name of this empire "came to be portrayed as the archetypal evil empire in early Jewish and Christian literature, the megacity representing imperial power and culture in all its oppressive splendor, the image of hubristic ambition and (ultimately doomed) human attempts to gain godlike power." In science fiction, the trope of an evil empire based in a self-indulgent and corrupt metropolis (e.g., the Galactic Empire in *Star Wars*) abounds. The many biblical threads that focus on Babylon coalesce, as Staples demonstrates, in Fritz Lang's 1927 film *Metropolis*, where a city deeply divided by socioeconomic class is run by a man who lives in the "new tower of Babel." By drawing on biblical imagery of ancient Babylon, *Metropolis* offers a scathing critique of affluence that is produced at the expense of the working class, while simultaneously critiquing human confidence in technology and ideas of continued human progress.

While previous chapters explore the ways that science fiction has taken up biblical themes in television, film, and literature, in "Messiah/Christ," Frank Bosman turns to how messianic themes and Christlike figures appear in science fiction video games. In biblical texts, a messiah is a powerful, divinely appointed figure who restores the kingdom of God. In science fiction works, messianic figures have a similar appeal, saving humanity or even the entire universe from the forces of evil. In his extended analysis, Bosman identifies the messianic hero as but one of several types of heroes in science fiction video games, all of whom enable players to experience the narratival adventure in different ways.

For example, a game with a "messianic hero" directly draws upon imagery inspired by the Christ-figure from Christianity as the gamer is led through a series of self-sacrificial actions (see, for example, the character Aurora in the game *Child of Light*). Games with a "christophoric hero" take this one step further; the gamer is provided the opportunity to voluntarily identify himself or herself as a messianic hero, choosing of his or her own accord a "(narratological) death of the game protagonist, that is, the player's avatar." For example, Bosman points to *Fallout 3*, a postnuclear war narrative in which the gamer has the choice to sacrifice his or her avatar to deliver others.

James F. McGrath's "Resurrection and Afterlife" begins by noting how, "if there is something that forms a common interest and pursuit across the domains of religion, magic, science, science fiction, and fantasy, it is surely the expression of a human desire to cheat, overcome, or at the very least postpone death." McGrath briefly outlines the diverse perspectives on afterlife found in the biblical texts and then traces the explicit and implicit use of resurrection and afterlife in science fiction. Here the focus might be on individual immortality or the survival of humanity more broadly, and authors interrogate the limits of human science, the possible effects of a reliance on technology, and potential relationships between mind, body, and/or soul. McGrath focuses his attention on *Battlestar Galactica* and the diverse ways that the show—from its original incarnation to its later spinoffs—have wrestled with questions of resurrection and afterlife.

In "Apocalypse," Kelly J. Murphy identifies the ways in which the genre of biblical apocalypse is used to criticize the present period of its authors, to call people to certain behaviors, to wrestle with the meaning of history, and, sometimes, to imagine a hopeful future. Murphy explores the ways in which these themes appear throughout the biblical books of Daniel and Revelation, as well as other ancient apocalypses. She then turns to the many ways that these themes have been threaded throughout contemporary apocalyptic and postapocalyptic science fiction. Often the future that contemporary science fiction writers picture is far messier than the ends imagined by the biblical writers. While some contemporary science fiction imagines a postapocalyptic world in which humans survive and perhaps even thrive, many of these stories are more pessimistic about human nature. This is particularly the case in how zombies are used in science fiction, and Murphy demonstrates this by turning to M. R. Carey's 2014 novel *The Girl with All the Gifts*.

Finally, in "Reading from the Twilight Zone: An Afterword," Christine Wenderoth reflects on why "biblical themes—Adam and Eve, Messiah/Christ, resurrection, apocalypse, and all the rest—transcend the pages of the Bible and enter our consciousness, our literature, our popular culture to stay alive and animate our explorations of the universe." To do this, she invokes the category of midrash in its broadest sense. Just as midrash builds on the biblical texts while also addressing gaps in them, science fiction builds on biblical themes and narratives, reshaping them for new contexts. Wenderoth calls readers to let *both* the Bible and science fiction speak—and to "let each speak to the other." After all, she writes, both are "here to help us to see the universe in all its mysterious, frightening, maddening, and awesome refractions."

Separately, each essay in this volume offers a unique look at a specific biblical story, corpus, or theme; read together, the essays highlight the many voices of the collection that has come to be called the Bible. In doing so, the contributors illustrate how the biblical texts wrestle in diverse ways with questions about the past, the then-present, and the future, always interrogating what it means to be human, what it might mean to be divine, as well as what might simply *be*—both seen and unseen. Each chapter individually explores how science fiction has taken up biblical stories and themes, often in radically new ways, and thus showcases how science fiction—much like the biblical material—wrestles with time and meaning. Together the chapters demonstrate that science fiction is not the obverse of the Bible. Rather, science fiction often draws on the biblical, even as it transforms it and makes it into something new.

Works Cited

Aichele, George, and Tina Pippin, eds. 1992. *Fantasy and the Bible. Semeia* 60.

———, eds. 1997. *The Monstrous and the Unspeakable: The Bible as Fantastic Literature.* Playing the Text 1. Sheffield: Sheffield University Press.

———, eds. 1998. *Violence, Utopia, and the Kingdom of God: Fantasy and Ideology in the Bible.* New York: Routledge.

"The Bible and Speculative Fiction." 2021. *JIBS* 3.1.

Crome, Andrew, and James F. McGrath. 2013. *Religion and Doctor Who: Time and Relative Dimensions in Faith.* Eugene, OR: Wipf & Stock.

Garber, David G., Jr. 2021. "Biblical Prophecy and Popular Fantasy and Science Fiction." Pages 143–290 in *The Oxford Handbook of the Bible and American Popular Culture.* Edited by Dan W. Clanton Jr. and Terry R. Clark. New York: Oxford University Press.

Gernsback, Hugo. 1926. "A New Sort of Magazine." *Amazing Stories* 1.1.

Grigg, Richard. 2018. *Science Fiction and the Imitation of the Sacred.* New York: Bloomsbury.

Hubble, Nick, and Aris Mousoutzanis, eds. 2013. *The Science Fiction Handbook.* Literature and Culture. New York: Bloomsbury.

Latham, Rob, ed. 2014. *The Oxford Handbook of Science Fiction.* New York: Oxford University Press.

Le Guin, Ursula K. 1979. *The Language of the Night: Essays on Fantasy and Science Fiction.* New York: Putnam.

"Margaret Atwood on Science Fiction, Dystopias, and Intestinal Parasites." 2013. Wired. https://tinyurl.com/SBLPress6708a1.

McGrath, James F., ed. 2011. *Religion and Science Fiction.* Eugene, OR: Pickwick.

———. 2016. *Theology and Science Fiction.* Cascade Companions. Eugene, OR: Cascade.

McKee, Gabriel. 2007. *The Gospel according to Science Fiction: From the Twilight Zone to the Final Frontier.* Louisville: Westminster John Knox.

Neese, Kevin C. 2016. *The Gospel according to Star Trek: The Original Crew.* Eugene, OR: Cascade.

Roberts, Adam. 2005. *The History of Science Fiction.* New. York: Palgrave Macmillan.

Seed, David. 2011. *Science Fiction: A Very Short Introduction.* New York: Oxford University Press.

Sheinfeld, Shayna. 2021. "The Old Gods Are Fighting Back: Mono- and Polytheistic Tensions in *Battlestar Galactica* and Jewish Biblical Interpretation." *JIBS* 3.1:1–19.

Simkins, Jennifer. 2016. *The Science Fiction Mythmakers: Religion, Science and Philosophy in Wells, Clarke, Dick and Herbert.* Critical Explorations in Science Fiction and Fantasy 54. Jefferson, NC: McFarland.

Suvin, Darko. 2016. *Metamorphoses of Science Fiction: On the Poetics and History of a Literary Genre.* Edited by Gerry Canavan. Ralahine Utopian Studies 18. New York: Lang.

Uhlenbruch, Frauke. 2015. *The Nowhere Bible: Utopia, Dystopia, Science Fiction.* Studies of the Bible and Its Reception 4. Boston: De Gruyter.

———, ed. 2016. *Not in the Spaces We Know: An Exploration of Science Fiction and the Bible.* Perspectives on Hebrew Scriptures and Its Contexts. Piscataway, NJ: Gorgias.

Wolfe, Gary K. 2005. "Coming to Terms." Pages 13–22 in *Speculations on Speculation: Theories of Science Fiction*. Edited by James E. Gunn and Matthew Candelaria. Lanham, MD: Scarecrow.

Adam, Eve, and Lilith

Krista N. Dalton

If you control the story of the world's beginnings, you control the language that orders knowledge. Nowhere is this more evident than in stories about the creation of humanity. Whether emerging *ex nihilo* from a thought or dream, brought up through a primeval ocean, or split from a dismembered primordial being, humanity is depicted as the apex of creation. Humans arrive and possess the land; their progeny gain dominance over the newly formed world. Such creation stories are foundational to our mythology because they explain ourselves and our relation to other beings. They help us to organize society and validate existing power structures, forming the basis of our knowledge about the world. For those influenced by the biblical mythos, for instance, the creation of Adam and Eve established a set of proverbial models. They represent the purest human form. Their time in the garden is a microcosm of a longed-for idyllic society. At the same time, their creation provides a prototype of difference. Adam is given dominion over all other creatures. This distinction marks humans as fundamentally different from other animal kinds. In one version of the tale, God also gives Eve to Adam as his subordinate, instituting a gendered hierarchy that persists to this day. The story thus contains naturalized categories and boundaries that have shaped the societies inheriting its mythos.

Artists and authors alike have drawn inspiration from this biblical myth and invoked its likeness through allusion, epithet, and rehearsal. In doing so, they have inherited the embedded power structures that come with it. In nineteenth- and twentieth-century science fiction, the creation myth in particular provided a lens for thinking through the prevailing concerns of the day, such as how to restore a damaged world, the right of humankind to colonize the galaxy, and what difference remains between humans and alien kinds (LeGuin 1979). Yet, even as these writers used the creation myth to imagine a technology-tinged landscape, some transformed the myth to provide a new vision of humanity. In doing so, some authors shifted and inverted the existing power structures of the story to create new ways of ordering the world and new ways of considering what exactly makes us human.

Adam, Eve, and Lilith in the Bible and Beyond

In the beginning God created humanity, the details of which are inconsistent in biblical literature. The discord stems from two versions of the creation story, often conflated in modern reception. In Gen 2–3 we are introduced to Adam and Eve, the central characters of the creation myth. While a mist hung heavy over the earth and neither shrub nor herb had yet appeared, God formed *Adam*, literally man, from the dust of the ground (*adamah*) (Gen 2:27). After breathing life into his clay golem (see b. Hag. 12a; b. Sanh. 38b), God planted Adam in a lush garden cultivated in Eden. Adam then watched as God coaxed trees and animals from the ground and birds from the air. God presented his creations to Adam, but while Adam named them, none was a suitable partner. Therefore, God set out to make Adam a helper:

> So the LORD God caused a deep sleep to fall upon the man, and he slept; then he took one of his ribs and closed up its place with flesh. And the rib that the LORD God had taken from the man he made into a woman and brought her to the man. (Gen 2:21–22)[1]

While Adam slept, God fashioned a companion from one of his rib bones, creating a woman from the substance of man, rather than from the dust of the ground. This connection marks her as different from the other animals, and Adam declares her a suitable partner at last, naming her *khavah* or "life" (Eve in the latinized spelling) (Gen 3:20). The two live in the garden until one day a serpent tempts the woman to eat from a forbidden tree. When they eat from a piece of its fruit, Adam and Eve attain the knowledge of good and evil. God fears that these enlightened humans might attain immortality, so he banishes them to the wild—the man cursed to till the ground and the woman subjected to the control of her husband.

---

1. All biblical citations are from the NRSV translation.

This etiological account contains enduring archetypes. Adam is the first of all creation, formed when the earth was but water and mud. He represents both the dawn of humanity and the dominion of men. He names each creature, including his wife, as he acts as God's steward in the garden. Eve is destined to be the "mother of all living" (3:20), the first *madonna* or Great Mother figure, who must push in agony from her womb. Yet in the throes of banishment, Eve is also diminished. The yoke of marriage tempers her potential as her husband rules over her according to divine decree.

The pairing of Adam and Eve in a gendered hierarchy has been a potent model for generations, yet the biblical text itself challenges this archetypal pairing. In Gen 1 we learn of a different account of creation, one spread over six days with humans only appearing on the sixth and final day:

> Then God said, "Let us make humankind [*adam*] in our image, according to our likeness; and let them have dominion over the fish of the sea, and over the birds of the air, and over the cattle, and over all the wild animals of the earth, and over every creeping thing that creeps upon the earth." So God created humankind [*adam*] in his own image, in the image of God he created them; male and female he created them. (Gen 1:26–27)

The dominion of humankind is more emphatically emphasized in this version. Humanity is the culmination of creation rather than the first and given authority over all creatures appearing earlier in the creation cycle. Most notably, no distinction is made between the creation of men and women. Both are created in the image of God simultaneously and given joint control.

Ancient Jewish authors noted the textual difference and wondered about the identity of the unnamed woman in Gen 1. Was she Eve? Surely not, because this woman was formed simultaneously with Adam and therefore could not come from Adam's rib. If she were not Eve, who was she? What happened in the sequence of creation? Rabbinic commentaries offered a few explanations. First, commentators suggested that it was actually Adam created in Gen 1, but he was initially created possessing both male and female attributes:

> Rabbi Yiremiah son of Elazar said: At the hour when the Holy One created the first person, he created him androgynous: "both male and female he created them." Rabbi Shmuel bar Nahman said: At the hour

> when the Holy One created the first person, he created him double-faced, and he sawed him [in half] and made him backs—a back here and a back there. They objected to him: But it is written, "And he took one of his ribs [*tselot*]" (Gen 2:21). He said to them: [it means] "one of his sides," just as one would say, "And for the side [*tselah*] of the tabernacle" (Exod 26:20). (Gen. Rab. 8.1 [my trans. based on Albeck and Theodor 1965])

Rabbi Yiremiah makes an intertextual comparison to support his position that Adam was split in two. Just as the Genesis account references ribs, or *tselot*, so also does a different biblical verse use the singular form of the word *tselah* to refer to the side of the tabernacle. Therefore, one can infer that the plurality in the verse in Genesis could be read as suggesting that Adam was split into two backs. This sawing in half of the androgynous creation has a strong parallel in Plato's *Symposium*, centuries earlier. There Aristophanes delivers a speech describing similar androgynous persons with two faces that were split in two when Zeus found humanity threatening to the gods (*Symp.* 189c–193d). The rabbis use the myth of double-faced humans to explain the mysterious discord between the two creation accounts in Genesis.

Other rabbinic commentators suggested that a different woman was created initially, only later to be replaced with Eve. One tradition suggested that the "first Eve returned to dust" upon the creation of the second Eve (Gen. Rab. 22.7). Another tradition sought to provide an explanation for the second Eve's creation and taught that the first woman repulsed Adam, prompting God to try again:

> And Adam said: "This at last [*zot hapa'am*]" (Gen 2:23). Rabbi Yehudah bar Rabbi said: At first God created her for him, but when he saw her covered in mucus and blood he was repulsed and kept her at a distance from him. Therefore, God created her for him a second time. As it is written, "This at last is bone from my bones"—this is she of this time [*pa'am*]. (Gen. Rab. 18.4 [my trans. based on Albeck and Theodor 1965])

The commentator explores the statement that Adam utters in the biblical text upon waking and seeing Eve, declaring "this at last is bone of my bones and flesh of my flesh" (Gen 2:23). If Adam says "this at last," what creation might have occurred prior to that moment to prompt such an emphatic declaration? A plain reading of the biblical text would assume Adam's statement refers to the creation of animals, whom God formed first as potential partners for Adam, but here the commentators link the prior creation to the woman in Gen 1. The commentators imagine that the birth of these first humans resembled that of the birth of a newborn. Covered in blood and mucus, Adam beheld Eve and felt revulsion. Therefore, God tried again, this time while Adam slept.

It is not until an early medieval text entitled the Alphabet of Ben Sira that commentators attach an identity to this first-attempt woman.[2] The narration begins with the biblical King Nebuchadnezzar seeking Ben Sira's help with a cure for his ill son. Ben Sira was a Hellenistic priestly sage attributed with writing the book of Sirach. This medieval fanfiction places the two characters into the same timeline in order to recount a story of Ben Sira's assistance to the king. Ben Sira gives the king an amulet inscribed with three angels and their names. When Nebuchadnezzar asks their purpose, Ben Sira provides the amulet's historiola:[3]

> After God created Adam, who was alone, He said, "It is not good for man to be alone" (Gen. 2:18). He then created a woman for Adam, from the earth, as He had created Adam himself, and called her Lilith. Adam and Lilith began to fight. She said, "I will not lie below," and he said, "I will not lie beneath you, but only on top. For you are fit only to be in the bottom position, while I am to be in the superior one." Lilith responded, "We are equal to each other inasmuch as we were both created from the earth." But they would not listen to one another. When Lilith saw this, she pronounced the Ineffable Name and flew away into the air. (Alphabet of Ben Sira 23a–b [Stern and Mirsky])

Here a distinction is made in the substance of Lilith's creation, representing a conflation of the Gen 1 and 2 accounts. The text explains that Lilith is created from the dust of the ground rather than Adam's rib bone, but she still arrives following Adam's initial creation. This similarity in substance renders them equals, yet Adam strives to impose a gendered hierarchy. Adam refuses to lie beneath Lilith during sex in a passive position, insisting that she is only fit to lie beneath him. Lilith refuses to consent to this aggressive sexual pairing and flees.

---

2. The Alphabet of Ben Sira was composed between the eighth and tenth centuries CE in three main parts: the first two contain alphabetically arranged proverbs and commentary, while the latter part contains the Tales of Ben Sira (Toledot Ben Sira). For analysis on the origins of the text, see Orr 2009.

3. The origin of cures is often linked to the larger cosmogonic myth, as Eliade (1963, 24–34) shows.

The narrative understanding of Lilith shifts when she pronounces the Ineffable Name and flies away. The letters יהוה, a name of God, routinely appeared in Jewish oaths and adjurations in the late ancient period. Cultic experts inscribed the letters on amulets and incantation bowls because of its ritual potency (see Urbach 1975, 124–34; Harari 2017). Lilith is thereby associated with the magical arts by virtue of her knowledge of its power. Lilith's pronouncement follows her rejection of Adam's authority, signaling her shift from Adam's human companion to that of a darker force:

> Adam stood in prayer before his Creator: "Sovereign of the universe!" he said, "the woman you gave me has run away." At once, the Holy One, blessed be He, sent these three angels to bring her back. Said the Holy One to Adam, "If she agrees to come back, fine. If not she must permit one hundred of her children to die every day. The angels left God and pursued Lilith, whom they overtook in the midst of the sea, in the mighty waters wherein the Egyptians were destined to drown. They told her God's word, but she did not wish to return. The angels said, "We shall drown you in the sea." "Leave me!" she said. "I was created only to cause sickness to infants. If the infant is male, I have dominion over him for eight days after his birth, and if female, for twenty days." When the angels heard Lilith's words, they insisted she go back. But she swore to them by the name of the living and eternal God: "Whenever I see you or your names or your forms in an amulet, I will have no power over that infant." She also agreed to have one hundred of her children die every day.[4] Accordingly, every day one hundred demons perish, and for the same reason, we write the angels' names on the amulets of young children. When Lilith sees their names, she remembers her oath, and the child recovers. (Alphabet of Ben Sira 23a–b [Stern and Mirsky])

Lilith reframes the purpose of her creation, not as a partner to Adam but as the wielder of demonic power over infants following childbirth.[5] By failing to submit to Adam's authority, Lilith's magical prowess is unleashed and must be restrained by divine decree. However, even God does not have total control over Lilith; the angels threaten Lilith into conceding power only in the presence of an amulet with their names. In the end,

---

4. According to a midrashic tradition, Lilith is so cruel as to destroy her own offspring (Num. Rab. 16.25).

5. The tradition of eight days for a male son stems from the period of time between birth and circumcision in Lev 12.

Lilith chooses her place as the great demon mother rather than as a partner to Adam.

This story constructs an etiology for earlier demonic lore. The earliest surviving mention of Lilith appears in Gilgamesh and the Huluppu-Tree, an ancient Sumerian poem dating to approximately 2000 BCE. In the poem Lilith is mentioned as a demoness who builds a house in a tree tended by the goddess Inanna, temporarily thwarting Inanna's intentions to harvest the wood of the tree for a throne. Later, when the hero Gilgamesh appears, Lilith flees to the desert. Similarly, in the biblical book of Isaiah, Lilith's dwelling place is described as a chaotic, desert land where the soil is infertile (Isa 34:14). Knowledge of Lilith's demonic power seems to have been widespread in the ancient Jewish community. She is listed among demons who visit women after childbirth in the Dead Sea Scrolls (4Q510 and 4Q511), and rabbinic texts depict her as one who preys on sleeping men:

> Rabbi Ḥanina said: It is prohibited to sleep alone in a house, and anyone who sleeps alone in a house will be seized by Lilith. (b. Shabb. 151b; see also b. Eruv. 100b)

Her name and presumed image also appear upon incantation bowls negating her power through legal divorce formulas (see Levene and Bohak 2012; Vilozny 2015). The Alphabet of Ben Sira merges these demonic associations with the creation myth, introducing not a primordial pair but a triad. Later kabbalistic tradition pairs Lilith with the demon Samael, framing Lilith as the true antipode to Eve (Zohar 3:124b–125a [RM]; Zohar 1:127b on Exod 12:38).[6] Her children become not just demons but humans of the "mixed multitude" (*erev rav*) who "pollute themselves" with forbidden women. The culmination of these traditions positions Lilith as the icon of otherness.

The mythologies of Adam, Eve, and Lilith are encoded with a naturalized order to the world. Adam is dominant masculinity. His wife must be his passive subordinate and never his equal. Lilith, who rejected domination, spends the rest of her days "living in the middle of the undertow" as Primo Levi (1988, 26) poetically described:

> But everything she does is useless: all her desires.
> She coupled with Adam, after the sin,

---

[6]. For the reception of this story in the Zohar, see Dan 1980, 17–40.

> But the only things born of her
> Are spirits without bodies or peace.

Eve, formed from Adam's rib rather than the same clay, is proclaimed his natural wife. While Lilith's progeny is destined to darkness and death, Eve is chosen as the mother of humanity. Eve and Lilith become the archetypal opposites: great mother of humanity versus mother of demons, a chaste wife versus a willful temptress, bearer of life versus bringer of death. The expected order is established.

Adam, Eve, and Lilith in Science Fiction

Origins are enthralling to the imagination. The creation myth contains within it the suggestion of what makes us human: enduring gender difference, primordial struggle with the gods, desire for knowledge and immortality, and distinctiveness over all other created beings. These themes have proved irresistible to science fiction writers to the point of cliché. Defined as a "shaggy God story," or a crudely reworked biblical myth, the Adam and Eve archetype abounds within the modern science fiction genre (Aldiss 1965, 125).[7] As the first humans charged with expanding the human race, their metaphorical significance resonates with the exploration of new humanoid or cyborg races in the midst of dystopian calamity. Numerous works invoke the imagery of this myth through the naming of characters, allusions to the Bible, and rewriting of the biblical story itself.

Mary Shelley's *Frankenstein* (1818), heralded as the forebearer of modern science fiction, makes frequent reference to Adam's creation, contrasting the purity of Adam to Frankenstein's monster. A young scientist distraught by the death of his mother performs a scientific experiment to animate nonliving matter. Repulsed by the monstrosity that emerges, the scientist flees. In a tense confrontation between the monster and his creator, the monster exclaims, "I ought to be thy Adam, but I am rather the fallen angel, whom thou drivest from joy for no misdeed" (Shelley 2013, 105). Later, the monster seeks out his creator and demands that he make him a female companion. He mourns his dissimilarity to Adam, who came forth "from the hands of God a perfect creature, happy and prosperous,"

---

7. Aldiss claimed that science fiction magazine editors "get approximately one story a week set in a garden of Eden spelt Ee-Duhn."

while from birth the monster was "wretched, helpless, and alone," without even Eve to console him (139).

Another nineteenth-century French author, Auguste Villiers de L'Isle-Adam, crafted a quite misogynistic tale about a fictionalized Thomas Edison who invented a female android replica in *The Eve of the Future* (1886). Her creation represents the perfection of womanhood, eliminating the mediocrity of her human counterpart while amplifying her beauty. Edison insists that the android will be superior: "ask yourself in the depths of your conscience if this auxiliary phantom-creature, which shall draw forth in you anew the desire to live, is not truly more worthy to bear the name of a human being than the living one" (de L'Isle-Adam 2013, ch. 8). Here the new creation is the inverse of Shelly's monster, surpassing the humanity of Eve rather than failing to live up to it.[8] The story helped popularize the term *android* and inspired notable films such as *Metropolis* (1927) and *Blade Runner* (1982).

These novels and their progeny imagine the challenges to humanness that arise when technology facilitates reproduction of nonhuman forms. Whether the androids surpass us, feel affinity toward society, or demand the same treatment as humans, their existence challenges the boundary between humans and other kinds—a boundary affirmed in the biblical creation myth itself. Eando Binder explicitly wrestled with this tension in a series of short stories featuring a robot named Adam Link (January 1939–April 1942).[9] In the first story, "I, Robot," Dr. Charles Link constructs the robot, teaching it to behave in a civilized (i.e., human) manner. He declares Adam the "first citizen of the new robot race" but cautions him about the prejudices he will face:

> But making you a full-fledged, legalized citizen among humans won't be easy, I'm afraid. People will fear you and hate you at first, perhaps. I will have to introduce you to the world gradually, and convince them you are entitled to all the rights and responsibilities of citizenship because of your humanlike mind. (Binder 2014, 14)

When Dr. Link accidently dies from a falling heavy object, his housekeeper accuses Adam of murder. It is not until Adam discovers a copy of Shelly's

---

8. On the boundary between human and android, see Hayles 2008.

9. The stories were republished as a novel in 1965. For the quotes here, see the reprint edition: Binder 2014.

Frankenstein that he understands the persistent mistrust of android forms. Later stories in the series join Adam with a robotic Eve, and the two struggle for acceptance. In these explorations into the future of scientific reproduction, the Adam and Eve myth becomes the paradigmatic human standard against which the scientifically formed creations are measured.

Following the devastation of World War II and the introduction of the atomic age, writers again returned to the biblical creation myth, not to consider robotic creations but to envision a future for a decimated human race. Often the central characters were explicitly named Adam and Eve or some variant thereof. For example, Robert Arthur's "Evolution's End" (1941) destroyed an entire species, leaving only Aydem and Ayveh to repopulate the earth. In Lester del Rey's "Into Thy Hands" (1945) two robots find each other in a dystopian landscape and identify themselves as Eve and Adam. Eve convinces Adam that knowledge is not necessarily evil but must be sheltered until humanity is ready for it. Other works save the naming as a final surprise revelation when a couple are fated to repopulate a world, such as *The Twilight Zone*'s "Probe 7, Over and Out" (1963) and "Two" (1961) or Isaac Asimov's 1965 short story "The Last Question." The invocation of the biblical creation myth through naming infuses the dystopian narrative with an ancient hope: if Adam and Eve could populate the world of old, a remnant of humans can do the same.

Strikingly absent from these stories is Lilith. Her part in the creation of the world is often neglected for her more monstrous memory. For example, Charles Williams's *Descent into Hell* (1937) depicts Lilith as a master illusion weaver who helps the protagonist create a doppelganger of a woman he desires. As he loses himself to his distorted self-love, he begins the descent to hell/madness, past the "grand gate of Gomorrah where aged Lilith incunabulates souls" (Williams 1973, 187). In C. S. Lewis's *The Chronicles of Narnia* (1950), Mr. Beaver reveals the true identity of the White Witch as a descendent of Lilith, who was one of the Jinn. To compound the monstrosity of Lilith's descendants, Mr. Beaver insists, "No, no, there isn't a drop of real human blood in the Witch'" (Lewis 2001, 147). The memory of Lilith's place as the human companion to Adam is replaced with that of her demonic nature.

Two notable examples, however, rework the myth of creation and include Lilith as a central character. George MacDonald's *Lilith* (1895) follows Mr. Vane, an intellectual bachelor, as he accidently steps through a magic mirror and is transported to a landscape of the unconscious. Vane meets Lilith, the princess of the industrial city-state of Bulika, who has stolen the waters of the world and forced her subjects to mine gems, transforming the rich agricultural landscape into an industrial wasteland. Various allusions to the myth appear throughout the text: Lilith has the "gait of a Hecate" (MacDonald 2012, 76), and Adam admits that Lilith's father is also his father (136). Lilith also slaughters the infants born in Bulika in order to preserve her mortality, fulfilling her mythic role as "the mortal foe" of Eve's children (120). MacDonald, though, crafts an ending of redemption. Vane and Lilith eventually accept Eve's offer of redemptive sleep, and Lilith undergoes a baptism by fire. Lilith's tortured body writhes as she encounters the darkness of her soul, "until at length she who had been but as a weed cast on the dry sandy shore to wither, should know herself an inlet of the everlasting ocean" (116).

C. L. Moore's "Fruit of Knowledge" (1940 [2015]) offers another revision of Lilith, set explicitly in the garden of Eden. The story begins with a woman gazing into a crystal pool as a cherub welcomes her as the newest arrival to the garden. The cherub asks for the woman's name, and she answers, "Lilith." The cherub stammers speechlessly, "Why, you … you're the Queen of Air and Darkness!" (2015, 200) and hurries to warn Adam of her evil. Moore's Lilith is created not by God but by Adam himself, emerging from his deepest desires. She inhabits the husk of a human body and spends passionate days with Adam. One morning she exits her human body in order to cleanse herself of her growing attachment to Adam, but when she returns her shell is filled with another woman. God has been watching and seized the opportunity of her absence to provide Adam with a more suitable wife. In rage, Lilith plots with the fallen angel Lucifer to bring about Eve's demise and win back Adam's attention, but Adam chooses Eve because she is from his own flesh. Together Adam and Eve eat of the forbidden fruit and are cast out of the garden, while Lilith's children are charged with forevermore haunting Eve's children in the night.

MacDonald and Moore both offer Lilith redemption—MacDonald through Christian baptism and Moore through humanizing Lilith's plight by showing how the odds were always stacked against her. Lilith appears infrequently throughout science fiction, in part because her tradition is less widely known and because she complicates the inspiring vision of new creation. But in many ways mythologies of Lilith are a prime complement to the postapocalyptic genesis. Lilith disrupts. Lilith embodies different ways of being.

Science fiction is, as Le Guin (1979, 156) insists, a "thought-experiment." Authors transport the world they know into a future less known and consider the consequences. The creation myth provides an intellectual space to consider the boundaries organizing the world. Adam and Eve represent the perfection of humanity and the resulting hard distinctions between humans and other kinds. Even Lilith is necessary to the order of the world, as Moore (2015, 218) concedes: "without the existence of such as Lilith, the balance of creation might tip over." As technology promises a future of change, authors returned to older myths not just to imagine new possibilities but to reassure themselves of the boundaries of their own world.

Octavia Butler's *Lilith's Brood*

"Are minority characters—black characters in this case—so disruptive a force that the mere presence of one alters a story, focuses it on race rather than whatever the author had in mind?" (Butler 1980). Octavia Butler raised this question in an essay entitled "The Lost Races of Science Fiction," and in it she unveils the persistence of whiteness in science fiction mythmaking. Audiences want to read the lives of "ordinary everyday characters," she was told by publishers and managers alike, which presumed that ordinary meant white. Butler's writing strove to disrupt this assumption, featuring black central characters in narratives that rethought the limits of ordinary. For her, the creation myth and its legacy in science fiction proved a powerful setting for dismantling racial boundaries, with Lilith playing the starring role.

Butler's *Dawn* (1987; see Butler 2012) is the first novel in the Xenogenesis trilogy later rereleased under the collection name *Lilith's Brood* (2000). The story begins as the African American heroine, Lilith Iyapo, awakes from a 250-year slumber upon an alien space ship orbiting the earth. Following a devastating nuclear war, the Oankali rescued the surviving humans and suspended them in sleep, only to awake a few at a time so as to study their bodies, thinking, and culture. In the meantime, the Oankali have cleansed the earth of its toxic radiation and restored it to a wild state, creating a diverse ecosystem of plant and animal life. Lilith will be among the first humans to return to the earth when the Oankali deem her ready, but she must accept their one condition: she must consent to mate with the Oankali.

Butler plays with the building blocks of the creation myth in this dystopian setting. In Butler's telling, new life begins with Lilith—not Eve—upon a spaceship. An alien species known for an irresistible impulse to heal reconstitutes the earth, pushing the primordial reset button of creation. Lilith is charged with awakening a small group of humans and teaching them survival skills, becoming both mother and father to the survivors. She is "to teach, to give comfort, to feed and clothe, to guide them through and interpret what will be, for them, a new and frightening world. To parent" (Butler 2012, 110). The garden of Eden transforms into an Oankali forest, a training ground and temporary home for the first awakened humans.

The choice of Lilith as the heroine is no coincidence. Butler explicitly references her mythology in the second novel, *Adulthood Rites* (1988, 28): "Lilith her name was. Lilith. Unusual name loaded with bad connotations. She should have changed it. Almost anything would have been better." Butler knowingly inverts the "shaggy God" premise by naming Lilith as the surrogate mother of humanity, harnessing the disruptive force of her myth in an act of reclamation. She celebrates Lilith's otherness, reconsiders the framework that deems her children as monstrous, and grapples with the myth's emphasis on sexual consent. Ultimately, Butler insists that there is no reason a black woman, or the mythical Lilith, cannot be the mother of humanity.

The poignancy of Butler's rejection of Eve has deep significance. The advent of ethnology and racial science in the nineteenth century aimed to determine the superiority of some races over others through a careful examination of their bodily characteristics. Theories of polygenesis, or the notion that human races descended from different origins, arose and complicated the religious perspective of a universal human descent from Adam and Eve. Biblical scholars invested in the maintenance of the institution of slavery began to exegete the text in such a way as to determine that Eve's tempter in the garden must have been a black man. Mason Stokes (1998, 722) explains, "If Eve's tempter was a black man (or a black woman), then original sin was not located in her eating of the apple, but in her far more grievous crime of heeding the seductive words of a black tempter."[10] In the legacy of racial difference in the American South, Eve represents both the purity and fragility of white women (Ware 2015). Dora Apel contends that Christian gender codes were appropriated in support of whiteness, cultivating a cultural understanding that white women are naturally pure vessels for reproduction. Apel (2004, 28) insists that "the construction of white female purity was dependent upon two images of blacks: black men

---

10. Stokes 1998 provides a survey of racist Eden mythos in biblical scholarship.

as bestial and black women as depraved." Southern husbands and brothers protected their vulnerable white women from the perceived danger manifest in black bodies.

Butler's choice of Lilith as her black heroine signals the innovation of her project: she writes to upend precious myths that have enabled systems of domination. One of those systems is male supremacy. The Oankali initially thought to awaken a man to lead the humans because they observed that humans were patriarchal. Instead, they chose Lilith, acknowledging the significance of their choice: "I believed that because of the way human genetics were expressed in culture, a human male should be chosen to parent the first group. I think now that I was wrong" (Butler 2012, 110). Lilith is also given power beyond the earthly realm, just like the mythological Lilith. The Oankali gift her with seemingly magical abilities through genetic engineering: "The Oankali had given her information, increased physical strength, enhanced memory, and an ability to control the walls and the suspended animation plants" (120). Unlike the mythological Lilith, who must flee from Adam in order to acknowledge her powers, this Lilith uses her gifts to fulfill her role as the leader of the humans. Lilith's otherness is reframed as strength.

Another system Butler tackles is the naturalized category of the human. Lilith's genetic enhancements cross the boundary between human and nonhuman, but as a result, others distrust her: "Some avoided Lilith because they were afraid of her—afraid she was not human, or not human enough" (2012, 181). When Lilith first learns of the Oankali's crossbreeding plans, she, too, shudders in horror: "Medusa children. Snakes for hair. Nests of night crawlers for eyes and ears" (41). When she learns she is pregnant, she whispers, "But it won't be a human.... It will be a thing. A monster" (246). These scenes of revulsion echo both the monstrosity of the mythical Lilith and modern racist depictions of African American women, using the trope of distrust for technological reproduction that animates science fiction. Whether Frankenstein or Adam Link or some other technological creation, the blurring boundary between human and alien kind startles humans, even as the very category of the human is itself a construct. Distinctions between who counts as human enough were made long before the advent of technology. Early colonizers regarded indigenous persons as "humanoid," nonhuman creatures resembling humans but not requiring any of the rights of humans and therefore justifying their displacement and enslavement. Butler scrutinizes the depths of prejudice by following the lives of Oankali-merged human descendants, her characters returning continually to the question of what constitutes enough humanness to justify fair treatment.

Finally, sexual consent is another major theme of the Lilith mythology that Butler explores. In the Alphabet of Ben Sira, the mythical Lilith refused to submit to Adam's sexual dominance, a choice enslaved black women in the American South did not have. In *Dawn*, Lilith has control of her sexual partners, choosing to accept the Oankali's request to mate. Lilith's choice to merge with an alien species is sharply contrasted with her rejection to sleep with one of her own kind. Soon after reawakening, Lilith meets a human man, but their reunion derails when he suggests that they sleep together. Lilith rejects his advances, but he escalates his proposition with brute force. With this rape scene Butler questions the moral superiority of so-called civilized humans. In this scene, human men are the animals, driven to rape and conquest.

Nevertheless, Butler does not let the Oankali off the hook. They are still bent on colonizing the earth and are coercive in their efforts to merge with humans. The Oankali emit enticing pheromones that make it unbearable for humans to leave their Oankali mates for more than a few days. They encode their sex as consensual because of the deep pleasure they elicit between human mates but blur the lines between consent and seduction. For example, Lilith's Oankali mate inserts his sensory tentacle into Lilith's human mate for the first time while he is unconscious. The Oankali also sterilize the humans without their consent, making them dependent upon the Oankali for survival and contributing to the normalization of child theft.

The possession of land followed by the reproduction of humans is a consistent plot in science fiction because science fiction has, as Greg Grewell (2001, 26) argues, "essentially borrowed from, technologically modernized, and recast the plots, scenes, and tropes of the literature of earthly colonization." Whether colonial narratives appear as local-galaxy exploration or repossession of dystopian-destroyed Earth, sexual control is a colonial tactic. Bringing the theme of sexual consent from the Lilith mythology to the colonizing narratives of science fiction and the legacy of African American enslavement in the Americas, Butler (2012, 178) champions a new vision through the voice of Lilith: "there will be no rape here.... Nobody here is property. Nobody here has the right to the use of anybody else's body."

Donna Haraway (2006, 140) classifies this type of writing as "cyborg writing," that is, writing that blurs the boundaries between human, animal, and machine in order to reimagine a more just society. Butler's

Lilith tests the categorical difference between human and alien species, enjoining the two genetically in a disruption of hierarchies of power. According to Haraway, cyborg writing explores bodily boundaries and social order in order to crack the "matrices of domination" (140). Minority writers have a special stake in disrupting naturalized identities, she contends, because "cyborg writing is about the power to survive, not on the basis of original innocence, but on the basis of seizing the tools to mark the world that marked them as other" (141). The desperate bid for survival from those with black bodies is personified in Butler's Lilith. Mythic memory chose Eve as the pure creation and marked Lilith as the demonic other, yet Butler rejects Eve's naturalized innocence for Lilith's will to survive.

At the heart of the creation myth is what Haraway (2006, 143) calls a "reproductive politics—rebirth without flaw, perfection, abstraction." In these plots, women assume the mother status and experience a loss of identity and autonomy, disappearing as selves in the service of populating the human race. Cyborg writers wrest away these mythologies and with them the structural power animating them. Thus, the story of creation can be retold without the naturalized interpretive framework; as Haraway writes, "the transcendent authorization of interpretation is lost, and with it the ontology grounding 'Western' epistemology" (120). Lilith can refuse to flee. Lilith can be the parent to humanity. The image of Lilith as the demonic mother preying on masculine fear can be replaced with that of a survivor who leads a new race of alien humans.

A wave of afrofuturist science fiction writers have followed from Butler's initial vision, including N. K. Jemisin (2012), Rivers Solomon (2017), Nnedi Okorafor (2011), and Colson Whitehead (2017). These writers employ a liberatory imagination that weaves mythology with scientific fiction in order to envision a world where people of color do not need to struggle to be regarded as human beings, where women do not need to struggle to be regarded as equal. They sit with the challenges to liberation by holding onto a futuristic vision of possibility. Much of the myth of Adam and Eve's creation has been invoked in order to justify systems of oppression. Afrofuturist writing takes those elements of oppression head on by challenging the naturalized assumptions of the story.

The persistence of the creation myth in science fiction and literature writ large lies in its facility to structure our knowledge of the world and ourselves. For minorities who have been fed a particular mythology emphasizing the difference of race or gender or sexuality or body types, the chance to imagine a new mythos means more than a good story. As Jemisin (2012) insists, "Myths tell us what those like us have done, can do, should do. Without myths to lead the way, we hesitate to leap forward. Listen to the wrong myths, and we might even go back a few steps." Butler participates in a long tradition of authors deploying the sacred myth in order to conceptualize new forms of creation. However, Butler does more than transpose her world into a technological future; she upends it and in so doing allows a path for new ways of ordering the world.

Representative Examples in Science Fiction

Arthur, Robert. 1941. "Evolution's End." *Thrilling Wonder Stories* (April).
Asimov, Isaac. 1956. "The Last Question." *Science Fiction Quarterly* (November).
Binder, Eando. 1939–1942. "I Robot." *Amazing Stories* (January 1939–April 1942).
———. (1965) 2014. *Adam Link, Robot*. Rockville, MD: Wildside Press.
Butler, Octavia. (1987) 2012. *Dawn*. New York: Open Road Media.
———. 1988. *Adulthood Rites*. New York: Warner.
———. 1989. *Imago*. New York: Warner.
Lewis, C. S. (1950) 2001. *The Chronicles of Narnia*. London: Harper Collins.
L'Isle-Adam, Auguste Villiers de. (1886) 2013. *The Future Eve*. Raleigh, NC: Baen Books. Kindle edition.
MacDonald, George. (1895) 2012. *Lilith: A Romance*. Charleston, SC: CreateSpace.
Moore, C. L. (1940) 2015. "Fruit of Knowledge." *The Best of C. L. Moore*. New York: Diversion Books.
Rey, Lester del. 1945. "Into Thy Hands." *Astounding Science Fiction* (August).
Shelley, Mary. (1818) 2013. *Frankenstein*. London: Penguin.
Williams, Charles. (1937) 1973. *Descent into Hell*. London: Farber & Farber.

Works Cited

Albeck, Chanoch, and Julius Theodor. 1965. *Midrash Bereshit Rabba: Critical Edition with Notes and Commentary*. Jerusalem: Wahrmann.
Aldiss, Brian W. 1965. "Dr. Peristyle." *New Worlds* 155:125.

Apel, Dora. 2004. *Imagery of Lynching: Black Men, White Women, and the Mob*. New Brunswick, NJ: Rutgers University Press.

Butler, Octavia. 1980. "The Lost Races of Science Fiction." *Transmission*. Repr. in *Garage Magazine* 15 (2018). https://tinyurl.com/SBLPress6708b1.

Dan, Joseph. 1980. "Samael, Lilith, and the Concept of Evil in Early Kabbalah." *AJS Rev* 5:17–40.

Eliade, Mircea. 1963. *Myth and Reality*. New York: Harper & Row.

Grewell, Greg. 2001. "Colonizing the Universe: Science Fictions Then, Now, and in the (Imagined) Future." *Rocky Mountain Review of Language and Literature* 55.2:25–47.

Harari, Yuval. 2017. *Jewish Magic before the Rise of Kabbalah*. Detroit: Wayne State University Press.

Haraway, Donna. 2006. "Cyborg Manifesto: Science, Technology, and Socialist-Feminism in the Late Twentieth Century." Pages 117–58 in *The International Handbook of Virtual Learning Environments*. Edited by Joel Weiss, Jason Nolan, Jeremy Hunsinger, and Peter Trifonas. Dordrecht, the Netherlands: Springer.

Hayles, Katherine. 2008. *How We Became Posthuman: Virtual Bodies in Cybernetics, Literature, and Informatics*. Chicago: University of Chicago Press.

Jemisin, N. K. 2012. "Dreaming Awake." https://tinyurl.com/SBLPress6708b2.

Le Guin, Ursula K. 1979. *The Language of the Night: Essays on Fantasy and Science Fiction*. New York: Putnam.

Levene, Dan, and Gideon Bohak. 2012. "Divorcing Lilith: From the Babylonian Incantation Bowls to the Cairo Genizah." *JJS* 63:197–217.

Levi, Primo. 1988. *Collected Poems*. Translated by Ruth Feldman and Brian Swann. London: Faber & Faber.

Okorafor, Nnedi. 2011. *Who Fears Death*. New York: DAW Books.

Orr, Gili. 2009. "The Medieval Alpha Beta de Ben Sira I ('Rishona'): A Parody on Rabbinic Literature or a Midrashic Commentary on Ancient Proverbs?" PhD diss., University of Amsterdam.

Solomon, Rivers. 2017. *An Unkindness of Ghosts*. New York: Akashic Books.

Stern, David, and Mark J. Mirsky. 1990. *Rabbinic Fantasies: Imaginative Narratives from Classical Hebrew Literature*. Philadelphia: Jewish Publication Society.

Stokes, Mason. 1998. "Someone's in the Garden with Eve: Race, Religion, and the American Fall." *American Quarterly* 50:718–44.

Urbach, Ephraim E. 1975. *The Sages*. Jerusalem: Magnes.

Vilozny, Naama. 2015. "Lilith's Hair and Ashmedai's Horns: Incantation Bowl Imagery in the Light of Talmudic Descriptions." Pages 133–52 in *The Archaeology and Material Culture of the Babylonian Talmud*. Edited by Markham J. Geller. Leiden: Brill.

Ware, Vron. 2015. *Beyond the Pale: White Women, Racism, and History*. London: Verso Books.

Whitehead, Colson. 2016. *The Underground Railroad: A Novel*. New York: Anchor Books.

The Tower of Babel

TOM DE BRUIN

The tower of Babel can be found in Gen 11:1–9, the first book in both the Christian and Jewish canon. For such a short narrative (nine verses, about 250 words in English) that is not referenced anywhere else in the Bible, the tower of Babel has claimed a place in collective imagination far outshining its relatively minor role in the Bible. The story functions as an etiology for linguistic and national diversity and as a warning against human arrogant audacity. The tower of Babel is found in science fiction both as a large literal tower and as a symbol for language and language diversity.

The Tower of Babel in the Bible and Beyond

The narrative of the tower of Babel occurs just after the worldwide flood that Noah and his family survived by building and sailing an ark (Gen 6:9–8:19). Following the flood, Noah cultivated grapes and became drunk (9:20–21). Ham, Noah's eldest son, uncovered his father's nakedness (9:22), which could be a literal act (voyeurism) or a euphemism (incest with either Noah or Noah's wife) (see Embry 2011). Ham and his descendants are cursed for this act, while his brothers are blessed (Gen 9:25–27). Genesis then names an impressive list of descendants for each of Noah's sons, demonstrating how the earth has been repopulated after the deluge (10:1–32). Among Ham's cursed offspring is his grandson Nimrod, the first great warrior on earth, a mighty hunter and king of Babel (10:8–11). Humanity is seen as unified, speaking one language and working together.

The unity of humankind functions as the introduction to the tower of Babel: humans wished to make a name for themselves so that they could remain as one. They decided to build a city and a tower in a plain in the land of Shinar, also known as Mesopotamia, which roughly corresponds with the southern border region of modern-day Iraq and Iran. Gathering here, they did not follow God's command to fill the earth. They chose rather to settle in one location. Making clay bricks and using bitumen as mortar, they (attempted to) build a tower that reached the heavens. In the cosmology of that time, the earth was seen as a flat disc and the heavens/sky as a dome above the sun and moon. Thus the tower is described as very tall but also reaching the domain of God. The tower and its city become a beacon to human autonomy, independence from the divine, and human control of nature through technological advancement. The narrative of the tower is retelling the narrative of civilization: taming the wilderness through human ingenuity. At the same time, the tower shows the human desire for permanence and fame and demonstrates the danger of hubris, pride, and arrogance. Humans wish to have a permanent name; mortals wish to approach the domain of the immortal; lesser beings attempt to become similar to God.

Human endeavor is meaningless in the presence of the almighty God, who easily reverses all of humankind's efforts. Humans wished to ascend to heaven, but God came down from heaven. Although the tower should have reached to heaven, only by descending can God see it. Noting their unity of nation and language, God realized that this tower was only the beginning of unified humanity's enterprise. God claimed that nothing humans wished to do would be impossible now and decided to confuse their languages so that they would not understand one another. Thus God created languages and the various nations. Although humankind wished to remain united, God scattered them over all the earth, and the construction of the city was abandoned. As the final nail in the coffin, while humanity wished to make a great name for themselves, the city received a terrible name. Citing a fictional etymology of the Hebrew verb *balal* (to confuse), the city was named Babel[1]—the same city over which Nimrod was king. The connection between Nimrod and the tower is not made in any explicit way in the Genesis account, but in later Jewish and Christian traditions a link is often made between chapters 10 and 11. Texts dating to the first centuries CE refer to Nimrod as the planner of the tower (e.g., Josephus, *A.J.* 1.113), and "ancient commentators read the two chapters together in

---

1. Babel is more commonly known as Babylon. The Hebrew name for the city is *babel*, which is usually translated as Babylon. Genesis 10–11 are the only places where the city is generally given as Babel in English Bibles. For more on Babylon in the Bible and in science fiction, see the essay by Jason Staples in this volume.

their unanimous identification of Nimrod as the principal architect of the Tower of Babel" (Callahan 2008, 147).

All in all, the tale of the tower of Babel functions as an etiology of nations and languages. I will call this theme the curse of Babel. While the biblical text is scarce on what exactly caused God to curse humanity (see Kugel 1998, 228–34), tradition soon gave some reasons: humanity wished to displace God; human civilization and technology was against the divine plan; humans wished to become creators themselves; humans became arrogant; and so on. It thus also came to be a warning against human endeavor, enterprise, arrogance, and hubris.

The Tower of Babel in Science Fiction

In science fiction the tower of Babel is picked up in various ways, from the very literal building of a New Tower of Babel in Fritz Lang's *Metropolis* (1927) to the crumbling tower of Babel in Josiah Bancroft's *Senlin Ascends* (2018a); from the naming of a planet in the *Star Trek* universe to the naming of the universal translator "Babel Fish" in Douglas Adam's *Hitchhikers Guide to the Galaxy* (1978).

Reviewing religion in science fiction, James McGrath (2016, 25) writes that "science fiction has a reputation for being antagonistic to religion; however, the reputation is not entirely deserved, and even where the description seems to fit, it often represents at best an oversimplification." This is an important note to make when it comes to Babel, as it stands in stark contrast to more reductive statements such as Juan-Luis Montero Fenollós's (2020, 270) "one of the most striking features of contemporary Babel is the total absence of God. The Tower has been laicized." Such a statement is easy enough to counter with an example—see, for instance, the discussion of Chiang's "Tower of Babylon" (1990) below—but working with Fenollós's conclusion can be productive. While clearly there are several works of science fiction that include God in their (re)telling of the tower of Babel, there are many more that replace the "religious" idea of a curse with a more "scientific" reason: a sickness or a machine.

In general, the reception of the tower of Babel has gone in one of two directions. The first takes up the theme of human audacity, enterprise, hubris, and arrogance—often combined with a bit of miscommunication thrown in for good measure. This is the heritage of the tower. The second direction is the curse, and it concerns the way the tower relates to language: imagery from the Genesis narrative, either explicit or implied, is used to discuss linguistics, the role of language, and translation. Naturally, there is some overlap between these two engagements with the tower, yet for the purposes of analysis I will try to keep them separate where possible. In what follows, I will elucidate these two themes, giving some key examples of science fiction that engage with them. I will examine literal towers of Babel first, followed by works that allude to the curse.

Towers of Babel

Several works of science fiction contain a literal tower. Two of these, *Metropolis* (1927) and "Bible Stories for Adults, No. 20: The Tower" (Morrow 1994), transpose the tower of Babel in time, using the imagery of the tower to discuss contemporary culture. For both of these the arrogant tower becomes a beacon of the upper class, and confusion of tongues allows for a discussion of the plight of the working class. Two others, "Tower of Babylon" (Chiang 1990) and *Senlin Ascends* (Bancroft 2018a), take place in a (pseudo)-ancient Near East. These two narratives use the tower more as a backdrop for their narratives and do less to develop the dominant themes of the tower.

Fritz Lang's 1927 dystopian *Metropolis*, written by Thea von Harbou, tells a tale of a futuristic divided society. Above ground live a class of elite industrialists, below masses of oppressed workers. The crowning glory of the upper-class city is the New Tower of Babel, which functions as a city hall. The narrative revolves around Freder's (the son of the city's master) pity for the workers, first piqued by his fascination or love for the working-class Maria. She functions as a prophet of sorts, preaching to the masses about the tower of Babel:

> Today I will tell you the legend of the Tower of Babel.... "Come, let us build us a tower whose top may reach unto the stars! And on the top of the tower we will write the words: Great is the world and its Creator. And great is Man!" ... but the minds that had conceived the Tower of Babel could not build it. The task was too great. So they hired hands for wages. But the *hands* that built the Tower of Babel knew nothing of the dream of the *brain* that had conceived it.

This speech, delivered on title cards as the film is silent, is intercut with images of a tower of Babel that does not look like the art deco industrialist building in the upper city but more like Peter Brueghel the Elder's *Little Tower of Babel* (1563). The tower of legend is thus not meant to be the New Tower. As Maria thus mixes the legend with the dystopian reality, her imagery refers, on the one hand, to the New Tower as it was dreamed up and built by the upper class and, at the same time, includes biblical references. Introducing the biblical narrative shows the major issues with the society of Metropolis and indeed with a classist society: unlike in Genesis, those who suggest building the tower will not actually be the ones who build it. This critique is strengthened in the following sequence, where we see imagery of the "brain" seeing a glorious tower, with beautifully written "BABEL" appearing on screen, followed by images of six thousand bald men, reminiscent of Egyptian slaves, toiling away at the building of the tower. They shout "BABEL" three times, in letters dripping with blood, then Maria continues:

> One man's hymns of praise became other men's curses. People spoke the same language but could not understand each other.

This class divide leads to a second innovation from the biblical narrative: rather than a confusion of languages, there is a confusion of meaning. As the workers rise up and storm the one dreaming up the tower, we see that the meaning of the tower depends on the audience. For the "brain" (the elite), the word Babel is a word of praise; for the "hands" (the lower class), a curse. The tower remains unfinished, and when the words "Great is the world and its Creator. And great is man" appear, the film interacts with the biblical narrative in a third way. The tower, a symbol of human enterprise, becomes a symbol for humanity's incapability. Exploitative class division causes the downfall of human achievement.

A second work that contains a literal tower of Babel is James Morrow's "Bible Stories for Adults, No. 20: The Tower." This story is extremely similar to the biblical one, but the curse is the complete opposite. It was published in 1994 in *The Magazine of Fantasy and Science Fiction* and was nominated for a Locus Award in 1995. Morrow's short story takes on the major themes of Genesis but reimagines them in 1980s New York. It centers on Michael Prete, the secretary of New York industrialist Daniel Nimrod—an obvious caricature of prominent business tycoon Donald Trump.[2] Prete

---

2. Indeed, in the postscript Morrow explains his preparation for writing this short story "I visited New York City, did some field work at the Trump Tower, came

sets up a meeting between Nimrod and the anonymous renter of the penthouse in Nimrod Tower. The tower itself is a bastion of multiculturality, from the "multiethnic security force" to the "polyglot shops" (Haynes 2002, 170), an obvious allusion to the dispersion of Babel. The renter in the penthouse introduces themself as the "Lord God of Hosts, the King of the Universe, the Architect of Reality, the Supreme Being, and so on" (Morrow 2014, 63). The tower, then, quite literally reaches to heaven. After exchanging gifts (Nimrod gives God a signed copy of his book *Paydirt: How to Make Your Fortune in Real Estate*; God signs a copy of the NIV), Nimrod tries and fails to make a deal to buy Saturn. Once God gets control of the conversation, the real reason for meeting becomes apparent: God is offended by Nimrod's vulgar arrogance: the plans for Nimrod Gorge and Nimrod Mountain were the final straw; again the allusion to humanity making a name for itself is obvious. When Nimrod refuses to back down, God brings up the topic of the biblical Babel. Nimrod complains how hard languages has made making deals, and God replies "I sympathize with your frustration.... In fact, there is probably only one thing worse than not being able to understand a person.... Being able to understand them completely" (Morrow 2014, 76). This is Morrow's reimagined curse of Babel, complete and utter understanding of the self and the other. Without "semantic doubt," realizing that "nothing is being lost in translation," civilization quickly falls apart as the downtrodden masses realize their lot (Morrow 2014, 83). Nimrod ends up like most Americans, operating "at a Stone Age level of efficiency" (Morrow 2014, 83). He is roaming New Jersey, haven stolen a hunting bow, looking for deer. Nimrod and humanity are back where they started in Gen 10: he is a mighty hunter, and they speak a single language. All in all, Morrow is critiquing American sensibilities of the 1980s, where diversity and cultural differences are imagined to be what is holding back societal development and unity. Babel's curse is in fact a blessing, as translation issues, giving the other the benefit of the doubt, and people not realizing the truth about themselves and their situations are exactly what is keeping society stable.

Both of these narratives use the tower of Babel to discuss class structures and social stability. Two other, more recent works also contain very literal towers: Ted Chiang's "Tower of Babylon" (1990) and Josiah Ban-

---

home, turned on the computer, kicked my cynicism into overdrive, and got to work" (Morrow 1994, 126).

croft's *Senlin Ascends* (2018a).[3] Bancroft's debut novel *Senlin Ascends* (originally self-published in 2013) tells of the eponymous protagonist's search for his wife in the tower.[4] In the narrative Senlin discovers that the iconic tower is not as majestic as it is made out to be. In this book Bancroft explores the topic of miscommunication through the imagining of the various levels of the towers as separate Ringdoms, which, though speaking a common tongue, have widely diverging cultural institutions. There is also a hint of another theme: as Senlin searches for his wife and struggles against the bureaucracy, customs, and laws of the Ringdoms, the futility of human endeavor becomes fronted.

The theme of futility is also the topic of Ted Chiang's 1990, "Tower of Babylon," winner of the 1991 Nebula. The novelette tells the tale of Hillalum, one of the builders of the ancient tower, just as they are reaching the vault of heaven. Throughout the narrative there are frequent discussions about whether God will approve of the building of the tower. Most builders and inhabitants of the tower are wildly optimistic, but Hillalum's constant doubt is foreboding. In the end, he is the first to break through the vault of heaven, only to discover he is back on earth. Humanity has created its greatest achievement: a tower from heaven to earth, which is ultimately futile:

> It was clear now why Yahweh had not struck down the tower, had not punished men for wishing to reach beyond the bounds set for them: for the longest journey would merely return them to the place whence they'd come. Centuries of their labor would not reveal to them any more of Creation than they already knew. Yet through their endeavor, men would glimpse the unimaginable artistry of Yahweh's work, in seeing how ingeniously the world had been constructed. By this construction, Yahweh's work was indicated, and Yahweh's work was concealed. Thus would men know their place. (Chiang 1990, 106)

---

3. There are more examples of short works that contain a literal tower that engage less with themes from the biblical myth. Better known among these include Robert F. Young's "Project Hi-Rise" (1978), which is about a union strike among the builders of the tower of Babel. God, it seems, has sent an organizer who incites the workers to strike, and when no resolution can be found, the building is abandoned. Another example is David D. Levine's "Babel Probe" (2007), which is about a probe sent back in time to examine the building of the tower.

4. The narrative of Senlin is further developed in the Books of Babel series (Bancroft 2018b, 2019, 2021).

Although the building of the tower may seem futile, Hillalum does see a point to the construction. Paradoxically, though they did not see more of creation than they already had, humanity now understands creation and its creator better. At the same time, the tower demonstrates the vanity of human pride.

Chiang's imagery of the tower as a testament to human vanity fits into a long tradition. In this tradition, towers are often seen as places where humans interfere with nature in some way, going beyond humanity's place in the world. These towers are often not specifically called Babel, but there is an implicit link to the narrative in this thematic reception. This theme is most obvious in film, a classic example of which is James Whale's *Frankenstein* (1931), where the creature is raised up to an opening in the top of the tower of the castle. More recent films imagine the tower as skyscrapers. The Tyrell Building (which is pyramid-shaped) is the place where synthetic humans are designed in *Blade Runner* (1982). In *Ghostbusters* (1984), the tower is a modern ziggurat meant to summon an apocalyptic demon. The tower houses the "Spiritual Switchboard" in *Freejack* (1992), which keeps the minds of the deceased alive until they can be put into a new host body. Finally, the robot uprising in *I, Robot* (2004) features robots designed and built in the US Robotics tower. In all of these examples, the tower hosts humans interfering with the limitations of humanity and mortality.

The Curse of Babel

The tower of Babel is literally present in some works, but the curse of Babel is a much more dominant theme in science fiction. The list of works that discuss language and confusion, and thus allude to Genesis, is seemingly endless. I will discuss some key examples, chosen because they are more explicitly linked to Babel or because they are well-known texts in the science fiction canon.

When it comes to popular science fiction, we cannot ignore what M. Keith Booker and Anne-Marie Thomas (2009, 9) call "the most important single phenomenon in the history of science fiction": *Star Trek*. Five television episodes split over three series engage with Babel: "Journey to Babel" (*The Original Series*, 1967), "Babel" (*Deep Space Nine*, 1993), and "Babel One," "United," and "The Aenar" (*Enterprise*, 2005).[5] The first and last are

---

5. The planet Babel features in a number of *Star Trek* transmedia publications; examples include Christopher Bennett's Enterprise novel *Tower of Babel* (2014); the "Return to Babel" quest in the *Star Trek Online* massively multiplayer online role-

strongly related, with the *Deep Space Nine* episode engaging most strongly with the curse. In "Journey to Babel," the original crew are taking a large group of nonhuman ambassadors to peace talks on the planet Babel. The theme of unification and dispersion is the most evident link to Genesis, as Daniel Bernardi (1997, 209) summarizes: "not unlike the biblical story, the Enterprise's journey to Babel, its mission to unite scattered races, is marred by the confusion of tongues—in this case, by peculiar-looking aliens with conflicting, disruptive, and sometimes violent motivations." As such this episode—and indeed the image of the united pre-Babel world—fits perfectly into Star Trek's humanist metanarrative of a unified humanity that is not marred by sexism or racism. The three-part *Enterprise* episode in essence reimagines the original episode and propagates very similar sensibilities and aesthetics. *Deep Space Nine*'s "Babel" takes a completely different route. A viral epidemic caused by a sabotaged food replicator is taking the station by storm: people are developing aphasia and dying from the accompanying fever.

Deep Space Nine shows a trend in some science fiction retellings of Babel: the curse is replaced by a more scientific "MacGuffin"[6] (Gross and Altman 1996, 43). In *Deep Space Nine* it is a virus that causes aphasia, but machines are also a possibility. For example, in the futuristic *Batman Beyond* animated series (known as *Batman of the Future* outside of the United States), the deaf villain Shriek makes a machine that causes speech to sound like gibberish ("Babel" 2000).[7] In Octavia Butler's Hugo and Locus award-winning short story "Speech Sounds" (1983), the narrator is not so sure about the cause for the worldwide communication-inhibiting pandemic. She calls it an "illness" but does not seem to know what it is. It

---

playing game (2010); and William Leisner's "A Less Perfect Union" (2008). The last details the naming of the planet after "the Biblical story in which the people of the Earth, all speaking a common language, had worked together to reach the heavens" (Leisner 2008, 76).

6. A MacGuffin is "any situation, goal, or device that sets a story in motion. [It is a]n element of a story that drives the plot, and about which the characters care a great deal, but that ultimately has little to do with the main action, story, or theme of the work and holds little interest for the audience" (Kroon 2010, 400).

7. Within the DC franchise, the comic book series *Justice League of America* ran a four-part series entitled *Tower of Babel*, which was published shortly after this *Batman Beyond* episode. In this series ecoterrorist Ra's al Ghul has a machine that does causes dyslexia rather than aphasia. Societal collapse ensues (Waid, Porter, and Geraci 2000a, 2000b, 2000c, 2000d).

could have been "the Soviets" or "a new virus, a new pollutant, radiation, divine retribution" (Butler 1983, 32). The illness had incapacitated people so fast that no one had time to find its cause. Although the first options the narrator names are scientific, the all-encompassing nature of the illness opens the door for a supernatural cause as well: a new curse of Babel.[8] In these narratives of aphasia, the role of language in culture and communication is discussed. Mirroring the curse's dispersion and fracturing of humanity, science fiction shows the precarity of human civilization by hypothesizing the removal of our ability to communicate. Societal collapse generally ensues.

Two well-known science fiction novels engage strongly with the concepts of language and the curse of Babel: Neal Stephenson's *Snow Crash* (1992) and Samuel R. Delany's *Babel-17* (1966). Both books are highly theoretical in the way they deal with language and linguistics; both see language as an infection, yet do so in completely different ways. Whereas Delany builds on the, for science fiction, very productive Sapir-Whorf hypothesis of linguistic relativity,[9] Stephenson seems to prefer a more universalist approach. As I will examine Delany's *Babel-17* in depth below, a short description of how he imagines the infectious influence of the titular language is useful. When the protagonist learns Babel-17, she discovers that she can think and analyze the world much more efficiently; at the same time, she develops a form of schizophrenia and becomes the saboteur of her own mission. Thus, in *Babel-17*, the *learning* of a new language has the power to change the way someone fundamentally envisions the world and indeed the self. Looking at *Snow Crash* in more detail now, it will become clear that it is not the learning of the language that infects but simply seeing it. Thus language is not a cultural or social construct but, as

---

8. Other contemporary works are more than willing to engage with the supernatural. In Syfy's show *Warehouse 13*, the protagonists use stones from the tower of Babel to communicate in a language that a hostile AI cannot understand ("13.1" 2010), and in the Disney Channel's *So Weird* a stone from the tower of Babel curses people with aphasia ("Babel" 2001).

9. See, for example, the construction of purpose-built languages in George Orwell's *1984* (1949) and Jack Vance's *The Languages of Pao* (1958), the "rhetoric diseases" that lead to nationalism and other -isms in Doris Lessing's *The Sentimental Agents in the Volyen Empire* (1983), the highly Saussurian semiotics of the Ariekei language in China Miéville's *Embassytown* (2011), or the temporally circular language of the heptopods in *Arrival* (2016) based on Ted Chiang's "Story of Your Life" (1998). Dunja Mohr's (2009) discussion of utopian and dystopian fiction is useful.

Walter Benn Michaels (2013, 68) refers to it, "a biological entity"; indeed, human bodies are "affected by 'information' they can't read."

Stephenson's *Snow Crash* describes a twenty-first-century, dystopian Los Angeles. Since the plot is too complicated to detail at length here, I will focus only on how Stephenson reimagines the tower of Babel and its curse, putting aside his critique of "contemporary consumer capitalism" (Booker and Thomas 2009, 106) and his discussion of "posthuman dangers" (Haney 2006, 128). The premise of the book is that the titular drug is causing people to babble: "ba ka na zu ma lay ga no ma la aria ma na po no a ab zu" (Stephenson 1992, 336). The drug takes on various forms, from the traditional injectable to a visual bitmap. In this visual form, the drug does not need physical access to a person: in the Metaverse, a simulated VR world where avatars of people interact, seeing an image of the drug will cause the user to "crash." There is no difference between the physical or the VR version. This is key to the plot: the virus has a biological and an informational infection method. It is revealed that the drug is actually a form of (computer) code that hacks the human brain. The language works on "a deep, pure level beyond ambiguity, mediation, and metaphor" (Kelly 2018, 70). The babbling is the speaking of a protolanguage, which is biologically defined: "a tongue that's based in the deep structures of the brain, that everyone shares. These structures consist of basic neural circuits that have to exist in order to allow our brains to acquire higher languages" (Stephenson 1992, 369). This is where Stephenson takes on a decidedly different view of language from that of Delany. Stephenson's postmodern writing demonstrates a disengaging of the link between signifiers and signifieds. Michaels elucidates this with one of Stephenson's own metaphors: "Like 'semen,' as Stephenson puts it, it's a 'carrier of information,' but, also like semen, or like a virus or the genetic code, it's not a carrier of meaning" (Michaels 2013, 124). In other words, the reaction to the carrier (i.e., getting pregnant and producing a biologically similar child) is not dependent on understanding the carrier. Words have a universalist power that is not dependent on the person hearing, speaking, or thinking them.

The protolanguage that hacks the brain is the language of Babel: Sumerian. Because this language runs on the brain like a computer program, it allowed the priest-kings to completely control the rest of society—there was no space for innovation. The fall of the tower of Babel, and thus of the mother language, was an actual historical event, instigated by the god/hacker Enki. He wrote a countervirus that caused the brain to no longer process Sumerian. This "Babel/Infopocalypse" was the beginning of human consciousness, of rationality, of civilization. In an attempt to maintain a pre-Babel society, the cult of Asherah—who is actually the biblical Eve—developed temple prostitution to spread a biological countervirus, akin to herpes. Judaism was the first to counter Asherah, with the creation of the torah and the sanctity of the written word. The command to "make an exact copy of me and read it every day" is evidence that Judaism is a "self-propagating entity … the Torah is like a virus" (Stephenson 1992, 374, 214). While kosher laws were a guard against the biological virus of Asherah, care for the written word was a guard against informational contamination. Although this portrayal of Judaism may be called "a powerful rereading of Jewish evolution and its influence on the birth of civilization" (Porush 1994, 567), Stephenson succumbs to supersessionism: "With its rigid adherence to laws stored in a temple, administered by priestly types vested with civil authority, it resembled the old Sumerian system, and was just as stifling. The ministry of Jesus Christ was an effort to break Judaism out of this condition" (Stephenson 1992, 375). However, it seems that Jesus's innovations were not without dangers: early Christian practices of glossolalia are seen to be viral outbreaks due to Christians "flouting [Jewish] tradition" (376). Stephenson's constant engagement with language, in both ancient and contemporary contexts, "forces its readership to question their basic assumptions about communication" (Hubble, Filtness, and Norman 2013, 67). The reader must constantly reevaluate how words and meaning relate, yet, as Nicholas Kelly (2018, 70) writes, "of course, Stephenson's fantasy of unmediated speech (in the form of code or some pre-Babelian language) is fantasy only." Although Stephenson posits a protolanguage where speaking and doing are innately the same, he deconstructs this with the interpretation of the fall of the tower of Babel. Humans may be little more than glorified computers, but "there is some defense against viral programming— … humans may choose their own programming, and … they may inoculate themselves" (Booker and Thomas 2009, 284). Thus, Stephenson's interpretation of Babel as the beginning of human consciousness and rationality, precisely because higher-level languages imply thought, thoroughly reinterprets the biblical story. The curse of Babel is, in fact, a blessing.

Samuel R. Delany, *Babel-17*

While Stephenson engages overtly with the tower in *Snow Crash*, Samuel R. Delany deals more extensively with its major theme: language and nations. "Race has," as Isiah Lavender III (2007, 197) aptly notes, "always been of concern to [science fiction], even—maybe especially—when it does not know that that was what it is talking about."[10] The tower of Babel and its curse fits this concern for race extremely well, and a few of the works discussed above engage overtly with issues of race and nationality. Thus although—besides in the name of the eponymous language—Delany does not refer to the tower of Babel, the work itself is a direct engagement with the heritage of Babel from the point of view of race and language. It is therefore extremely suitable for a longer discussion here.

Published in 1966, *Babel-17* is one of Delany's earliest novels and the first to win him a major science fiction award. It won the Nebula in 1967 and was a finalist for the Hugo. Writing just after the golden age (1937–late 1950s) of science fiction, Delany is often seen as "the first African-American science fiction writer" (Delany 1998), which—though not entirely correct—shows the importance of Delany's work and how rare African American authors were in the "largely Jewish, highly liberal" science fiction community of the time (Delany 1998). Although written in the 1960s, *Babel-17* resonates with many contemporary critical theories of race and gender; as L. H. Stallings (2015, 228) argues, it "precedes … new materialisms in feminism, Afrofuturism, and critical race theory." As such Delany is often included, together with musicians such as Sun-Ra and activists such as Sojourner Truth, in lists of influential black speculative thinkers, often called Afrofuturists.[11]

Delany is also representative of a shift in science fiction in the 1960s and 1970s, where a group of authors moved their emphasis to the "'soft' sciences (such as psychology and sociology) rather than the 'hard' physical sciences (physics, biology, mathematics)" (Higgins and Duncan 2009, 129). These so-called New Wave writers "sought to instill science fiction with greater social and political relevance, more mature subject matter, and higher literary qual-

---

10. The inherent link between science fiction and race is further emphasised by the first sentence of Lavender's article: "The blunt thesis underlying Afrofuturism is that *all* black cultural production in the New World *is* sf" (Lavender 2007, 187).

11. See, for example, Jayna Brown's (2021) analysis of utopian thinking in black thinking and culture. For considerations on how the concept of Afrofuturism is applicable to Delany, see also Stallings 2015 and Lavender 2007.

ity than what they perceived to be the case in Golden Age science fiction" (Booker and Thomas 2009, 327). This shift to the soft sciences is clear in *Babel-17*, where, although the book is a space opera containing war, action, spies, aliens, various futuristic technologies, danger, and space battles,

> Delany has worked a number of important transformations upon the simple space-opera formula. His protagonist, for example, is not a macho male roustabout, but rather a female poet. The most dangerous weapon in the work is not an SF gadget but a mysterious invented language. The real villain of the piece is not a mad scientist or an evil empire but rather the inability of one group of human beings to communicate with another group. (Malmgren 1993, 7)

Communication and language, then, become the key theme and plot device to the novel. In this extended discussion of *Babel-17*, I will summarize the work and demonstrate how it engages with the reception of the tower of Babel in Western history. I will look at how Delany engages with the curse of Babel to discuss and deconstruct Western rationalism and epistemology from the point of view of race.

In a universe besieged by war between the Alliance and the Invaders, Rydra Wong is the most famous poet of her age. She is enlisted by the Alliance to decode a series of radio messages in an unknown language, Babel-17. From the get-go, it is clear that Wong is a gifted communicator with a knack for languages. Having assembled a crew and after some travels, Wong discovers that she has learned the language; thinking in Babel-17, she experiences the world differently:

> She looked down at the ... not "webbing," but rather a three-particle vowel differential, each particle of which defined one stress of the three-way tie, so that the weakest points in the mesh were identified when the total sound of the differential reached its lowest point. By breaking the threads at these points, she realized, the whole web would unravel. Had she flailed at it, and not named it in this new language, it would have been more than secure enough to hold her.... Thinking in Babel-17 was like suddenly seeing all the way down through water to the bottom of a well that a moment ago you'd thought was only a few feet deep. She reeled with vertigo. (Delany [1966] 2009, 96)

This scene, the first where Wong is able to experience the world through Babel-17, underlies the entire book. Shifting to this new language shows

Wong a "a new reality in which obstacles are overcome, dangers neutralized, conflicts resolved" (Malmgren 1993, 10). The language is perfectly exact and fundamentally analytical, so much so that "it almost assures you technical mastery of any situation you look at" (Delany [1966] 2009, 188). The language thus is the epitome of objectivity and can be placed in a long Western tradition of a "search for a perfect language" (Eco 1995). Ria Cheyne (2008, 387) discusses how there has been a Western desire from the seventeenth century onward "to rediscover the pre-Babel language" (and thus God's plan for humanity), "a universal and ... philosophical language" that would "mirror reality." Delany's Babel-17 represents this language. Admittedly, it has some peculiarities: the word for the Alliance is literally "one-who-has-invaded" (Delany [1966] 2009, 188); but these appear to be on purpose. The language has been weaponized in this way. Far more disconcerting is the discovery that Babel-17 lacks the first- and second-person. The language is absolutely objective, without any allowance of the subject or subjectivity. As such, it seems to be the zenith of Western epistemology, a completely objective form of thought and communication.

As Wong learns more of Babel-17, the powers and dangers of the language become clearer. Delany places the power of language in the context of "double consciousness" (Rutledge 2000, 132). The term, first used by William Du Bois in 1903 (Pittman 2016), is used to describe the way a person can survive in two cultures by developing two consciousnesses (Lavender 2007, 196). Delany mixes this with linguistic theory, when Wong explains, "when you learn another tongue, you learn the way another people see the world, the universe" (Delany [1966] 2009, 20). Key to this developing of multiple ways of seeing and interacting with the world is the concept of subjectivity and self-criticism. Epistemologically both ways of seeing the world cannot be simultaneously true. Babel-17, however, is a language that does not allow subjectivity or the concept of the self: "The lack of an 'I' precludes any self-critical process. In fact it cuts out any awareness of the symbolic process at all—which is the way we distinguish between reality and our expression of reality" (Delany [1966] 2009, 188). In Babel-17 thinking or speaking is not simply putting one's experience of reality into words; it *is* reality. The language, then, overrides the self, it "overlays his or her reality with an alien perception" and ultimately causes Wong to unwittingly sabotage her own mission (Lavender 2007, 196). Babel-17 does not allow double consciousness but overwrites one's culture with the dominant one. Thus the language and the aliens are figured as white, seen in their "desire for power and territory" and their language "that forcibly initiates people into the alien culture and controls them by eliminating their identities" (Lavender 2007, 196). As such Delany puts post-Enlightenment Western thinking up for grabs. The desire for objectivity itself, or in the terms of Babel, the desire for a uniform humanity, seems to be fundamentally problematic.

Yet Delany's book contains an ambiguous relationship to objectivity and unification. The work begins with an epigraph attributed to Mario Pei:

> Nowhere is civilization so perfectly mirrored as in speech. If our knowledge of speech, or the speech itself, is not yet perfect, neither is civilization. (Delany [1966] 2009, vii)

This quote demonstrates another key part of Delany's interaction with the tower of Babel. As Western civilization yearned for a perfect language, they also yearned for the perfect civilization. Dunja Mohr (2009, 227) argues that a Western desire for a pre-Babel language was inherently linked to the desire for utopia: "utopias focused on the retrieval of the imaginary and idealized protolanguage erased in the biblical Babylonian confusion, envisioning that the different languages symbolically originating at the tower of Babel coalesced into one language of linguistic excellence everyone can understand." The inverse is also true, with nefarious, constructed languages playing a large role in dystopian novels (229). This strong connection between language and utopia is similarly present in Pei's epigraph above and underlines an ambivalence in *Babel-17*. As Wong learns Babel-17, she loses more and more control of herself. Having lost her double consciousness and having become forcibly initiated into the alien culture, she battles this loss of selfhood. In this she reflects "the classic battle of the mid- to late 1960s in which minorities successful in the mainstream culture had to fight the charge of the larger Black community that they were losing the double consciousness battle" (Rutledge 2000, 132). Babel-17 is clearly not Pei's perfect language that will bring about the perfect civilization; the falling of the tower of Babel is still not reversed. Together with Butcher, a native speaker of the language who becomes her lover, Wong rediscovers her selfhood within Babel-17 in relation to him; together they improve the language: "we have Babel-17 corrected—perhaps I should call it Babel-18—which is the best tool conceivable to [stop the war]" (Delany [1966] 2009, 192). This new language, which presumably has the analytical strengths of Babel-17 but also contains the self and subjectivity, it seems, *does* have the power to create perfection.

The important question arises as to what exactly Wong and Butcher have done to correct Babel-17. Stallings (2015, 237) has recently argued that this is related to their identities as poet and criminal: "The artist and criminal might be said to be products of the environment or society, but the criminal is constructed out of human ethics and the artists out of aesthetics." Wong is portrayed throughout the novel as a gifted communicator—especially in understanding the Other. When she gathers her crew together to form a rather literal organism with a nervous system, a brain, nose, ear, and eye, "she serves as the Imagination of the assemblage" (Malmgren 1993, 11). Butcher, on the other hand, is the archetypical criminal and indeed responsible for the attacks on the Alliance that sparked the entire plot. The language Babel-17 is strongly related to both of these functions. The purely objective and analytical nature of the language precludes any imagination or poetics: "with intelligence, there can be no building or creating: it can only be for gathering and observing for purposes of colonization, domination, and control by an institute or agency" (Stallings 2015, 231). Butcher, it turns out, is solely a criminal because of Babel-17. Having no concept of the self and no self-critical process, he has no concept of ethics; he simply does. Babel-17 functions as "a preset program for the Butcher to become a criminal and saboteur" (Delany [1966] 2009, 215)—not just for Butcher but for any speaker of the language. Thus Wong and Butcher represent issues with the analytical language: imagination and ethics.[12] Pure objective analysis does not allow for creation or for ethical reflection.

Delany's perfect Babel-18 must then include creativity and ethics. Just as *Rydra Wong* helped Butcher differentiate between *right and wrong* (the similarity between her name and phrase must be intentional), Babel-18 demonstrates the need for ethics to guide objective enquiry, as Stallings (2015, 232) points out: "ethics have been created and ignored by scientific communities for centuries; whether it is scientific racism, eugenics, or biological terrorism." Rationalism and Western epistemology, where knowledge is the result of objective scientific enquiry, is therefore flawed. It is, just like

---

12. Stallings (2015, 232–33) argues that aesthetics and ethics are opposed forces, being linked to the arts and science, respectively. She argues that Delany wishes to argue for a new mode of enquiry based on aesthetics rather than ethics. My analysis of the text takes a different focus. While, in my view, Delany does question some ethical constructs (e.g., monogamy; see Stallings 2015, 236), ethics itself does not appear to be the issue.

Butcher, "a preset program" to become criminal. Babel-17 hearkens back to the tower of Babel, a building created in a narrative revolving around dubious ethics, a building that was made simply because humans could, a bastion to a unified and *specifically uniform* humanity. Babel-18 represents a post-Babel language, one of difference and diversity; yet it is also a pre-Babel language, one of unity. The inclusion of poetics, symbolized by Wong's skill in understanding the Other, allows for the language to "bridge the gap between Self and Other" (Malmgren 1993, 12). As "a multicultural broker of acceptance, tolerance, open-mindedness, and difference," she models how humanity can use language to "break through the historical conditioning of a racialized America" (Lavender 2007, 197). The perfect civilization built on the perfect language becomes a combination of pre-Babel unity and post-Babel diversity. As Mohr (2009, 236) argues, "perfected communication that does not erase but multiplies perceptions is then ultimately his utopian goal."

All in all, the tower of Babel plays a variety of roles in science fiction. The biblical themes of unity and dispersion, language and civilization, human endeavor and arrogance are productive in various ways. The physical tower of Babel stands to illuminate class structures and social stability, as we see in *Metropolis*. Yet it also brings up the dangers of human arrogance and hubris, as Ted Chiang's "Tower of Babylon" highlights. The curse of Babel reminds us how fragile civilization is. "Speech Sounds" and *Deep Space Nine* show that the smallest interference in humanity's ability to communicate can destroy society almost overnight. Finally, in *Snow Crash* and *Babel-17*, Babel becomes a fruitful tool to discuss the role of language in engaging with and envisioning the world. Delany's *Babel-17* shows the power science fiction has as a lens to reimagine reality. As Booker and Thomas (2009, 126) note, Delany "demonstrates the promise of sf as a vehicle for the representation of cultural perspectives that differ from the white, male, middle-class mainstream of Western culture." Returning to Lavender's (2007, 197) claim that "race has always been of concern to [science fiction]," Delany's vision of the difference-embracing, ethically driven Babel-18 shows a different tower of Babel, one through we which we may be "encouraged and enabled to refigure the world in which we live … and maybe even change it."

Representative Examples in Science Fiction

"13.1." 2010. *Warehouse 13*. Directed by Chris Fisher. Written by Ian Stokes. Syfy.

"The Aenar." 2005. *Star Trek: Enterprise.* Directed by David Straiton. Written by Michael Sussman and André Bormanis. UPN.

Bancroft, Josiah. 2018a. *Senlin Ascends.* Books of Babel 1. London: Orbit Books.

———. 2018b. *Arm of the Sphinx.* Books of Babel 2. London: Orbit Books.

———. 2019. *The Hod King.* Books of Babel 3. London: Orbit Books.

———. 2021. *The Fall of Babel.* Books of Babel 4. London: Orbit Books.

"Babel." 1993. *Star Trek: Deep Space Nine.* Directed by Paul Lynch. Written by Michael McGreevey and Naren Shankar. Syndicated.

"Babel." 2000. *Batman Beyond.* Directed by Curt Geda. Written by Stan Berkowitz. Kids' WB.

"Babel." 2001. *So Weird.* Directed by Pat Williams. Written by Richard Clark. Disney Channel.

"Babel One." 2005. *Star Trek: Enterprise.* Directed by David Straiton. Written by Michael Sussman and André Bormanis. UPN.

Babylon 5. 1993–1998. Created by J. Michael Straczynski. Syndicated.

Bennett, Christopher L. 2014. *Tower of Babel.* Star Trek Enterprise: Rise of the Federation 2. New York: Pocket Books.

Blade Runner. 1982. Directed by Ridley Scott. Written by Hampton Fancher and David Peoples. Warner Bros.

Butler, Octavia. 1983. "Speech Sounds." *Asimov's Science Fiction Magazine* (December):26–41.

Chiang, Ted. 1990. "Tower of Babylon." *Omni* (November):50–68.

Delany, Samuel R. (1966) 2009. *Babel-17.* SF Masterworks. London: Gollancz.

Elwood, Roger. 1990. *The Wandering.* Old Tappan, NJ: Power Books.

Frankenstein. 1931. Directed by James Whale. Universal.

Freejack. 1992. Directed by Geoff Murphy. Written by Ronald Shusett and Stuart Oken. Warner Bros.

Ghostbusters. 1984. Directed by Ivan Reitman. Written by Dan Aykroyd and Harold Ramis. Columbia.

Hall, Tom. 1993. *Doom.* MSDOS. iD Software.

The Hitchhiker's Guide to the Galaxy. 1978. Written by Douglas Adams. BBC Radio 4.

I, Robot. 2004. Directed by Alex Proyas. Written by Jeff Vintar and Akiva Goldsman. Twentieth Century Fox.

"Journey to Babel." 1967. *Star Trek: The Original Series.* Directed by Joseph Pevney. Written by D. C. Fontana. NBC.

Leisner, William. 2008. "A Less Perfect Union." Pages 1–172 in *Infinity's Prism* by William Leisner, Christopher L. Bennett, and James Swallow. Star Trek Myriad Universes. New York: Pocket Books.

Levine, David D. 2007. "Babel Probe." *Darker Matter* 1.

Lewis, C. S. 1945. *That Hideous Strength: A Modern Fairy-Tale for Grown-Ups*. Cosmic Trilogy. London: Bodley Head.

Metropolis. 1927. Directed by Fritz Lang. Written by Thea von Harbou. Universum Film.

Morrow, James. 1994. "Bible Stories for Adults, No. 20: The Tower." *The Magazine of Fantasy and Science Fiction* (June):112–26.

Orwell, George. 1949. *1984*. London: Secker & Warburg.

Pratchett, Terry. 1976. *The Dark Side of the Sun*. Gerrards Cross: Colin Smythe.

Star Trek Online. 2010. Windows. Atari.

Stephenson, Neal. 1992. *Snow Crash*. New York: Bantam.

"United." 2005. *Star Trek: Enterprise*. Directed by David Straiton. Written by Michael Sussman and André Bormanis. UPN.

Waid, Mark, Howard Porter, and Drew Geraci. 2000a. "Tower of Babel 1:Survival of the Fittest." *JLA* 43. DC Comics.

———. 2000b. "Tower of Babel 2: Seven Little Indians." *JLA* 44. DC Comics.

———. 2000c. "Tower of Babel 3: Protected by the Cold." *JLA* 45. DC Comics.

———. 2000d. "Tower of Babel 4: Harsh Words." JLA 46. DC Comics.

Wright, John C. 2019. *Nowither: The Drowned World*. The Unwithering Realm 2. Superversive Press.

———. 2019. *Somewhither*. The Unwithering Realm 1. Superversive Press.

Young, Robert F. 1978. "Project Hi-Rise." *The Magazine of Fantasy and Science Fiction* (November):22–32.

Works Cited

Arrival. 2016. Directed by Denis Villeneuve. Written by Eric Heisserer. Paramount.

Bernardi, Daniel. 1997. "'Star Trek' in the 1960s: Liberal-Humanism and the Production of Race." *Science Fiction Studies* 24:209–25.

Booker, M. Keith, and Anne-Marie Thomas. 2009. *The Science Fiction Handbook*. Chichester: Wiley-Blackwell.

Brown, Jayna. 2021. *Black Utopias: Speculative Life and the Music of Other Worlds*. Durham, NC: Duke University Press.

Callahan, Allen Dwight. 2008. "The Strength of Collective Man: Nimrod and the Tower of Babel." Pages 147–62 in *African American Religious Life and the Story of Nimrod*. Edited by Anthony B. Pinn and Allen Dwight Callahan. New York: Palgrave Macmillan.

Cheyne, Ria. 2008. "Created Languages in Science Fiction." *Science Fiction Studies* 35:386–403.

Chiang, Ted. 1998. "Story of Your Life." Pages 257–314 in *Starlight 2*. Edited by Patrick Nielsen Hayden. New York: Tor.

Delany, Samuel R. 1998. "Racism and Science Fiction." *The New York Review of Science Fiction* 120.

Eco, Umberto. 1995. *The Search for the Perfect Language*. The Making of Europe. Oxford: Blackwell.

Embry, Brad. 2011. "The 'Naked Narrative' from Noah to Leviticus: Reassessing Voyeurism in the Account of Noah's Nakedness in Genesis 9.22–24." *JSOT* 35:417–33.

Fenollós, Juan-Luis Montero. 2020. "Imagining the Tower of Babel in the Twenty-First Century: Is a New Interpretation of the Ziggurat of Babylon Possible?" Pages 269–86 in *Receptions of the Ancient Near East in Popular Culture and Beyond*. Edited by L. Verderame and Agnès Garcia-Ventura. Atlanta: Lockwood.

Gross, Edward, and Mark A. Altman. 1996. *Captains' Logs Supplemental: The Unauthorized Guide to the New Trek Voyages*. Boston: Little, Brown.

Haney, William S. 2006. *Cyberculture, Cyborgs and Science Fiction: Consciousness and the Posthuman*. Consciousness, Literature and the Arts 2. Amsterdam: Rodopi.

Haynes, Stephen R. 2002. *Noah's Curse: The Biblical Justification of American Slavery*. Religion in America Series. Oxford: Oxford University Press.

Higgins, David M., and Roby Duncan. 2009. "Key Critical Concepts, Topics and Critics." Pages 125–42 in *The Science Fiction Handbook*. Edited by Nick Hubble and Aris Mousoutzanis. Literature and Culture Handbooks. London: Bloomsbury.

Hubble, Nick, Emma Filtness, and Joseph Norman. 2013. "Major Science Fiction Authors." Pages 31–74 in *The Science Fiction Handbook*. Edited by Nick Hubble and Aris Mousoutzanis. Literature and Culture Handbooks. London: Bloomsbury.

Kelly, Nicholas M. 2018. "'Works Like Magic': Metaphor, Meaning, and the GUI in Snow Crash." *Science Fiction Studies* 45:69–90.

Kroon, Richard W. 2010. *A/V A to Z: An Encyclopedic Dictionary of Media, Entertainment and Other Audiovisual Terms*. Jefferson, NC: McFarland.

Kugel, James L. 1998. *Traditions of the Bible: A Guide to the Bible as It Was at the Start of the Common Era*. Cambridge: Harvard University Press.

Lavender, Isiah, III. 2007. "Ethnoscapes: Environment and Language in Ishmael Reed's 'Mumbo Jumbo', Colson Whitehead's 'The Intuitionist', and Samuel R. Delany's 'Babel-17.'" *Science Fiction Studies* 34:187–200.

Lessing, Doris. 1983. *The Sentimental Agents in the Volyen Empire*. London: Jonathan Cape.

Malmgren, Carl. 1993. "The Languages of Science Fiction: Samuel Delany's *Babel-17*." *Extrapolation* 34:5–17.

McGrath, James F. 2016. *Theology and Science Fiction*. Cascade Companions. Eugene, OR: Cascade.

Michaels, Walter Benn. 2013. *The Shape of the Signifier: 1967 to the End of History*. Princeton: Princeton University Press.

Miéville, China. 2011. *Embassytown*. London: Pan Macmillan.

Mohr, Dunja. 2009. "'The Tower of Babble'? The Role and Function of Fictive Languages in Utopian and Dystopian Fiction." Pages 225–48 in *Futurescapes: Space in Utopian and Science Fiction Discourses*. Edited by Ralph Pordzik. Spatial Practices 9. Amsterdam: Rodopi.

Morrow, James. 2014. *Bible Stories for Adults*. Boston: Houghton Mifflin Harcourt

Pittman, John P. 2016. "Double Consciousness." In *The Stanford Encyclopedia of Philosophy*. Edited by Edward N. Zalta. Metaphysics Research Lab, Stanford University. https://tinyurl.com/SBLPress6708c1.

Porush, David. 1994. "Hacking the Brainstem: Postmodern Metaphysics and Stephenson's SnowCrash." *Configurations* 2:537–71.

Rutledge, Gregory E. 2000. "Science Fiction and the Black Power/Arts Movements: The Transpositional Cosmology of Samuel R. Delany Jr." *Extrapolation* 41:127–42.

Stallings, L. H. 2015. "'Think Galactic. Or Your World Is Lost': The Boundaries of Science and Art and Samuel Delany's New Poetics." *African American Review* 48:225–38.

Vance, Jack. 1958. *The Languages of Pao*. New York: Avalon Books.

Noah's Ark

NICOLE L. TILFORD

If the world was coming to an end and you could save only one thing, what would it be? Variations of this parlor game have been circulating for millennia, and for good reason. Not only is the question an interesting way to pass the time, but it also speaks to a larger desire to understand humanity's relationship to the rest of the cosmos. Are humans special? Do they alone deserve to survive the end of the world, or are they part of a larger ecosystem that must be preserved? If humans are worth saving, is each individual important, or is it the collective potential of the species that is valuable? Can humanity really survive any challenge it encounters?

Ark narratives, both ancient and futuristic, attempt to provide answers to these questions. While the nuances vary, the basic plot remains the same: a select group gathers on an ark in an attempt to survive an unprecedented disaster. The imagined disasters reveal much about the present anxieties of the authors and their intended audiences: whether they are concerned about pollution, disease, war, natural disaster, and so forth. So does the ending. Ark narratives rarely have a happy ending. Even if part of the group survives, conflicts abound, culture is lost, and moral sacrifices are made along the way. Perhaps most importantly, not everyone survives. People are prevented from joining the ark, groups splinter, and individuals die en route. Who ultimately survives is telling and often reveals more about the social anxieties of the narratives' intended audiences than the imagined disaster does. Ark narratives are generally not optimistic stories about humanity's survival against overwhelming odds in some nebulous future; rather, they are pessimistic tales about social exclusion in humanity's present.

The Ark in the Bible and Beyond

Genesis 6–9 is one of the earliest recorded versions of an ark narrative. Warned by a deity that the world will be destroyed by an unprecedented flood, one righteous man builds a large vessel and places his family and a few select animals on it. Together, they weather a great storm until, at last, the occupants of the ark are able to disembark and repopulate the land.

On the surface, the biblical text reflects common anxieties about water among ancient Near Eastern communities. Although there were some larger settlements, much of the ancient Near East consisted of small agrarian and pastoral communities who relied upon stable weather patterns for survival. Too little or too much rain could be disastrous for a community. Consequently, water was a symbol not only of life but also of death. Thus, in ancient Egypt, whose principal river ebbed and flowed in fairly predictable yearly cycles, water was a force of divine order. Farther north, however, where rivers were far less predictable, water was a symbol of destructive renewal. These northern regions produced multiple narratives (e.g., Ziusudra, Gilgamesh, Atrahasis) in which great floods destroy almost all of humanity, thereby paving the way for the formation of a new civilization. While some scholars maintain that such traditions record the communal memory of one massive flood somewhere in the Black Sea region (see, e.g., Ryan and Pitman 1998), it is more likely that these traditions reflect a common anxiety about localized flooding.[1] Regardless, the biblical text follows the trend of the northern traditions, using shared anxiety over water's destructive powers to frame its narrative.

However, one does not need to read the biblical text too carefully to see that there is a greater concern at play in the narrative. Although water is clearly the destructive agent, the flooding is not a random natural event. Rather, a deity sends the flood to punish humans for their actions. Herein lies the true anxiety at the heart of the narrative: certain people could corrupt the community and bring the deity's wrath down upon it. If it happened in the past, it could happen again. The audience must thus be careful, lest its members include individuals deemed unacceptable by the deity.

The biblical narrative in Gen 6–9 does not identify which specific people the audience should be concerned about. The first few verses con-

---

1. For more on explanations of ancient Near Eastern flood narratives, see Pleins 2003.

demn the so-called sons of God who mate with human women and sire a race of mighty men (Gen 6:1–2). The Hebrew text is unclear as to who these sons of God were or where they came from. Early Greek translations understood them to be giants (LXX Gen 6:1–4), while other early interpreters understood them to be divine beings, angels perhaps, who disobeyed the deity by lusting after human women (e.g., Jub. 5; 2 Bar. 56).[2] Regardless, there is expressed anxiety over an outside group mingling with regular humans. Such anxiety fits well with concerns found elsewhere in the Hebrew Bible, where authors fret over the people chosen by God, be they Israelites, Judeans, or early Jews, mixing with their ancient Near Eastern neighbors (see, e.g., Num 25; Deut 23:3–6; Ezra 9). Immediately after the union of the sons of God with human women, the Genesis text notes that "the wickedness of humankind was great in the earth" (Gen 6:5),[3] thereby implying that the offspring of such unions—blended social units—are morally reproachable.

A few verses later, the Genesis story states that "the earth was corrupt ... [and] filled with violence" (Gen 6:11). Scholars typically read this statement as a second explanation for the deity's anger: here, violence, not illicit sex, brings about the flood.[4] Early interpreters, however, understood violence to be a direct result of the aforementioned union; that is, violence was one characteristic of the illicit offspring (e.g., 1 En. 6–11). This is linguistically defensible. The Hebrew term for wickedness that is used here, *ra'ah*, is a generic term covering all sorts of activities that the speaker deems evil, of which violence (Heb. *hamas*) could be one. Yet, whether a literary seam or clarification, the condemnation is clear: violence is a reprehensible activity that ought to be avoided.

---

2. For more on early interpretations of the biblical ark narrative, see the essays in Stone, Amihay, and Hillel 2010.

3. Biblical translations follow the NRSV.

4. Due to certain discrepancies in the text (e.g., different divine names, different totals for the number of animals who enter the ark, different conclusions), scholars typically argue that the biblical ark narrative is, in fact, two or more narratives that have been spliced together. For more information, see Pleins 2003, 26–30. While I agree with that assessment, for our purposes it is enough to recognize that, from an early date, the biblical ark narrative has been read as a cohesive story with a unified theme and that it is this cohesive narrative that inspired science fiction renditions of the ark narrative. I will therefore focus on the ark narrative as a relatively cohesive whole.

According to the text, because humanity was wicked and violent, the deity intervened before humans destroyed all life on the earth. Yet, there was also something about humanity worth saving: Noah. According to the text, Noah was a "righteous" man (Gen 6:9; 7:1). The Hebrew term used to describe Noah here, *tsadik*, is the antithesis of *ra'ah* and serves as a generic term covering all sorts of activities that the speaker deems good. The text is unclear what actions make Noah worthy of praise, though presumably in the final narrative his actions include obedience to God and offering appropriate sacrifices (see Gen 6:22; 8:20). Early interpreters similarly emphasize Noah's righteousness, though typically without any clarifying details (e.g., Wis 10; Josephus, *A.J.* 1.75). The biblical ark narrative thus provides a positive albeit vague affirmation of humanity's potential. As the ancestor of the postdiluvian human race, Noah models the behavior that the intended audience should emulate. The intended audience *can* rise above humanity's wicked nature, as long as they do so in a manner that is deemed acceptable by the text's intended community.

This point is reinforced when the deity chooses to save Noah and his immediate family and promises never again to flood the earth (Gen 8:21–22). Unlike the divine promises in later biblical texts (e.g., Gen 15; 2 Sam 7; Jer 33), this promise is not limited to one group of people. All humanity is to be spared from future deluge. Such a seemingly universal promise, however, is tempered by the fact that most of humanity has been destroyed by this point in the narrative. Humanity will be spared as long as it is made in the image of the flood's sole survivor, Noah. The biblical ark narrative uses Noah to urge the audience to avoid wickedness and be righteous instead.

The Ark in Science Fiction

Times may change, but the question remains the same: If the world was ending, what would be worth saving?[5] Living in a world of advanced weaponry and degrading environmental conditions, contemporary science fiction authors in particular have wrestled with this question and have looked to the biblical ark narrative as a model for humanity's survival. The scenarios they depict are remarkably similar: the fate of humanity or a race similar to it is threatened by an external force or the ill-devised activities of human beings. The disasters therefore reflect a range of modern anxieties:

---

5. An earlier version of this section appeared as Tilford 2014.

External Force
- rogue planets: e.g., Edwin Balmer and Philip Wylie, *When Worlds Collide* (1933)
- supernova: e.g., Arthur C. Clarke, *The Songs of Distant Earth* (1986)
- invading aliens: e.g., *Titan A.E.* (2000)
- virus: e.g., Ken Catran, *Deepwater Black* (1997)
- solar flares: e.g., "The Ark in Space," *Doctor Who* (1975)
- a great flood: e.g., Stephen Baxter, *Flood* (2009)

Human Activity
- war: e.g., James P. Hogan, *Voyage from Yesteryear* (1982)
- pollution: e.g., *WALL-E* (2008)
- overpopulation: e.g., *Pandorum* (2009)
- depletion of resources: e.g., *Battle for Terra* (2007)
- mad scientist: e.g., *Sky Captain and the World of Tomorrow* (2004)

In response to the threat, an ark of some sort is built to safeguard humans, animals, and/or vegetation until disaster passes. On occasion, this ark is a boat like Noah's that floats on the water (e.g., Stephen Baxter, *Ark* [2009]; Harry Dayle, *Noah's Ark: Survivors* [2013]; *Downsizing* [2017]). Other times, the ark is a train that circles the globe (e.g., *Snowpiercer* [2020–]) or an underground bunker that safeguards its occupants until the earth is safe to occupy once again (e.g., Laura Martin, *The Ark Plan* [2016]). More often, however, the arks that these authors construct are intended to save their inhabitants from a world that is rendered permanently uninhabitable. As such, these science fiction arks no longer float on water; rather, they fly through space (e.g., Vernor Vinge, "Long Shot" [1972]; *The 100* [2014–2020]). Regardless of format, such arks, like their biblical counterpart, enable their authors to reflect upon the nature of the human race and what, if anything, is worth saving from it.

Noah, of course, had it easy. There was only one righteous family in the whole land—his own. Naturally he would choose to save them. Science fiction narratives present a more difficult choice. Billions of people on a world, only a handful of seats on an ark. Whom to choose?

Within these narratives, the apocalyptic event itself often resolves some of this tension. In Edwin Balmer and Philip Wylie's classic novel *When Worlds Collide* (1933), for instance, the majority of Earth's population is wiped out by earthquakes, tidal waves, and volcanic eruptions before the arks are ready to be boarded, and thousands more are killed in the riots that ensue as people fight to board the completed rockets. Similarly, in the popular *Battlestar Galactica* series and its reboot (1978–1979, 2004–2009), an attack by killer robots leaves billions dead before the series even begin.

Still, people survive, and space on the ark is limited. A choice has to be made. The resulting occupants are not simply characters designed to propel the narrative forward; rather, they reflect the values of the authors— in other words, these characters reflect the kinds of people the authors deem to be valuable in society and, by extension, those deemed not valuable. The young frequently have an edge in the selection process. Children board the ark first or get the last seat on overfilled rockets fleeing disaster (e.g., *Battlestar Galactica*, "Saga of a Star World" [1978]). As one example, the sole survivor of the planet Krypton is the young Kal-El, who is sent to Earth in a pod where he will grow up to be the legendary Superman (see, e.g., Siegel, "Superman" [1938]). Humanity is born innocent, and innocence is worth saving.

Lotteries are also used. In the *Stargate SG-1* episode "Lifeboat" (2003), the series's protagonists encounter a ship occupied by three thousand cryogenically frozen people from the doomed planet of Ardana. Most of these people, it is revealed, do not have any particular skill or innate qualities to recommend them; they were selected at random. Some people are simply in the right place at the right time. Thus, the survivors in Harry Dayle's *Noah's Ark: Survivors* (2013) are those who happened to have booked a cruise in the one spot on the planet left untouched by a ravaging comet. In such cases, simply being human is enough, which suggests that there is something innately redemptive in the whole human race.

Many arks, however, are planned in advance of the apocalypse, and their occupants are chosen with care. Sometimes, ideological or religious affiliation is paramount. Thus, the occupants of the massive ark in *Raised by Wolves* (2020–) are those considered to be true believers of the Mithraic god; their enemies, the atheists, are left to fend for themselves and end up building a smaller ark occupied by a few human embryos and two android caregivers. The elite of society are frequently chosen: the world's leading politicians, scientists, artists, and businessmen—the so-called best of humanity, or at least the ones with enough money to pay for their survival (e.g., Balmer and Wylie, *When Worlds Collide* [1933]; *Moonraker* [1979]). In Garrett Putman Serviss's "Second Deluge" (1911–1912), the classic science fiction story that seemingly introduced the ark trope to the genre, the Noah figure draws up a list that details exactly which occupations of people to include on his ark, how many of each, and the number of family members who would be allowed to join them. The occupations on this list—various types of scientists, statesmen, artists, teachers, agricultural workers, and mechanics—are those occupations that the author deems valuable in his own society; tellingly, most working-class occupations, such as shop owners, secretaries, and factory workers, do not make the cut. The television series *Salvation* (2017–2018) mimics this selection procedure when a rich inventor commissions a think tank to generate a similar list. Despite decades between the two narratives, the list put forth by the majority of the think tank is not all that different from the one drawn up by Serviss's Noah figure, though the minority voice does push for more inclusivity. The overwhelming implication is that those people in society who are more productive—either as producers of wealth or of culture—are more valuable.

Often, genetic variety is paramount. If a child is chosen, the parent must stay behind (Baxter, *Ark* [2009]). Large families need not apply (Serviss, "Second Deluge" [1911–1912]). The magic number according to some authors is between 80 and 160; this number of unrelated individuals provides enough genetic diversity to repopulate the human race, provided that individuals are willing to mate with multiple partners and produce multiple offspring (e.g., Balmer and Wylie, *When Worlds Collide* [1933]; *Salvation* [2107–2018]; but see Fecht 2014 for the scientific improbability of this low number). Such considerations privilege heterosexual individuals. Homosexuals, if considered by authors at all, are sometimes permitted entry, but they, too, must be willing to reproduce in traditional fashions (e.g., Baxter, *Ark* [2009]). In more recent narratives, nonbinary individuals find space on arks (e.g., *The 100* [2014–2020]), suggesting a gradual change in how sexuality is viewed in today's society. However, heterosexuality remains the norm for these authors and thus for their arks.

The selection of individuals, especially when drawn from the elite, is frequently a matter of contention. Riots break out as desperate people attempt to claim reserved spaces (e.g., Balmer and Wylie, *When Worlds Collide* [1933]; Baxter, *Ark* [2009]). Conflict ensues when the family of those chosen do not obtain their allotted seats (*Stargate: Atlantis*, "The Ark" [2007]). Tensions rise when the elite attempt to claim the best living spaces, food, and luxuries at the expense of those around them (e.g., *Battlestar Galactica*, "Saga of a Star World" [1978]). Not everyone agrees that the elite are more worthy of survival.

Douglas Adams's *The Hitchhiker's Guide to the Galaxy* (1978, 1981, 2002) parodies this situation, casting those designated as *undesirables* in Golgafrincham society—hairdressers, television producers, insurance salesmen, management consultants, security guards, account executives, and so forth—out into space in the B-Ark so that the rest of society may live in relative peace. Ironically, the rest of the population is destroyed by a disease soon after, such that those deemed most useless in Golgafrincham society are left to perpetuate the species. They cannot even invent a wheel or make a fire without becoming bogged down in paperwork. Such a tale, while humorous, provides a scathing critique of the bureaucratic system of contemporary England. It suggests that, when individuals become too focused on rules and regulations and forget the purpose of their endeavors, the species is doomed.

Ray Bradbury makes a similar move in his more serious tales, "Way in the Middle of the Air" (1950) and its sequel, "The Other Foot" (1951). In the first story, a group of African Americans use rocket ships to flee the prejudices of a pre–civil rights South. Their white neighbors look on in consternation but are unable to stop the exodus. When the earth is decimated by war at the beginning of the second story, that same African American community must decide whether to accept their former white neighbors into their new colony on Mars. Debate ensues, guns are readied, but ultimately the community chooses to forgive the sins of the past. Set in the era of Jim Crow laws and black-separatist movements, these two stories critique the racial tensions of the early twentieth century. They force the reader to reconsider the assumption that some are more deserving of life than others simply because they are born into a certain class or have a certain skin color.

Regardless of who is selected, science fiction arks must be quite sizeable to carry any substantial number of people. Garrett Putman Serviss's terrestrial ark in "Second Deluge" (1911–1912), for instance, is eight hundred feet long and one hundred feet high, while the space arks in *Stargate SG-1*'s "Scorched Earth" (2000) and the *Battlestar Galactica* reboot series (2004–2009) are so large that they fill the skies. Such arks would be technologically and financially prohibitive to our own civilization, let alone earlier generations.

Some authors solve this dilemma by eliminating the human occupants altogether. Knowledge, not people, is important, they argue. Thus, in the *Star Trek: The Next Generation* episode "The Inner Light" (1992), the crew encounters an ark in which the memories and scientific knowledge of a long-dead alien race are preserved for posterity. Similarly, the ark in Karen Thompson Walker's novel *The Age of Miracles* (2012) serves merely as a "message in a bottle.... Among the final contents were the sounds of waves crashing on a beach, human voices speaking greetings from around the world, images of extinct flora and fauna, a diagram of the Earth's exact location in the universe." No human cargo here, just the memories and knowledge of an extinct race. There is a certain intellectual honesty in these narratives: for these authors, all people are equal—equally unimportant, that is; culture is paramount.

Other authors solve the issue of size and cost by reducing the human occupants to their basic building blocks. Humans themselves are not on the ark, but there is enough DNA of the doomed race that the species may be re-created when a new home world is found. Thus, the occupants of the ark in Vernor Vinge's short story "Long Shot" (1972) are human embryos, while the occupants of the ark in *Stargate SG-1*'s "Scorched Earth" (2000) are genetic samples of a doomed alien race (see also *Space 1999*, "Mission of the Darians" [1975]; *Titan A.E.* [2000]). Arthur C. Clarke's seedships in *The Songs of Distant Earth* (1986) contain not only the DNA needed to reinvent the human race on a distant planet but 10 percent of the world's literature to help them do so. Ironically, the biblical text upon which so many of these science fiction arks are based was not included in this archive, since religious texts and their derivative works were excluded lest they "reinfect virgin planets with the ancient poisons of religious hatred, belief in the supernatural, and the pious gibberish with which countless billions of men and women had once comforted themselves at the cost of addling their minds" (1986, 115–16).

Even those narratives that include actual humans on the arks often view the occupants more as vessels for human DNA than as individuals. As one female protagonist in Balmer and Wylie's *When Worlds Collide* (1933, 45) reflects, she and her companions are but "bits of biology, bearing within us seeds far more important than ourselves—far more important than our prejudices and loves and hates." In such cases, that which is worth preserving about humanity is again not the individual human itself but the collective possibility of humanity.

An interesting twist on this idea can be found in Jack Williamson's story, "The Fortress of Utopia," which was first published in the November 1939 issue of the pulp magazine *Startling Stories*. The cover of the issue depicts what might be considered a standard science fiction ark, complete with animals calmly boarding a spaceship two-by-two while soldiers ward off a frantic mob. The depiction is reminiscent of what one finds in traditional paintings of the biblical scene (e.g., Edward Hicks, *Noah's Ark* [1846]), and the reader would likely have expected to find a fairly straightforward ark narrative within the issue's pages.

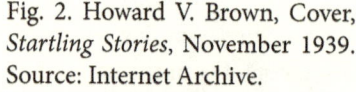
Fig. 1. Edward Hicks, *Noah's Ark*, 1846. Source: Wikimedia.

Fig. 2. Howard V. Brown, Cover, *Startling Stories*, November 1939. Source: Internet Archive.

Yet Williamson's story is anything but straightforward. Faced with the destruction of the planet, the protagonists in the story do not immediately build an ark. Rather, they erase the memories of every human being on the planet and reprogram them with just enough knowledge that humanity can, after several generations, find a solution to the coming disaster. After various failed ark attempts, humans transform the earth itself into a spaceship capable of moving out of the way of impending danger. In this narrative, the individuality of each human is irrelevant, as is most of the collected art, culture, and history of humanity; it is simply the physical bodies of the race as a whole that must survive. It is unclear whether the cover artist intended to set the audience up so that Williamson could subvert their expectations or whether the artist simply could not find another way to portray the story. The result, however, is a narrative that clearly plays with readers as they consider what to save.

However, as the commander of one of these science fiction arks states, "it is not enough to survive. One has to be worthy of survival" (*Battlestar Galactica*, "Resurrection Ship: Part 2" [2006]). The events that occur after these science fiction arks launch often make one question whether those selected are really worth saving. Space arks in particular test the limits of humanity. People die. Arks explode. Stasis pods fail. Prolonged voyages, close quarters, inadequate food rations, limited water, rampant disease, technical difficulties, dwindling energy supplies—all conspire to reduce humanity to its most animalistic impulses. Deprived of the comforts of home, people go mad (*Pandorum* [2009]). They forget their past (*Star Lost* [1973]). They hoard goods (e.g., Baxter, *The Ark* [2009]). They attack peaceful worlds (*Battle for Terra* [2007]). They attack one another (e.g., Balmer and Wylie, *After the Worlds Collide* [1934]). They resort to savagery and cannibalism (e.g., *Space 1999*, "Mission of the Darians" [1975]). In multiship fleets, arks that are incapable of keeping up with the rest of the fleet are left behind (*Battlestar Galactica*, "Resurrection Ship: Part 2" [2006]). The weak are abandoned. Social order collapses. Freedoms are lost. Humanity disappears. Only animals survive. As the antagonists in the *Battlestar Galactica* reboot claim, perhaps humanity really does deserve to die.

Some authors seem to agree. In the film *Seeking a Friend for the End of the World* (2012), for instance, a hastily constructed ark explodes upon departure. The protagonists can but wait along with the rest of the world for the end to come. Similarly, in the *Loki* episode "Lamentis" (2021), the residents of an alien moon are doomed when their sole ark is destroyed by an exploding planet. Science fiction arks represent what each author believes to be the most important aspect of humanity: its individuality, its collective history, its genetic possibility. More importantly, these arks represent hope, a chance that humanity will survive even in the direst circumstances; when they fail, hope fails with them.

Doctor Who and the Ark

One long-running British television series, *Doctor Who*, contains three separate ark narratives, a testament to both the trope's interest and its flexibility. The series features a nearly immortal human-like alien, the Doctor, who travels through space and time having all sorts of (mis)adventures with various companions. Every so often, the Doctor dies and regenerates into a new form, typically as a white British male. To date, there have been thirteen such regenerations, with the most recent incarnation at the time of this essay's composition breaking the previous pattern and taking the form of a white British female. The ark narratives occur during the first, fourth, and eleventh incarnations of the Doctor (or seasons 3 and 12 of the original series and season 5 of the post-2005 reboot series).

As Peter B. Gregg (2004, 650–51) points out, *Doctor Who*, like any television series, is the product of many agents: producers, actors, designers, corporations, and so on. The producers are perhaps most influential, making the final decisions on what will be said, who will be cast, and how the plot will proceed. But writers, actors, and editors also influence the direction of any given episode, as do the corporations that fund the series (here, the British Broadcasting Corporation) and the audience (here, a mixture of children and adults). Episodes are therefore constrained by a variety of interests: a desire to be entertaining, have a compelling message, attract high ratings, and be educational. For an episode to be successful, Gregg notes, it must balance these competing interests, while appealing to its audience's expectations. It cannot "stretch genre conventions or comment on contemporary social issues" in a way that "alientate[s]" its audience (651). Each ark narrative, then, can be said to reflect the specific fears and hopes of its particular generation, rather than any one individual.

"The Ark"

The first ark narrative is split into four episodes, "The Steel Sky," "The Plague," "The Return," and "The Bomb," all collectively referred to as "The

Ark" serial. These four episodes originally aired in March 1966 and reflect the tensions of that era. Although the serial had impressive scenery for its day and included an unprecedented number of live animals, the costumes were deplorable and the script melodramatic, such that today the serial is not typically viewed as a highlight of the series.[6]

In the first two episodes, the first Doctor (played by William Hartnell) and his companions are transported ten million years into the future, where they encounter a generation ship filled with humans and a benign alien race, the Monoids, who serve as their helpers.[7] These two groups have left a dying Earth, which is being pulled slowly into the sun. The disaster reflects the common pessimism of science fiction writers in the 1950s and 1960s, who, having suffered the shock of multiple world wars and the continued escalation of international tensions, mused that the end of the world was inevitable. As in much science fiction from the United Kingdom of the time (see Mann 2001), the disaster in the *Doctor Who* serial is presented as natural in origin and thereby beyond human control.

The solution, however, is entirely in humanity's control. This was, after all, also the era of the space race, where new technologies opened up the real possibility of space travel. If humanity could only put aside its differences, band together, and use human ingenuity to harness technology toward positive ends, these science fiction creators mused, it might survive any disaster.

The first two episodes of the *Doctor Who* serial reflect this optimism: humans unite to construct a great spaceship to carry survivors to a distant planet where they may begin civilization anew. Recognizing that space is limited, the ark preserves millions of people and animals in miniature, with only a small contingent of full-sized humans to act as caretakers until the ship arrives at its destination. Although the humans who remain in charge of the ark are homogenous (the cast appears entirely white and British), the leader of the ark states that the entire human race is stored in miniature, which suggests that people of all races ultimately survive the apocalypse and have a vital role to play in the preservation of the species. The resulting society on the ark is relatively benign, with humans and Monoids coexisting in harmony.

---

6. See fan reviews at Callahan n.d.

7. A generation ship is a spaceship designed to travel extremely long distances in space. Because of the distance, it is assumed that generations will be born and die on the ship before the ship arrives at its destination.

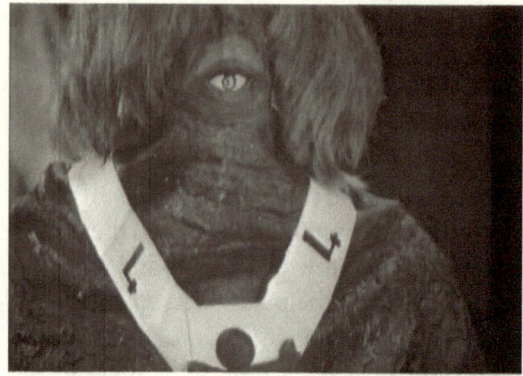

Fig. 3. Monoid. "The Bomb." *Doctor Who*. BBC. 1966.

It is not, however, perfect. Although apparently treated well, the Monoids—who have dark skin, dark hair, and dark clothing and wear collars around their necks—are the subservient race. They have been allowed to join the voyage in exchange for their servitude, but they are treated little better than slaves, a fact that the first two episodes take for granted. Their numbers include doctors, lawyers, and technicians, but they are allowed to speak only through gestures. They are, in other words, essentially silent, a characteristic that, as Vanessa de Kauwe (2013, 146) points out, "render[s] them powerless," with no "social, legal and political representation." When disaster strikes, the death of a Monoid is considered tragic; the death of a human, however, is catastrophic. Such imbalance is literally cast in stone: the first episode witnesses the beginning of the construction of a tremendous statue that will take over seven hundred years to build. Although intended to commemorate the voyage and constructed entirely by the Monoids using labor-intensive methods, the statue portrays only a single human male. Humans are ultimately all that matter on the ark.

Moreover, justice on the ark is harsh. A small mistake is punishable by death or miniaturization. The ark's inhabitants justify these harsh punishments by arguing that even a small imbalance in the ark's ecosystem would result in death for the entire species. As the commander of the ark states, "What happens to me is not so important. Or you for that matter, or any one of us ... but the voyage and the eventual landing of our descendants on the planet Refusis—that's it! That's the only thing that's important" ("The Plague"). Like other science fiction ark narratives surveyed above, the individual person is not important, only the collective possibility of the human species.

It is this latter perspective that drives the narrative's plot. The Doctor's unexpected arrival threatens the precarious balance on the ark. Unwittingly, one of the Doctor's companions carries with her a common cold virus, which quickly decimates the inhabitants of the ark. The occupants, it turns out, have no built-up immunity to the virus, because the common cold had been cured centuries prior to the ark's construction. The resulting confusion, anger, and death seem to mark the end of the mission, and the inhabitants begin to wonder why they even bothered to leave Earth.

This is not the first time *Doctor Who* had incorporated a plague into its narrative. As pointed out by one *Doctor Who* blogger, the subplot is almost a "carbon copy" of the plot from a season one serial, the "Sensorites," in which the Doctor must rush to find a cure for a deadly disease while his companion stands trial (Steve 2017). Given the increasing popularity of pestilence narratives in the late 1950s and 1960s, it is not surprising that the producers would recycle the plot here. It provided a convenient source of conflict that was sure to interest viewers.

Striking in this episode, however, is the recognition that the Doctor's careless wanderings can have unintended consequences. Like the missionaries and explorers of the 1600s, the Doctor could carry a disease across space and time to the detriment of those he encounters. The recognition, perhaps, would have provoked viewers to consider the travels of the Doctor in a new light; the travels were not simply benign expeditions but potentially dangerous in their own right. This recognition, however, is short-lived, as the Doctor dismisses the worry with the haughty declaration that he and his companions were "usually very healthy" ("The Plague"). The Doctor is not concerned with the consequences of his actions. Luckily, the disease is also short-lived, since the Doctor is able to find a cure and save the ark. Crisis is averted, and the trio continue on their adventures, leaving the ark to continue on its merry way.

Within the first two episodes, therefore, one finds both anxiety about the inevitable destruction of the earth and optimism that human ingenuity can overcome such an obstacle. Yet one also finds hints, not fully explored, that the Doctor's travels are not as innocent as they first appear and that the survival of the human race carries with it some inherent racial inequality. Sadly, the latter two are not solved by human ingenuity. (After all, the inequality remains, and the cure for the disease was found by the alien Doctor, not human medical practitioners.) Some things, it seems, remain beyond human control.

Although the conflict seems to resolve in the second episode, the 1966 serial does not end with the Doctor's departure. In the third and fourth episodes, the Doctor and his companions return seven hundred years later to find a very different ark. Due to a mutation in the cold virus, the human caretakers have become weak. The Monoids have taken control of the ship and rule with an iron fist. As a colonial group in transition, they have abandoned their native customs in favor of those of their former oppressors; they even develop a voice box on their collar so they can speak English (Kauwe 2013, 151). The humans, on the other hand, are now slaves, locked in a small room when their service is not needed.

The first two episodes present the Monoids as subservient but never use slave language. Only near the end of the fourth episode is it even acknowledged that the humans once treated the Monoids as slaves. The viewer could almost be forgiven for missing the connotations. In the latter two episodes, however, the viewer cannot mistake the nature of the relationship between the two races. The language of slavery is highlighted prominently within the dialogue of the first five minutes, with terms such as "slaves," "masters," and "overlords" being used directly and with disdain. Apparently, it is fine for one race to enslave another when humans are in charge, but when the Monoids take over, such arrangements are no longer palatable.

Whether the producers intended such discrepancy is unclear. The change in social order could simply be a plot device designed to explore another obstacle that human ingenuity must overcome, yet the timing of the episodes is telling. The 1950s and 1960s witnessed a rise in racial tensions across the globe. In the United Kingdom, for instance, black immigrants from British-controlled regions in the Caribbean were increasingly moving to England, where they were met with hostility and viewed as second-class citizens. Laws were enacted to restrict immigration, and speeches were made by prominent politicians that incited fear that Britain was losing its "cultural" (i.e., white) identity (see Samanani 2018). That this serial shows greater sympathy to the white humans than their dark-costumed alien overlords likely reflects this political tension, with the producers siding with the majority population.

The ending of the fourth episode largely reinforces this perspective. The Doctor, with the help of the native inhabitants of the ark's destination and a civil war among the Monoids, frees the enslaved humans, and a peace accord is reached. The voyage's monumental statue—which under the Monoid rule had been recast in Monoid likeness—is blown up. The human caretakers, Monoids, micro-size cargo, and native inhabitants are able to build a new life together. Here it is important to point out that the native inhabitants of the ark's destination are invisible. Due to a fluke cosmic flare, they no longer have physical form. Because of this, they have no race, or rather, they are postracial. Thus, while continuing to focus on the experiences of the white humans, the serial establishes a new civilization composed of three species: one white, one dark, and one invisible.

Presumably, the three species will coexist equally on their new home world. However, the contempt in which the humans and Monoids hold each other suggests that it is the threat of retribution from the invisible natives that will ultimately preserve the peace, not any true understanding between the species (Crome 2013, 199). The message for Britain seems to be that only the invisible hand of the law would help the United Kingdom achieve an uneasy peace between the races. Such a law, the Race Relations Act of 1965, was enacted a few short months prior to the serial's airing. This act prohibited racial discrimination, and additional laws would be passed in subsequent years that clarified the extent of the protections afforded therein. The legal system, like the invisible aliens, would eventually save Britain from its old prejudices.

The final two episodes of the serial therefore bring the viewer to a different conclusion than the first two episodes. Fear of the earth's destruction is long forgotten, to be replaced by fear of racial instability. Like the disease of the first two episodes, this challenge cannot be overcome by human ingenuity. It takes the intervention of the alien Doctor once again, along with a group of invisible aliens, to force the humans to live peacefully with their Monoid neighbors. There is something worth saving about humanity, but it is not human ideals, social order, or ingenuity. It is simply the collective presence of the species.

"The Ark in Space"

Doctor Who returned to the ark theme in the "Ark in Space," which originally aired in four parts in January and February of 1975. Unlike the earlier "Ark" serial, to which this episode makes no reference, the individual episodes are unnamed. Despite early disputes over the script, the final serial was well received, with the episodes drawing as many as 13.6 million viewers when the serial first aired (Sullivan 2015).

The serial begins when the fourth Doctor (played by Tom Baker) and his companions arrive on Nerva, a space station orbiting Earth several thousand years in the future. As with the ship in the previous serial, the

Nerva is an ark designed to save its occupants from a dying world. This time, the cataclysm was caused by solar flares, which wiped out all life on the planet. Thus again, fear of natural disaster underlies the plot.

And, once again, the solution stems from human ingenuity, a point that the Doctor makes clearly:

> Homo sapiens. What an inventive, invincible species. It's only a few million years since they've crawled up out of the mud and learned to walk. Puny, defenseless bipeds. They've survived flood, famine, and plague. They've survived cosmic wars and holocausts, and now here they are amongst the stars, waiting to begin a new life, ready to outsit eternity. They're indomitable. Indomitable! ("The Ark in Space: Part 1")

Everything has been meticulously planned, from the automated systems to the extensive databases storing the totality of human knowledge to the cryogenically frozen plants, animals, and humans. Unlike the previous serial, there are no caretakers. The ark occupants remain in frozen animation with only the computer to keep watch over them. The humans chosen to occupy the ark are also limited in number. Although said to represent all races, only a few hundred humans are preserved, each with a specific set of skills and chosen for the genetic value they would bring to the new civilization. Again, then, that which is worth saving is not individual human beings but the collective possibility of humanity: "human culture, human knowledge, human love and faith" ("The Ark in Space: Part 3").

As with the earlier ark narrative, outsiders threaten the balance of the new civilization. The inhabitants of the ark have been carefully chosen from a curated gene pool that has been "balanced, cross-matched, compat[8]-evaluated" ("The Ark in Space: Part 1"); the initial selection has been made with care, and the future breeding partners have been planned out long in advance. Although similar eugenic projects receive poor evaluations in science fiction (see Kirby 2007), here the selective breeding is touted as optimal for the survival of the human race. Any random deviations could be catastrophic. Thus, so-called regressives—those with undesirable genetic traits—are limited in number, since they threaten the genetic stability of the new colony. When the Doctor and his companions arrive and begin reviving the occupants, they themselves are classified as regressives,

---

8. Shorthand for *compatibility*.

largely due to their antiquated speech patterns; they are therefore met with suspicion and promised quick extermination.

Before the Doctor and his companions can be killed, however, the Nerva's commander (pointedly called Noah by his subordinates) is infected by a Wirrn, an alien lifeform that has invaded the station. The adult version of this lifeform, found dead in the first episode, looks like a giant green wasp without wings, while its young look like large green slugs. Once attached to a human, the young share the knowledge and slowly absorb the body of the host. The viewer is clearly intended to feel horror at this process, suggesting that the survival of human knowledge (in this case, within the Wirrn) is not enough; human form must also survive.

Fig. 4. Wirrn-Human Hybrid. "Ark in Space: Part 3." *Doctor Who*. BBC. 1975.

Although fear of natural disaster looms in the backstory, the primary fear of the serial revolves around the Wirrn-human hybrid. It is no accident that the infected crew member is the leader of the ark. In the years leading up to the episode, the United Kingdom had experienced a series of political scandals and economic upheavals that shook the people's faith in their government. The infected commander, and the diseased ship he leads, are the evil monsters the British people fear their government to be (Gregg 2004, 652–53).

The Wirrn-human hybrid represented another fear as well. Giant insects have long caused panic in science fiction narratives, with writers drawing upon a primordial human fear of crawling creatures to create bone-chilling narratives (see Stableford 2006, 156–60). Here, however, the invasion by insects takes on a new dimension when the infection they cause threatens the carefully planned genetic purity of the new colony. More than mere monsters, they become symbols of the dangers posed by contemporary scientific advancements.

Since the 1950s, scientists had been making steady advancements in the field of genetic engineering, and science fiction writers had been capitalizing on the fears the resulting theories aroused. In the 1960s and 1970s, however, scientists began conducting experiments to see how DNA from different species could be combined to make a new hybrid species. Theory became reality in 1972 when scientists successfully produced the first recombinant DNA molecule. This ushered in a new wave of science fiction and horror narratives on the subject (Kirby 2007, 96). Although not the result of a human experiment, the Wirrn-human hybrid reflects the fear that such manipulation could deprive humanity of its essential core. The human race could become inhuman monsters, containing the knowledge of humanity without its indomitable spirit.

The horror is heightened when viewers discover that the invasion is not a cosmic fluke. Earlier in the serial, there are hints that humans exist in colonies outside of Earth. The Doctor and his companions are mistaken for colonials with no understanding of their history, and there is said to be a group of regressives on one of the colonies. The viewer finds out in the fourth episode that, while the occupants of the ark slept, a group of humans from one of these colonies attacked the Wirrn home world, slaughtering their breeding stock and nearly exterminating the race. The attack on the Nerva was therefore an act of revenge, designed to destroy the humans while ensuring the survival of the Wirrn. The Wirrn-human hybrid may not be the result of human science gone awry, but it is the direct result of human activities nonetheless. Humans may be the engineers of their own salvation, but they are also capable of engineering their own destruction.

The colonial nuances here are interesting. On the one hand, the colonial efforts of humans on the Wirrn home world are applauded. They are "space pioneers" who have "succeeded." Any sympathy the viewer may feel for the Wirrn is negated by their unwavering malevolence toward humans. Even the Doctor's weak assertion that "there's plenty of room in the galaxy for us all" falls flat as he works hard to destroy the Wirrn once and for all. Humans are his "favorite species," after all, and the colonies serve a purpose in helping to seed humanity among the stars ("The Ark in Space: Part 4").

On the other hand, human colonies are portrayed as backward places, with improper speech and faulty genes. They are therefore not considered as homes for genetically pure humans. The occupants of the ark would rather sleep for five thousand years than relocate to one of the colonies. Moreover, the remaining occupants of Earth would rather take their chances in thermic shelters, where they eventually die, than relocate. The narrative makes no mention of any attempt to build ships to relocate Earth's inhabitants. Although the racial tensions mentioned above were slowly changing, one cannot help but hear some of the same white-British nationalism here that one finds in the first ark serial. Although the viewer is assured that "all colors, all creeds" are represented on the ark ("The Ark in Space: Part 1"), the cast, whether in cryogenic pods or revived, is entirely white, the alien colored.[9] To be human is to be of Earth. To be worthy of survival, one must be white British.

Nuances aside, the narrative resolves when the Doctor, with the help of his companions and the station's crew, succeed in destroying the Wirrn. Unlike the first narrative, the humans take an active role in their salvation, using electricity, bravery, and misdirection to trick the Wirrn into leaving on a small transport ship. There, the infected station's commander uses what remains of his humanity to blow up the transport and save the human race. The indomitable human spirit the Doctor praised at the beginning of the serial survives.

Within these four episodes, therefore, one again finds anxiety about the inevitable destruction of Earth and optimism that human ingenuity can overcome any external challenge. One also sees an insecurity about race, this time clearly defined in terms of genetics and colonial location. Rather than fear of disease, however, one finds a fear of insects, which brings the serial more into the realm of science fiction horror than the previous serial. Still, this serial reaffirms the notion that the collective possibility of humanity is worth saving, even if individual people and their unique qualities are not.

"The Beast Below"

The third *Doctor Who* ark narrative consists of a single episode, "The Beast Below," which aired in April 2010.

In this episode, the eleventh Doctor (played by Matt Smith) and his companion arrive on a space ship a thousand years in the future. As before, a group of humans have set off to search for a new world because their own has been destroyed. The imagined disaster is once again natural; some unspecified solar event has caused the earth to burn. This time, however, human ingenuity fails. Although many nations take to the skies

---

9. Originally, the script writer intended one of the station's crew to be black, but he was overruled during production, and the role went to a white actress instead (Sullivan 2015). What a difference that casting might have made.

in ships, the principal population of the narrative, the United Kingdom, is powerless to save themselves … until, that is, a giant star whale appears. Then, human ingenuity kicks in: the whale is trapped and forced to carry the British people to safety. Unlike the previous two narratives, there is a great deal of fatalism in this episode. Humans live and die according to the whims of nature, and there is a clear limit to human ingenuity.

Fig. 5. Star Whale. "The Beast Below." *Doctor Who*. BBC. 2010.

This narrative is also much more localized in scope. Gone are the bright pristine corridors of the previous two narratives and the utopian façade they represent. Gone is the promise that all peoples of Earth have a place on the ark. This ark is dark and dirty, its population limited to the people of England and Northern Ireland. Yet, this ark is also more diverse than its predecessors. Children join the cast, as do minorities. The population of the ark are not specialists; they are ordinary people who go about their day attending school, drinking tea with friends, and riding bicycles. The leader of the ship is a black queen, tenth in a long line of Elizabeths who ruled the kingdom, and many of her crew are either minorities or human-machine hybrids. This ark does not promise racial equality; it assumes it. No doubt this shift is possible due to societal changes in the British population. Since the 1980s, Britain, like other Western nations, had increasingly embraced the varied cultural identities of its populous, with public policy generally reinforcing the notion that a diverse population is a positive development

(Samanani 2018, 7). This *Doctor Who* narrative is pitched to an audience comfortable with this diversity. The desired diversity is not preached as an ideal; it is simply taken for granted.

However, not all is well on this voyage. People live in fear of making a mistake and being sent "below," where unnamed horrors are said to await them. The people, even the queen, have forgotten the truth about the ship's propulsion, that a star whale carries them to safety. They have forgotten that the crew of the ship tortures the creature on a daily basis to ensure its continued cooperation. Upon coming of age and once every five years thereafter, each citizen is reminded of this truth and is given a choice: protest the treatment of the creature or forget about it. Those who protest are fed to the whale; those who choose to forget return to their normal lives, accepting that the harsh treatment of the whale is necessary to secure the continued survival of the United Kingdom. Important here is the recognition that the blame cannot be placed on a single ruler or governing body; the entire population makes the choice again and again to treat the creature harshly. As the Doctor says sarcastically, it's "democracy in action" ("The Beast Below").

Unlike the previous two narratives, this episode recognizes that life beyond humans has value. The other two narratives did preserve animal life, either in vast gardens or in cryogenic chambers. Yet, they were present in the background as mere props. The serials did not consider why the inclusion of animals on the ark was important or what function they served. Moreover, the alien species on the earlier arks were seen as obstacles to overcome, not beings with their own valid needs and feelings. In this ark narrative, however, the viewer is encouraged to pity the star whale. Although they feel justified in their actions, the humans know that the whale has feelings and that they are wrong to treat it harshly.

This awareness is heightened when the Doctor discovers the presence of the star whale. The Doctor immediately recognizes that the treatment is wrong but also feels limited in his options. If he frees the creature, humans will die. If he lets the treatment continue, the creature will suffer immensely. He eventually decides to cause severe brain damage to the creature, effectively killing it so it no longer feels pain but continues to serve as the ship's propulsion. Like his previous incarnations, the Doctor still sides with humans, though at least he exhibits great anguish in doing so, making it clear to the viewer that such behavior—putting human needs above all else—is reprehensible. Again, the change in perspective reflects changes in British mentality over the intervening decades. Just as there was more racial sensibility in Britain by this point, so there was more eco-sensibility.[10] Humanity was no longer the center of the universe; humans had come to be seen as part of a larger ecosystem that must be protected if the human race is to survive.

Fortunately for the star whale, the Doctor's companion recognizes that the star whale does not eat children who are sent below. Indeed, the star whale appeared in the first place when it heard the children of Earth crying in fear. These two facts lead to the realization that the star whale volunteered to help the British people and would likely continue to do so without external motivation if given the chance. The companion therefore frees the whale, who acts as anticipated. The two species, human and whale, continue in harmony, neither living in fear or in pain. Unlike the previous serials, then, the resolution stems completely from the initiative of a human being. The Doctor plays an ancillary role. Yet, the solution relies not on human ingenuity but on human compassion. Humans are worth saving, provided that they act justly toward the natural world around them.

Within this episode, therefore, one again finds anxiety about the inevitable natural destruction of Earth. However, much of the superficial optimism of the previous serials disappears. There is more racial diversity, and the ending is more satisfying, with two species living in relative harmony. But this happy ending is not guaranteed. Most humans and even the alien Doctor are content to put human needs above all else, even if it means torturing an innocent creature. Human ingenuity cannot save the day. Only a random act of kindness can preserve the human race. The message is clear, even if the certainty that humans will enact it is not.

Conclusion

The arks described in this essay are fictions. They represent what *could be*. And yet, they are more than simple stories. They reflect their authors' darkest fears and their most ardent hopes. They are social commentaries on how humans treat each another and the world around them, and the answer is not always pretty. Yet, for most of these authors, there is something worth redeeming about the human race, some righteousness worth

---

10. For more on ecology and the development of science fiction, see the essays in Canavan and Robinson 2014.

holding on to. These fictitious stories beg the audience to consider what that righteousness is and what people today might do to help it survive in the world.

The world is coming to an end. What will you save?

Representative Examples in Science Fiction

Novels and Short Stories

Adams, Douglas. 2002. *The Ultimate Hitchhiker's Guide to the Galaxy*. New York: Del Rey.

Balmer, Edwin, and Philip Wylie. 1933. *When Worlds Collide*. New York: Stokes.

———. 1934. *After the Worlds Collide*. New York: Stokes.

Baxter, Stephen. 2008. *Flood*. London: Gollancz.

———. 2009. *Ark*. New York: New America Library.

Bradbury, Ray. (1950) 1977. "Way in the Middle of the Air." Pages 89–102 in *The Martian Chronicles*. Grand Master ed. New York: Bantam.

———. 1951. "The Other Foot." Pages 43–57 in *The Illustrated Man*. Garden City, NY: Doubleday.

Catran, Ken. 1997. *Deepwater Black: The Complete Story*. London: Hodder Children's.

Clarke, Arthur C. 1986. *The Songs of Distant Earth*. New York: Ballantine.

Dayle, Harry. 2013. *Noah's Ark: Survivors*. Leigh-on-Sea: Shelfless.

Hogan, James P. 1982. *Voyage from Yesteryear*. New York: Ballantine Books.

Martin, Laura. 2016. *The Ark Plan*. New York: Harper.

———. 2017. *Code Name Flood*. New York: Harper.

Serviss, Garrett Putman. 1911–1912. "Second Deluge." *The Cavalier*.

Vinge, Vernor. 1972. "Long Shot." *Analog Science Fiction/Science Fact* 89.6:159–70.

Walker, Karen Thompson. 2012. *The Age of Miracles*. New York: Random House.

Williamson, Jack. 1934. "Born of the Sun." *Astounding Stories* 13.1.

———. 1939. "The Fortress of Utopia." *Startling Stories* 2.3.

Radio

Adams, Douglas, and John Lloyd. 1978. *Hitchhiker's Guide to the Galaxy*. "Fit the Sixth." BBC Radio.

Comics

Balmer, Edwin, and Philip Wylie. 1940–1941. *Speed Spaulding*. San Mateo Times.

Siegel, Jerry, et al. 1938. "Superman." *Superman*. Action Comics #1.

Films

Battle for Terra. 2007. Directed by Aristomenis Tsirbas. Written by Evan Spiliotopoulos and Aristomenis Tsirbas. Menithings Production.

Downsizing. 2017. Directed by Alexander Payne. Written by Alexander Payne and Jim Taylor. Paramount Pictures.

Moonraker. 1979. Directed by Lewis Gilbert. Written by Christopher Woods. Eon Productions et al.

Pandorum. 2009. Directed by Christian Alvart. Written by Travis Milloy. Constantin Film Produktion.

Seeking a Friend for the End of the World. 2012. Written and directed by Lorene Scafaria. Mandate Pictures.

Sky Captain and the World of Tomorrow. 2004. Written and directed by Kerry Conran. Paramount Pictures.

Titan A.E. 2000. Directed by Don Bluth and Gary Goldman. Written by Hans Bauer and Randall McCormick. Twentieth Century Fox Film Corporation.

WALL-E. 2008. Directed by Andrew Stanton. Written by Andrew Stanton and Pete Docter. Disney Pixar.

When Worlds Collide. 1951. Directed by Rudolph Maté. Written by Sidney Boehm. Paramount Pictures.

TV Series/Episodes

The 100. 2014–2020. Produced by Jason Rothenberg. Bonanza Productions Inc.

"The Ark." 2007. *Stargate: Atlantis*. Directed by William Waring. Written by Brad Wright and Robert C. Cooper. MGM Television.

"The Ark in Space." 1975. *Doctor Who*. Directed by Rodney Bennett. Written by Robert Holmes. British Broadcasting Corporation.

Battlestar Galactica. 1978–1979. Produced by Glen Larson. Larson Productions.

Battlestar Galactica. 2004–2009. Produced by Ronald D. Moore et al. R&D TV et al.

"The Beast Below." 2010. *Doctor Who.* Directed by Andrew Gunn. Written by Steven Moffat. British Broadcasting Corporation.

"Black Market." 2006. *Battlestar Galactica.* Directed by Hames Head. Written by Ronald D. Moore. R&D TV et al.

"Episode 1.6." 1981. *Hitchhiker's Guide to the Galaxy.* Directed by Alan J. W. Bell. Written by Douglas Adams. British Broadcasting Corporation.

"For the World Is Hollow and I Have Touched the Sky." 1968. *Star Trek: The Original Series.* Directed by Tony Leader. Written by Rik Vollaerts. Paramount Television.

Galactica 1980. 1980. Produced by Glen Larson. Larson Productions.

"The Inner Light." 1992. *Star Trek: The Next Generation.* Directed by Peter Lauitson. Written by Morgan Gendel. Paramount Television.

"Lamentis." 2021. *Loki.* Directed by Kate Herron. Written by Bisha K. Ali. Marvel Studios.

"Lifeboat." 2003. *Stargate: SG-1.* Directed by Peter DeLuise. Written by Brad Wright and Jonathan Glassner. MGM Worldwide Television Productions.

"Mission of the Darians." 1975. *Space 1999.* Directed by Ray Austin. Written by Johnny Byrne. Incorporated Television Company.

Raised by Wolves. 2020–. Directed by Aaron Guzikowski et al. HBO Max.

"Resurrection Ship: Part 2." 2006. *Battlestar Galactica.* Directed by Michael Rymer. Written by Ronald D. Moore. R&D TV et al.

"Saga of a Star World." 1978. *Battlestar Galactica.* Directed by Richard A. Colia and Alan Levi. Written by Glen Larson. Larson Productions.

Salvation. 2017–2018. Produced by Alex Kurtzman et al. CBS Television.

"Scorched Earth." 2000. *Stargate: SG-1.* Directed by Martin Wood. Written by Brad Wright and Jonathan Glassner. MGM Worldwide Television.

Snowpiercer. 2020–. Produced by Scott Derrickson et al. TNT.

Star Lost. 1973. Written by Harlan Ellison. CTV Television Network.

"The Steel Sky," "The Plague," "The Return," and "The Bomb." 1966. *Doctor Who.* Directed by Michael Imison. Written by Paul Erickson and Lesley Scott. British Broadcasting Corporation.

Works Cited

Callahan, Daniel. n.d. "BBC: The Ark." *The Doctor Who Ratings Guide.* https://tinyurl.com/SBLPress6708d1.

Canavan, Gerry, and Kim Stanley Robinson. 2014. *Green Planets: Ecology and Science Fiction*. Middleton, CT: Wesleyan University Press.

Crome, Andrew. 2013. "'There Never Was a Golden Age': *Doctor Who* and the Apocalypse." Pages 189–204 in *Religion and* Doctor Who*: Time and Relative Dimensions of Faith*. Edited by Andrew Crome and James F. McGrath. Eugene, OR: Cascade.

Fecht, Sarah. 2014. "How Many People Does It Take to Colonize Another Star System?" *Popular Mechanics*. https://tinyurl.com/SBLPress6708d7.

Gregg, Peter B. 2004. "England Looks to the Future: The Cultural Forum Model and *Doctor Who*." *Journal of Popular Culture* 37:648–61.

Kauwe, Vanessa de. 2013. "Through Coloured Eyes: An Alternative Viewing of Postcolonial Transition." Pages 143–57 in *Doctor Who and Race*. Edited by Lindy Orthia. Bristol: Intellect.

Kirby, David A. 2007. "The Devil in Our DNA: A Brief History of Eugenics in Science Fiction Films." *Literature and Medicine* 26:83–108.

Mann, George. 2001. "The History and Origins of Science Fiction." Pages 1–26 in *The Mammoth Encyclopedia of Science Fiction*. Edited by George Mann. London: Little Brown.

Pleins, J. David. 2003. *When The Great Abyss Opened: Classic and Contemporary Readings of Noah's Flood*. Oxford: Oxford University Press.

Ryan, William, and Walter Pitman. 1998. *Noah's Flood: The New Scientific Discoveries about the Event That Changed History*. New York: Simon & Schuster.

Samanani, Farhan. 2018. "Race in Britain: Inequality, Identity, Belonging; 1–2 November 2018 Conference Briefing." Cumberland Lodge.

Stableford, Brian. 2006. "Entymology." Pages 156–60 in *Science Fact and Science Fiction: An Encyclopedia*. New York: Routledge.

Steve. 2017. "The Plague (The Ark Episode 2)." *Time Space Visualiser*. https://tinyurl.com/SBLPress6708d3.

Stone, Michael E., Aryeh Amihay, and Vered Hillel. 2010. *Noah and His Books*. EJL 28. Atlanta: Society of Biblical Literature.

Sullivan, Shannon Patrick. 2015. "Serial 4C: The Ark In Space." *Doctor Who: A Brief History of Time (Travel)*. https://tinyurl.com/SBLPress6708d4.

Tilford, Nicole L. 2014. "The Ark in Space: *Battlestar Galactica* and Other Seed Ships." Noah's Flood: Ancient Stories of Natural Cataclysm. https://tinyurl.com/SBLPress6708d6.

The Handmaid

RHONDA BURNETTE-BLETSCH

Margaret Atwood's *The Handmaid's Tale* (1985) imagines a near future in which the United States has been replaced by a Bible-based theocracy called Gilead. The novel and its adaptations make use of a wide array of biblical texts and images.[1] Most frequently cited is a text in which the barren Rachel decides to use her handmaid Bilhah as a reproductive surrogate (Gen 30:1–4):

> When Rachel saw that she bore Jacob no children, she envied her sister; and she said to Jacob, "Give me children, or I shall die!" Jacob became very angry with Rachel and said, "Am I in the place of God, who has withheld from you the fruit of the womb?" Then she said, "Here is my maid Bilhah; go in to her, that she may bear upon my knees and that I too may have children through her." So she gave him her maid Bilhah as a wife; and Jacob went in to her. (NRSV)

On ceremony days in Gilead, a commander removes a Bible from a locked chest and reads this passage to his assembled household before ritually raping a handmaid while she lies upon the knees of his wife.

This despicable practice is intended to address an infertility crisis brought about by nuclear radiation, climate change, and exposure to toxic chemicals. Such a fictional focus reflects real concerns about the ways

---

1. The novel has been adapted into a film (1990) and a Hulu series (2017–) by the same name. Atwood has also published a sequel entitled *The Testaments* (2019). Atwood prefers to call her dystopias "speculative fiction" rather than science fiction, because they do not present futuristic technology or unprecedented cultural situations. As she points out, all the atrocities mentioned in *The Handmaid's Tale* have occurred historically at least once (Atwood 2011, 8). This essay was written prior to the release of seasons 4 and 5 of the Hulu series.

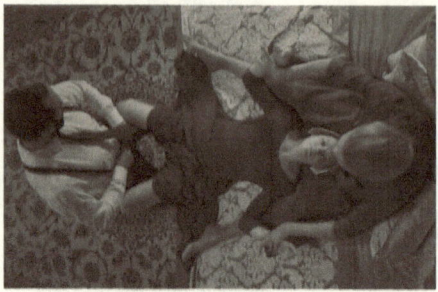

Fig. 1. The ceremony or ritualized rape of a handmaid. "Offred," *The Handmaid's Tale*, Hulu, 2017–.

in which modern technologies and changing environmental conditions could affect reproductive patterns in the future. More importantly, the proposed solution—rounding up fertile women to serve as handmaids for wealthy, powerful childless couples—reflects real concerns about the ways in which women, especially poor and minority women, are often exploited by wealthier segments of society. Atwood's tale and others like it draw upon the narratives of Genesis to reflect upon the ethics of surrogacy, polygamy, and other such reproductive practices and the power dynamics such practices embody.[2]

The Handmaid in the Bible and Beyond

Although Atwood cites the Rachel and Bilhah text, the tension between wives and handmaids in *The Handmaid's Tale* more closely resembles the tempestuous relationships of the Sarah-Hagar tradition. Bilhah has no voice in Genesis, which would perhaps make her the ideal handmaid in Gilead.[3] Despite hints of a more complicated backstory (Gen 35:22; 49:4), Bilhah and Leah's handmaid Zilpah remain undeveloped characters.[4] Each bears Jacob two sons, who become the eponymous ancestors of four Israelite tribes. Conversely, in the Sarah-Hagar account we find round characters, multiple voices, and competing theologies that invite diverse

---

2. An impressive volume of essays on the Bible in Atwood's work was published by Rhiannon Graybill and Peter J. Sabo in 2020. However, none of these authors examines *The Handmaid's Tale* as a modern revision of the Sarah-Hagar story.

3. In the third season of the Hulu series, the mouths of handmaids in Washington, DC, are actually sewn closed to ensure their silence.

4. Readers are only told that Jacob's son Reuben sleeps with Bilhah and later loses his birthright for this reason. Jubilees 33 elaborates Bilhah's role in the story by making it clear that she was an unwilling participant in this tryst.

interpretations. Therefore, I propose that it is more fruitful to consider the works of Atwood and her adapters as a chapter in the reception history of Gen 16 and 21.

It is possible to read the Sarah-Hagar tradition in a variety of ways. As Norman Gottwald (1995, 257) has noted, no reader comes to a text "naked" but is instead "outfitted with preunderstandings and pretexts that shape what we see and what we emphasize in the Bible." Because each interpreter has a distinct social location, many interpretations are conceivable, and none is disinterested. Reading with others unlike ourselves makes us aware of our own biases and helps us see different interpretive possibilities in a text.[5]

If many interpretations are possible, then the adjudication of readings is political. The powerful can "assert and propagate [their] interpretation over all others" (Weems 1991, 33), while readings of the marginalized are suppressed. Privileged readers have tended to identify with more powerful characters and interpret biblical texts to their own advantage. There is a long history of Caucasian interpreters who envisioned Hagar as the "uppity" or "hypersexual" black slave of her white mistress Sarah.[6] Likewise, Christian supersessionist readings have long cast Hagar as Israel and Sarah as the church (Heard 2014, 274). In both of these interpretive traditions, commentators are quick to blame Hagar while excusing Abraham, Sarah, and the God who sends a slave back to an abusive mistress.[7] Such interpretations conceal injustice within the text while reinforcing a privileged worldview.

---

5. Nicole Simopoulos (2007, 63–72) shows how different social locations and life experiences shape interpreters' perceptions of the Sarah-Hagar story. She found that upper-middle-class Caucasian women tended to identify more closely with Sarah and understand Hagar as a homewrecker, but those who had experienced divorce also sympathized with Hagar's loneliness and despondency in Gen 21. Latina women, who had moved from Mexico and Central America to Northern California, empathized with Hagar's sense of displacement as an Egyptian living in a foreign land. Black South African women tended to understand Hagar as an exploited woman and to resent Sarah's abusiveness.

6. See, for example, the collected texts about Hagar in Taylor and Weir 2006, 107–254.

7. These characters are initially introduced in Gen 11 as Abram and Sarai, but for convenience I will use their more familiar names throughout this chapter. Furthermore, although a complex composition history lies behind these chapters, I am concerned here only with the final form of the text that is available for adaptation.

Feminist and womanist interpreters have challenged privileged readings of the Sarah-Hagar tradition, drawing attention to ways in which both women are trapped by cultural ideologies and biological circumstance. Yet, Sarah reveals her complicity in the abusive patriarchal system when she decides to achieve her own security at the expense of a lower-status, ethnically other woman.[8] The matriarch's desire to secure her own well-being blinds her to Hagar's suffering.

Sarah is introduced as a barren woman (Gen 11:29–30), a motif that runs throughout the ancestral narratives (see also Gen 25:21; 30:1–2). Most of the matriarchs in Genesis have difficulty bearing children and are depicted as desperate to do so at any cost. The Hebrew word *aqarah* ("barren"), which literally means "uprooted" or "lacking roots," calls to mind the tenuous social position of childless women in patriarchal societies (Pabst 2003, 10). It is used only for female infertility, as there is no indication that the biblical world recognized male sterility. The desperation of these literary characters for offspring recognizes that a woman's social status and security in the ancient world depended upon childbearing. Barrenness conferred shame and lowered a woman's social standing.

Sarah's marginality as a childless matriarch in a patriarchal culture is evident in her repeated absence from theophanic episodes and Abraham's willingness to sacrifice her twice over, first in Egypt (Gen 12:10–16) and then in Gerar (20:1–2). However, as the wife of a wealthy patriarch (13:2), she is also a privileged woman. She owns the Egyptian slave Hagar, whose lower status is cemented by ethnicity. Because the name Hagar in Hebrew suggests "the stranger" (*hagger*), it is possible that this is not the slave woman's actual name. She may simply be known among Abraham's people as "the Stranger" or "the Outsider." As a privileged female, Sarah chooses to exploit the body of this slave as a reproductive surrogate to raise her own status and secure her position in Abraham's lineage. Hagar's agreement to this scheme is not required or considered of any consequence.

Both the Code of Hammurabi and ancient Nuzi law allow a barren woman to give a slave to her husband for the purpose of bearing a son she might claim as her own (Okoye 2007, 173). According to these texts, any son born under such an arrangement must be adopted by the barren wife and cannot be disinherited.[9] Moreover, the surrogate remains a slave in the

---

8. Williams 1991, 36; Weems 2005, 10–11; Gafney 2017, 38.
9. The laws do not specify what would happen to daughters born to the handmaid.

household she served and can never be cast out. Scholars disagree whether these laws reflect the legal backdrop of the Genesis narratives, since many details in the Bible do not seem to fit this precise scenario.[10] Scholars also disagree over whether Hagar's status changes once she is given to Abraham as a reproductive surrogate. Does she remain a slave, or does she, at least temporarily, become a secondary wife? Genesis 16 repeatedly describes Hagar as a "handmaid" (*shiphkhah*), but verse 3 stipulates she was given to Abraham "as a wife" (*lishah*) (Trible 1984, 11).[11]

If Hagar's social status was elevated, it was short-lived. Once she conceived, her mistress "became small" (*qalal*) in her eyes. This is yet another ambiguous expression. Was Hagar angry with Sarah because she had forced her to serve as a sexual surrogate? Did she feel superior to her mistress because of her own ability to conceive when Sarah could not? Or did the jealous Sarah simply perceive a slight where none was intended?[12] Here, as elsewhere, the social location of the interpreter tends to determine the reading. With Abraham's permission, Sarah responds to the slight by "dealing harshly" (*innah*) with her Egyptian handmaid. Ironically, this same verb will be used of Pharaoh's treatment of the Israelites (Exod 1:11), suggesting that the flight of Hagar, the Egyptian, from Sarah should be understood in parallel with Israel's later exodus from Egypt. Like Israel, Hagar flees from oppression into the wilderness, where she encounters an angel of Yahweh.

Sympathetic readers might feel elation on behalf of the runaway slave woman, but she is immediately sent back to Abraham's camp. The use of the terms "handmaid" and "mistress" reminds us of Hagar's rightful place in this society, and the directive in Gen 16:9 to "submit" (*innah*) echoes Sarah's previous harsh treatment. One could easily read this text, as was likely intended by the Israelite author, as proof of God's favor for the Israelites over the Ishmaelites. Alternatively, womanist interpreter Delores

---

10. Leah is not childless when she offers her handmaid to Jacob (Gen 30:9), and the handmaids continue to be recognized as the mothers of their children (21:10; 33:1–2; 35:23–26; 37:2; 46:18, 25). Ishmael and Hagar are cast out (Gen 21), and the children of Bilhah and Leah seem to have a lower status that the biological children of Rachel and Leah (Gen 33:1–2).

11. The same expression is later used in relation to Bilhah (Gen 30:4) and Zilpah (30:9). Here also the evidence of a status change is unclear. The women continue to be called *shiphkhah* in later chapters (32:22; 33:1, 2, 6). The expression *lishah* might simply mean "as a woman [to impregnate]."

12. We hear about this offense from Sarah's perspective (Jacobs 2007, 147).

Williams (1993, 19–20) argues that, by returning to Sarah, Hagar temporarily sacrifices control of her own destiny to ensure her survival and that of her child. Likewise, Toba Spitzer (1998, 10) argues that the angel's use of a *hithpael* form ("cause yourself to submit") indicates Hagar's continuing agency even in choosing to return to her mistress.

Hagar also receives a covenant promise reminiscent of the one given Abraham. She, too, will have countless descendants who will be required to endure slavery before the promise is fulfilled (cf. Gen 15:12–16). Most commentators view Hagar's covenant as inferior to Abraham's; after all, who wants a son who is "a wild ass of a man" and lives "at odds with all his kin" (Gen 16:12)? However, it may be that the dominant interpretive tradition has shaped the negative translation of this verse. Christopher Heard (2014, 277–79) points out that other biblical occurrences of this animal metaphor are largely positive, connoting freedom, isolation, and a wilderness habitat. Moreover, the grammar of verse 12 just as easily indicates nearness to kin as it does opposition.[13] Given that these words appear in the context of a blessing, it seems logical to opt for a more positive translation describing Hagar's son as destined to be a free man who will live cooperatively in the midst of his own kin group.

Seeing and hearing are important motifs in Hagar's theophany. She is instructed to name her son "God will hear" (Ishmael) because the Lord has heard her affliction (cf. Exod 2:24–25; 3:7). Hagar responds to this encounter with God beside a wilderness "spring" (*ayin*, literally "eye") by becoming a theologian. While naming the location of a theophany is a common biblical occurrence, only Hagar dares to name God. Her theological formulation, El-roi ("God of seeing"), is born of Hagar's personal experience and appears nowhere else in scripture. This is a God who hears and sees Hagar and promises her a future.

The theological perspective espoused by Abraham and Sarah is quite different. In Gen 21, God seems to place the interests of Sarah and her child over those of Hagar and Ishmael. Sarah, now with her own biological son Isaac recently weaned, witnesses Ishmael doing … something. The verb (*mtskhq*), a participial form of Isaac's name, is usually trans-

---

13. The expression in question is *yado be-kol*, usually translated "his hand [will be] against everyone." Heard argues that in such expressions the meaning of the preposition *be* depends on the associated verb and can be positive (Gen 21:18) or negative (1 Kgs 11:26). Since a verb is lacking here, either an adversative or cooperative meaning is possible.

lated "playing" or "mocking."[14] However, the pun seems to indicate that she sees Ishmael "Isaacing" or potentially standing in the place of Isaac (Okoye 2007, 170–71; Robinson 2013, 208). Enraged, Sarah demands that Abraham "drive out [*garesh*] this slave woman [*amah*] with her son" to ensure Isaac's exclusive right to inheritance. Using the same verb that later describes Israel's dispossession of the indigenous inhabitants of Canaan (Exod 33:2) underlines Hagar and Ishmael's outsider status. Sarah labels Ishmael the son of Hagar (not Abraham) and replaces the term "handmaid" (*shiphkhah*) from Gen 16 with what seems to be a more derogatory expression. In her anger and disgust, Sarah resorts to a dehumanizing discourse that marks Hagar and Ishmael as abject and insists that they not be counted as a part of Abraham's lineage.[15] While the slave and her child resided in Abraham's household, group boundaries remained fluid. Sarah protects her own interests by forging a firm boundary that requires Hagar and Ishmael be expelled into the wilderness. According to the narrator, God sides with Sarah over Hagar and convinces Abraham to do so as well.

Hagar once again experiences a theophany in the wilderness constructed around the motifs of hearing and seeing. At first, she finds *no* spring (eye) and asks *not* to look upon the death of her child. But when Hagar weeps, God hears.[16] The promise of progeny is repeated, and God opens her eyes to see that water is nearby. Like Abraham, Hagar is assured of her offspring's future prosperity at a time when it seems most unlikely. She regains agency in the story, filling a skin with water, giving Ishmael a drink, and later securing him an Egyptian wife. God is with Ishmael, although he and his mother are basically written out of the biblical story going forward (Gen 25:9, 12–18).

Why was Ishmael not allowed a share of the inheritance, as were the sons of Bilhah and Zilpah? Genesis 12–50 constructs Israel's national iden-

---

14. The words "with her son Isaac," which are lacking in Hebrew manuscripts, are imported from the Septuagint.

15. Drawing on the work of Judith Butler, Sarah Ahmed argues that emotions such as anger or disgust can be used to construct and reinforce community boundaries. See this discussion in Claassens 2013, 3–4.

16. Strangely, God hears the voice of Ishmael, not Hagar. Hagar's weeping is a pathos-filled counter to Sarah's laughter (Gen 18:12; 21:6), yet both actions could be seen as small acts of resistance against a patriarchal social structure (Claassens 2005, 299–302).

tity based on a shared myth of common origins and divine destiny. Identity formation and boundary maintenance are major concerns of the ancestral narrative. What does membership within the covenant community entail? Who is part of this chosen people, and, perhaps even more importantly, who is not? Hagar is Egyptian, whereas Bilhah and Zilpah originate from within Laban's household. Despite their lower social class, they likely share an ethnic and religious background with Rachel and Leah.[17] Because of Hagar's abject otherness, Ishmael is ultimately excluded. In a patriarchal society such as ancient Israel, the bodies of women become mechanisms of inclusion and exclusion in the construction of community boundaries. Female bodies are used for similar purposes in *The Handmaid's Tale* and other works of science fiction.

The Handmaid in Science Fiction

Very few works of science fiction have appropriated the ancestral narratives of Genesis so thoroughly and explicitly as have Atwood and her adaptors. To situate *The Handmaid's Tale* among other texts in the reception history of Gen 12–50, it will be necessary to cast a wide net. As I have argued elsewhere (Burnette-Bletsch 2007, 129–60), biblical reception can take various forms, including direct citations, paraphrases, paradigms, allusions, echoes, and analogues. Analogues refer to works whose family resemblance with a biblical text is unintentional but nonetheless fruitful for interpretation. What follows are science fiction works that deal with reproduction and surrogacy in ways reminiscent of Gen 12–50.

Octavia Butler's time-travel slave narrative, *Kindred* (1979), intentionally uses the name Hagar to appropriate the biblical tradition. The novel's modern-day black protagonist, Dana, finds herself repeatedly called back in time to a nineteenth-century Maryland plantation where she encounters her ancestors: Alice, a black freewoman, and Rufus, the white planter who forces Alice into slavery and concubinage. Recalling their names from genealogical records in her family Bible, Dana realizes that she must ensure the birth of their daughter, her own great-grandmother, Hagar. Alice chose the name Hagar for their child, over the objection of Rufus, suggesting that she sees a parallel between her own

---

17. Rabbinic tradition holds that Bilhah and Zilpah were Laban's children by concubines and thus were half-sisters of Rachel and Leah (Kadari 2009).

sexual exploitation and that of the biblical handmaid. The intertext adds richness to Butler's exploration of power, gender, and race in the antebellum South.[18]

Like Atwood, Sheri S. Tepper sets her own feminist novel, *The Gate to Women's Country* (1988), in a dystopian future. The Pacific Northwest has become a political matriarchy, with most men living outside the city walls in hypermasculine garrisons. However, to the south live the Holylanders, members of a patriarchal, fundamentalist society with Old Testament underpinnings. The misogynistic Holylanders practice polygamy and value women only for their reproductive ability. Although the novel does not directly cite biblical narratives, the allusions are clear. Both Genesis and (more overtly) Euripides's Greek play *Iphigenia in Aulis* serve as intertexts that illustrate the dangers of patriarchy in contrast to life in Women's Country, which is quietly working toward its own eugenic solution to the problem of male violence.

Joanne Ramos's debut novel *The Farm* (2019) deals with socioeconomically coerced surrogacy in a capitalistic society. Poor and immigrant women are recruited to live at a highly controlled commercial facility where they serve as baby hosts for wealthy clients. Some of these clients are infertile, and others simply want to avoid the inconvenience of pregnancy. While Genesis is never directly cited as a source for the novel, the story weaves together issues of gender, race, and class in a manner reminiscent of the biblical account.

Finally, the young adult novel *Only Ever Yours* by Louise O'Neill (2014) describes a dystopian future plagued by infertility in which only males are born naturally. Females (called Eves) are genetically produced in a lab and raised to serve as child-bearing wives, sexual concubines, or the "chastities" who indoctrinate the next generation of Eves. O'Neill's debt to *The Handmaid's Tale* is obvious, although she chose to use Gen 2–3 as her biblical intertext.

This handful of examples demonstrates the potential use of biblical handmaid accounts in science fiction explorations of race, class, and gender. Hagar's status as a slave and ethnic outsider renders the Sarah-Hagar tradition an especially suitable intertext for stories of slavery and

---

18. Forced parentage is also a theme in Butler's Xenogenesis trilogy in which some survivors of a nuclear-devastated Earth reluctantly agree to an interbreeding program with alien colonizers to ensure the survival of their species. Aside from the title, this trilogy has little overt connection to Genesis.

colonization. As in the biblical text, the bodies of poor and minority women are exploited in these works by a wealthier, more privileged segment of society.

Atwood's *The Handmaid's Tale*

Atwood's novel and its adaptations use the Genesis ancestral narrative along with other biblical texts to create a future theocracy in which women are denied personal agency and control over their own bodies.[19] Gilead defines women by their relationship to men as indicated by an assigned uniform: wives (blue: companionship), aunts (brown: enforcers), handmaids (red: childbearing), marthas (green: domestic labor), jezebels (scantily clad: sex workers), and unwomen (gray: manual labor).[20] These categories deprive women of rounded, complex identities and trap them in roles determined by age, fertility, and class.[21] While aunts and wives enjoy some privileges, all of these women are trapped in socially prescribed roles. They are all answerable to men and lack independent authority.

Like Genesis, Gilead links fertility with divine blessing. Fathers are promoted. Wives who become mothers through surrogacy are honored. The childless Serena, wife of prominent commander Fred Waterford, lacks such honor. Serena's endless toil in the garden symbolizes her desperation to nurture a new life. "The attentive mother," Fred observes when he finds her working in the greenhouse (season 2, episode 9). However, Serena's horticultural labors are in vain. "The gray mold is back," she responds listlessly. "I already lost a tray of cuttings." Infertility is always a woman's fault; the word "sterility" is forbidden. Wives and handmaids are indoctrinated

---

19. Atwood draws heavily on historical and literary precursors, such as American Puritanism and George Orwell's *1984*, but was also inspired by the rise of religious political conservativism during the Reagan era. See Clarke 1995, 237–38.

20. In the novel, lower-class women, called econowives, wear striped clothing indicating that they perform all "female services" for their husbands. In the series, econowives wear blue-gray clothing.

21. Race is handled differently in the novel and its adaptations. In the original novel, Atwood imagines Gilead as a Caucasian society in which people of other races are deported to the colonies. In the Hulu series, non-Caucasian women appear among the lower classes in Gilead as handmaids, jezebels, marthas, econowives, and unwomen. the series also casts some black actors in the role of "eyes" and one junior commander.

to see infertility as a personal failing, since state ideology claims that God grants children only to the worthy.

For handmaids, the oft-quoted phrase "give me children or I will die" has a more literal meaning. If no pregnancy occurs within three postings, they will be declared unwomen and sent to the colonies (i.e., wilderness) to serve as forced labor under lethal radioactive conditions. Reduced to ambulatory wombs, handmaids are denied even their own names. Their designations change with each posting, indicating the lack of a fixed identity and temporary ownership by their assigned commander ("Of-xx"): June becomes Offred, Emily becomes Ofglen, and Janine becomes Ofwarren. As with Hagar, their assigned names suggest otherness, lack of personal agency, and the absence of a personal identity.

The assigned name of Atwood's main character, Offred, resembles the word "offered," suggesting that she is a kind of sacrifice. Indeed, Aunt Lydia teaches the handmaids to see their reproductive vocation as a divinely mandated self-sacrifice. They offer their bodies upon the altar of the state so that Gilead might continue. As Lydia often reminds them, they are sinners ("selfish," "ungrateful," "sluts"), and bearing children provides their only opportunity for redemption (cf. 1 Tim 2:15). Yet, like Hagar, Offred and the other handmaids have very limited agency.

Aunts indoctrinate the handmaids at Rachel and Leah Centers, ironically named for the biblical matriarchs rather than Bilhah and Zilpah. The biblical handmaids' names are effaced and replaced by those of Jacob's wives. Real and threatened violence creates docile bodies. Janine loses an eye for insolence. An aunt beats the soles of June's feet with frayed wire when she attempts to run away. These harsh corporal punishments serve as deterrents against further resistance. Agency is further discouraged by brainwashing and persistent infantilization. Aunt Lydia calls the handmaids "girls" (1985, 31), wives offer them cookies for good behavior (1985, 121; season 1, episode 2), and marthas force them to beg for a match (1985, 218).

Conformity is ensured by a system of constant surveillance. Bright red uniforms make the handmaids maximally visible. They are assigned walking partners, ostensibly for mutual protection but actually to spy on one another. Since an unguarded remark might be reported or overheard, handmaids learn to police their own speech and behavior. As Aunt Lydia says, "The Republic of Gilead ... knows no bounds. Gilead is within you" (1985, 25; season 2, episode 2). Secret police, called the "Eyes of God," represent state surveillance. God and, by extension, the government are always watching. Given these realities, the common greeting, "under His eye," gains an ominous connotation that subverts the positive seeing motif in Hagar's theophanies (Gen 16:13). To be seen by Gilead's God is dangerous, not comforting.

The social ideology of Gilead does not permit alliances between women of different classes. The tumultuous relationship between June and Serena mirrors that between Hagar and Sarah. The novel's protagonist hopes to find an older sister or motherly figure in her commander's wife but is disappointed (1985, 17). The Hulu series makes Serena much younger and, therefore, a potential peer for June. Yet, short-lived détentes only highlight the usual acrimony in their relationship. Serena's higher social position allows her to strike June when she feels disrespected (Gen 16:6). "There's biblical precedent," the latter notes wryly (season 1, episode 8; 1985, 18).

Antagonism goes both ways, especially in the Hulu series, which recreates the protagonist as a more outwardly resistant character. While June lacks Serena's authority, she uses what power is at her disposal to defy her mistress. Repeatedly ordered by Serena to pick up a knitting needle, the heavily pregnant handmaid claims to have felt a cramp. Surely Serena would not want to put the child at risk, she asks (season 2, episode 6). June's thinly veiled contempt clearly implies that her mistress has "become small" in her eyes (Gen 16:4). Serena notices and retaliates by treating her handmaid harshly. Like Abraham, Fred usually allows his wife to exert authority over the handmaid. Better the women despise one another than cooperate in challenging the patriarchy! When they do briefly join forces in the Hulu series (season 2, episode 8), Fred intentionally shames Serena by beating her with a belt in front of June to drive a wedge between them once more.

Like the impregnation ceremony, domestic abuse is biblically justified in Gilead. Before beating Serena, Fred reads aloud an amalgam of biblical texts as if they constitute a single passage:

> Wives, submit yourselves unto your own husbands, as unto the Lord [Eph 5:22]. And ye husbands dwell with them according to knowledge giving honor unto the wife as unto the weaker vessel [1 Pet 3:7a].... But if we confess our sins, He is faithful and just to forgive us [1 John 1:9a]. (season 2, episode 8)

Selective sampling of scripture allows the leaders of Gilead to craft a self-serving theocratic state purportedly around biblical tenets (Walker 2019,

77–78).[22] Biblical interpretation is the sole purview of the male ruling class (Sons of Jacob) and their collaborators (aunts). They cherry pick verses, often mixing together disparate texts or even deliberately misquoting, to advance their own interests at the expense of others. Gilead maintains power through control of information. Reading and writing are prohibited for women (with the sole exception of aunts), which prevents challenges to the authorized interpretation of scripture. Interpretive closure leads to biblical language that is either trivial (stores named *Loaves and Fishes*, *All Flesh*, etc.) or oppressive. A monolithic text is a dead text that loses the interpretive potential to inspire resistance.[23]

Examples of biblical sampling and misquotation abound. Pseudobiblical quotations, such as "To each according to her ability, to each according to his needs" or "They also serve who only stand and wait," form part of the handmaids' training.[24] Men cannot be blamed for sexual assault because "all flesh is weak," although June mentally corrects this to "all flesh is grass" (1985, 48). Handmaids must forgive resentful wives because "they know not what they do" (1985, 49). Handmaid training includes an altered form of the Beatitudes: "Blessed are the merciful. Blessed are the meek. Blessed are the silent." June notes the omission of "inheriting the earth" and suspects that the saying about silence was made up entirely (1985, 94; season 1, episode 1). Fred later justifies misogyny and violence with a misquotation of Prov 22:14: "'The mouth of a woman is a deep pit, he that falls therein will suffer.' You are the misery of man. All of you" (season 2, episode 14).[25]

---

22. Janine's weaning ceremony (season 1, episode 9) combines quotations from Luke 1:48 ("For he has regarded the low estate of his handmaid and behold from henceforth all generations shall call you blessed"), Gen 33:6 ("And the handmaidens came near, they and their children and they bowed themselves"), 2 Sam 2:6 ("The Lord now show you kindness and faithfulness and I too will show you the same favor"), and Num 6:24 ("The Lord bless thee and keep thee"). A similar sampling of disparate scripture passages occurs in the prayer meeting of season 3, episode 3.

23. This idea is represented in the novel by the literalization of biblical metaphors (e.g., the Whirlwind as a car model) and the Soul Scrolls office where rote prayers are mechanically generated for the faithful (Atwood 1985, 166–67).

24. The first quotation derives from Karl Marx's *Critique of the Gotha Program*. The second comes from John Milton's sonnet "When I Consider How My Light Is Spent."

25. The actual quotation condemns an adulteress rather than women in general.

In Gilead, the Bible is kept under lock and key like an incendiary device. As June asks, "Who knows what we'd make of it, if we ever got our hands on it?" (1985, 91). Nonetheless, the women of Gilead do engage in hermeneutics of their own. The Hulu series makes this more explicit. June often recognizes misuses of scripture and quotes biblical passages from memory as a form of resistance. When Aunt Lydia reminds her that the meek are blessed, she responds defiantly, "'And blessed are those who suffer for the cause of righteousness, for theirs is the kingdom.' I remember," earning herself an electric shock (season 1, episode 3). Serena attempts to reform Gilead's laws so that their daughter might be permitted to read. She and other wives crash a council meeting where Serena makes her argument and reads from the prologue of John's Gospel (season 2, episode 14). She loses a finger due to this infraction. The series also introduces Eden, a young female character who possesses a contraband Bible covered in marginal notes. She is initially committed to her duty as a potentially fertile wife in a loveless arranged marriage, but she eventually runs afoul of Gilead's laws by running away with a young guard. Once captured she justifies her refusal to repent and save herself by citing scripture (Isa 43:2; 1 Cor 13). Eden bravely faces execution as a fresh-faced martyr clinging to her own beliefs.

These scenes nod toward the multivalent nature of biblical texts. Interpreters in different social locations understand texts and, thus, the biblical God differently. In opposition to the official theology of Gilead, June constructs her own theology. When Serena celebrates her handmaid's pregnancy as the answer to their prayers, June protests incredulously, "You think I prayed to bring a baby into this house?" (season 1, episode 10). When Serena insists that their situation is God's will, June protests "No one knows the things of God" (season 2, episode 10). Hiding out in a newspaper office as a fugitive, June builds an altar and prays for the reporters who had been massacred there (season 2, episode 2). When she orchestrates an underground railroad to smuggle children out of Gilead, she understands this operation as a biblical exodus.[26] Just as Hagar expe-

---

26. The closing voiceover of season 3 paraphrases Exod 2:3: "And the Lord said, 'I have seen my people in bondage, and I have heard their cry. I know their sorrows. And I am come to deliver them from the hand of evil men, and to lead my people out of that sorrowful place to a land flowing with milk and honey.'" Similarly, the female protagonists in *The Handmaid's Tale*'s sequel reinterpret the story of the Levite's concubine (Judg 19) to justify resistance (Atwood 1985, 77–80, 302–3).

riences God differently than Sarah and Abraham, June theologically parts ways with the official religion of Gilead. Many interpreters have noted that the protagonist of Atwood's novel resists her situation by reclaiming language through Scrabble and her inner monologues. Likewise, June resists in the Hulu series by reclaiming biblical interpretation.[27]

Like Hagar, June lives in a society that allows more privileged women to exploit her body as a reproductive surrogate. The bodies of handmaids become a natural resource in service of the state. While all the women of Gilead are trapped in socially prescribed roles, wives and aunts enjoy special privileges in exchange for their complicity with the system. Even more parallels may be drawn from the Hulu series. Like Hagar, June runs away from Gilead during her pregnancy but ultimately returns to ensure the safety of her newborn child (season 2, episode 11). She eventually smuggles the infant out of Gilead but again chooses to return in order to save her kidnapped older daughter. Like Hagar, June constructs a theology from her own experiences in which a benevolent God sees and sides with people like her. Atwood's novel, and even more so its Hulu adaptation, features a hermeneutical situation where biblical interpretations of the powerful can be challenged by the theological intuition of the oppressed.

Representative Examples in Science Fiction

Atwood, Margaret. 1985. *The Handmaid's Tale*. New York: Houghton Mifflin.
———. 2019. *The Testaments*. New York: Doubleday.
Butler, Octavia. 1979. *Kindred*. Boston: Beacon.
The Handmaid's Tale. 1990. Directed by Volker Schlöndorff. Written by Harold Pinter. Cinecom Pictures.
The Handmaid's Tale. 2017–. Created by Bruce Miller. Hulu.
Ramos, Joanne. 2019. *The Farm*. New York: Random House.
Tepper, Sheri S. 1988. *The Gate to Women's Country*. New York: Bantam.

---

27. The series explains June's proclivity toward religious faith by giving her a Catholic father. Her father is entirely absent in the novel.

Works Cited

Atwood, Margaret. 2011. *In Other Worlds: SF and the Human Imagination.* New York: Anchor.

Burnette-Bletsch, Rhonda. 2007. "The Bible and Its Cinematic Adaptations: A Consideration of Filmic Exegesis." *JBR* 1:129–60.

Claassens, Juliana. 2005. "Laughter and Tears: Carnivalistic Overtones in the Stories of Sarah and Hagar." *PRSt* 32:295–308.

———. 2013. "Just Emotions: Reading the Sarah and Hagar Narrative (Genesis 16, 21) through the Lens of Human Dignity." *Verbum et Ecclesia* 34:1–6.

Clarke, Elizabeth. 1995. "How Feminist Can a Handmaid Be? Margaret Atwood's *The Handmaid's Tale.*" Pages 235–50 in *The Discerning Reader: Christian Perspectives on Literature and Theory.* Edited by David Barratt, Roger Pooley, and Leland Ryken. Grand Rapids: Baker.

Gafney, Wilda C. 2017. *Womanist Midrash: A Reintroduction to Women of the Torah and the Throne.* Louisville: Westminster John Knox.

Gottwald, Norman. 1995. "Framing Biblical Interpretation at New York Theological Seminary: A Student Self-Inventory on Biblical Hermeneutics." Pages 251–61 in *Social Location and Biblical Interpretation in the United States.* Vol. 1 of *Reading from This Place.* Edited by Fernando F. Segovia and Mary Ann Tolbert. Minneapolis: Fortress.

Graybill, Rhiannon, and Peter J. Sabo, eds. 2020. *"Who Knows What We'd Make of It, If We Ever Got Our Hands on It?": The Bible and Margaret Atwood.* Biblical Intersections 18. Piscataway, NJ: Gorgias.

Heard, Christopher. 2014. "On the Road to Paran: Toward a Christian Perspective on Hagar and Ishmael." *Int* 68:270–85.

Jacobs, Mignon R. 2007. *Gender, Power, and Persuasion: The Genesis Narratives and Contemporary Portraits.* Grand Rapids: Baker.

Kadari, Tamar. 2009. "Zilpah: Midrash and Aggadah." *Jewish Women: A Comprehensive Historical Encyclopedia.* Jewish Women's Archive. https://tinyurl.com/SBLPress6708e1.

Okoye, James C. 2007. "Sarah and Hagar: Genesis 16 and 21." *JSOT* 32:163–75.

O'Neill, Louise. 2014. *Only Ever Yours.* London: Quercus.

Pabst, Irene. 2003. "The Interpretation of the Sarah-Hagar Stories in Rabbinic and Patristic Literature: Sarah and Hagar as Female Representations of Identity and Difference." *Lectio Difficilior* 1. https://tinyurl.com/SBLPress6708e2.

Robinson, Bernard. 2013. "Characterization in the Hagar and Ishmael Narratives." *SJOT* 27:198–215.
Simopoulos, Nicole M. 2007. "Who Was Hagar? Mistress, Divorcee, Exile, or Exploited Worker: An Analysis of Contemporary Grassroots Readings of Genesis 16 by Caucasian, Latina, and Black South African Women." Pages 63–72 in *Reading Other-Wise: Socially Engaged Biblical Scholars Reading with Their Local Communities*. Edited by Gerald O. West. SemeiaSt 62. Atlanta: Society of Biblical Literature.
Spitzer, Toba. 1998. "Where Do You Come from and Where Are You Going? Hagar and Sarah Encounter God." *The Reconstructionist* 63:8–18.
Taylor, Marion Ann, and Heather E. Weir, eds. 2006. *Let Her Speak for Herself: Nineteenth-Century Women Writing on the Women of Genesis*. Waco, TX: Baylor University Press.
Trible, Phyllis. 1984. *Texts of Terror: Literary Feminist Readings of Biblical Narratives*. Philadelphia: Fortress.
Walker, Seth. 2019. "Remix in Gilead." Pages 77–89 in *The Handmaid's Tale and Philosophy*. Edited by Rachel Robison-Greene. Chicago: Open Court.
Weems, Renita J. 1991. "Do You See What I See? Diversity in Interpretation." *Church and Society* 82:28–43.
———. 2005. *Just a Sister Away: A Womanist Vision of Women's Relationships in the Bible*. Revised and updated. Bloomfield: Walk Worthy.
Williams, Delores S. 1993. *Sisters in the Wilderness: The Challenge of Womanist God-Talk*. Maryknoll, NY: Orbis.

The Utopian City

STEVEN J. SCHWEITZER

> If the war was over tomorrow, Zion's where the party would be.
> —Tank, *The Matrix* (1999)

The concept of an ideal city plays an important role in both biblical tradition and science fiction. The biblical tradition envisions a restored, future idealized city for the righteous across its various genres and time frames, but particularly within prophetic literature. This eschatological hope for a utopian dwelling place typically stands in contrast with the perceived desperate circumstances of the present. Across various science fiction works, this theme of the ideal city serves a similar function, both as a source of hope and as an example of contrast to a deficient present reality. Science fiction often uses the ideal city to create a utopian context only to subvert that expectation through the subsequent revelation that the utopian city is really dystopian in nature. The city of Zion in *The Matrix* trilogy provides one example of how this theme is manifest in both traditional and unexpected ways.

The Utopian City in the Bible

The first mention of a city in the Bible occurs early in the book of Genesis. Cain, son of Adam and Eve, departs from his parents after committing the first murder (of his brother Abel). Cain's wife bears him a son, Enoch. Genesis 4:17 states that Cain "built a city"[1] and named it after his son. While this association of the first murder and the first city through the figure of Cain has led to a long history of interpretation of the city itself as evil, this is not the only possibility. As the passage continues, another

---

1. All biblical citations are from the NRSV.

descendant of Cain, Jabal, is the first one to "live in tents and have livestock," while his brother Jubal is the first to "play the lyre and pipe" and his half-brother Tubal-cain is the first to forge "bronze and iron tools" (Gen 4:19–22). Surely, all these elements of "civilization" (nomadic lifestyle, domestication of animals, music, and metallurgy) are not to be viewed negatively simply because of their association with the lineage of Cain. Perhaps, in each case, the intention is to show hope—that even from great evil, good is possible, and humanity can still improve its condition. As the biblical tradition unfolds, such a recurring hope for an idealized city can be easily identified, and this city is most often associated with Jerusalem or, as it is also known, the city of David or the city of Zion.

The name Zion seems to have originally been associated with a Canaanite fortress within the city of Jebus, which according to biblical tradition David conquered soon after his coronation as king (2 Sam 5:6–10). The city became David's capital and was called Jerusalem. The link between the "city of Zion" and the "city of David" was thereby established, particularly in subsequent prophetic literature and the book of Psalms. The relocation of the ark of the covenant (symbolizing God's presence among the people) to the city (2 Sam 6:1–19) and the construction of the temple by David's son Solomon (1 Kgs 6–8) infuse this city with special political, religious, and cultural meaning as well as the notion of it being sacred space. The book of Deuteronomy refers to the city as the "place that the Lord your God will choose" (Deut 12:5, 11, 14, 21, 26), where God's name would dwell (12:11), and the book of Psalms refers to it as the "city of the great King," that is, God (48:1–3).

The destruction of the Jerusalem temple and the city itself by the Babylonians in the sixth century BCE therefore presented a theological problem for the ancient Israelites. If the God of Israel was supreme, how could God's chosen dwelling place be destroyed by those regarded as sinners? The answers offered by the biblical prophets transformed the earlier Zion traditions into an eschatological, utopian hope. The book of Ezekiel argues that God's presence, in the form of the "glory of the Lord," had abandoned the city and the temple prior to its destruction (Ezek 10–11), understood as a response to Israel's sins. This divine action is then reversed in Ezekiel's eschatological vision by the coming of the glory of the Lord to the future temple in the restored city (43:1–5). With God's return to the people, the city—in the midst of the reconstituted land of Israel—is thus able to flourish agriculturally (48:15–20) as holiness is restored (44:4–14) and temple sacrifices by the appropriate personnel resume (44:15–46:24).

While Ezekiel focuses on the temple and the land, the brief inclusion of the ideal city as part of this restored community is consistent with the expansion of this concept found in other postexilic texts.

The book of Isaiah decries the "city of chaos" (that is, Jerusalem) left desolate (24:1–13), but it maintains a promise that one day the city will become "a quiet habitation, an immovable tent," with God as king (33:20–22). The prophet proclaims that the city shall be rebuilt by the Persian king Cyrus, acting in response to God's prompting, and the exiles will be free to return (45:13), bringing comfort to the people and the redemption of Jerusalem (52:7–10).[2] The ruins and foundations will be rebuilt by those symbolically known as "the restorer of streets to live in" (58:12), that is, people promoting social justice. In this ideal city, foreigners will rebuild the walls, and nations will "bring … their wealth" (60:10–14). Such wealth will be amassed and readily available to all, so that gold and silver are as common as bronze and iron (60:17). Violence will be removed (60:18), and the sun will not set because God is the light of the city (60:19–20). The city walls shall be named "Salvation" and the gates called "Praise" (60:18). The book concludes with a utopian vision of "a new heavens and a new earth," with a completely restored Jerusalem as the central city to which all nations look and come with joy. Long life will be normative for its inhabitants, and the land's produce and harvests will be plentiful as "all flesh shall come to worship" God in Zion (65:17–25; 66:12–14, 22–23).[3]

The New Testament book of Revelation draws heavily on the imagery from the Hebrew Bible in creating its utopian vision of the future. The imagery and themes related to the ideal city in the books of Ezekiel and Isaiah are incorporated and recast by this later Christian apocalyptic text. At the end of the cataclysmic series of events in the book, the final two chapters transition to "a new heaven and a new earth" with the "holy city, the new Jerusalem"[4] descending to earth out of heaven (21:1–2). Rather

---

2. While this restoration happened in a limited way in the late sixth century BCE under Cyrus and the Persian rulers who followed him, the utopian visions of the ideal city were not realized historically. This failure to see the manifestation of such visions produced further eschatological visions and hope for a more complete restoration yet to come.

3. The book of Zechariah (especially the oracles in chapters 8, 12, and 14) contains similar prophetic visions of a utopian future, centered on the city of Jerusalem. See Schweitzer 2006 for discussion of these utopian themes in this prophetic text.

4. See the "New Jerusalem" texts among the Dead Sea Scrolls (2Q24; 4Q554–555; 5Q15; 11Q18) and the Temple Scroll (11Q19–20) found at Qumran that also draw on

than the righteous being transported to heaven, heaven comes to earth. This new city is where God dwells, so that God comes to the people and lives among them. For the righteous who are in the city, death no longer has hold, and suffering no longer exists (21:3–4).[5] The author, John, is given an angelic tour of the cubically shaped city, with its jeweled wall, its gates of pearl, its streets of pure gold, and its miraculous fruit trees. As with Isaiah, there is no sun, as God is the light in this city. Nations bring their wealth, and holiness is pervasive (21:9–22:5).[6]

In each of these biblical examples, the utopian city of the eschatological future is associated with the presence of God among the people and includes not only the restoration of the city's previous conditions but also the concept of an ideal existence for those who inhabit the city, whether in terms of longevity, absence of pain and suffering, continual light, abundance of produce and the fecundity of the land, or great wealth and prosperity.

It is important to note that in each case the ultimate result is peace (*shalom* in Hebrew)—not just the absence of war, but a state of wholeness and right relationships. This peaceful and holistic existence occurs following a final battle in which the nations attack Jerusalem/Zion and God defeats the enemy and establishes a new reign as the righteous and just king.[7]

The biblical tradition employs the concept of the ideal city as part of a utopian construct of the future. The city (Zion/Jerusalem) is besieged but will be delivered as a result of divine intervention. Enemies are defeated, and an era of peace commences. This age is evidenced by prosperity, agricultural abundance, access to wealth, safety and security, holiness of the city's inhabitants, and joy (suffering and pain and sometimes death itself no longer exist). The biblical tradition lacks details as to how these conditions will be instituted and how they will be maintained into the perpetual future. No mechanisms or processes are described. Human existence in this future utopian city is idealized.

---

the visions in Ezek 40–48 and share striking similarities with the depiction of the New Jerusalem in Rev 21–22.

5. Note the difference between long life in Isa 65 and the removal of death in Rev 21, as the latter vision extends the scope of the earlier oracle.

6. On the New Jerusalem in Revelation, see Koester 2020, 112–19.

7. See the "final battles" in Ezek 38–39; Isa 63:1–6; 66:15–17; Rev 19:11–20:15. Compare Zech 12:1–13:9; 14:1–21.

The Utopian City in Science Fiction

Darko Suvin (1976, 58) calls science fiction the "literature of cognitive estrangement." That is, science fiction uses unfamiliar settings and characters to estrange readers from their usual assumptions. While certainty a broad definition, other theorists have taken Suvin's starting point and worked to clarify. For example, James Gunn defines science fiction as

> the branch of literature that deals with the effects of change on people in the real world as it can be projected into the past, the future, or to distant places. It often concerns itself with scientific or technological change, and it usually involves matters whose importance is greater than the individual or the community; often civilization or the race itself is in danger. (Gunn 2005, 6)

My own understanding emphasizes the otherness posed by a science fiction work: science fiction is a genre that presents an alternative reality that is better or worse than the present context using temporal or spatial displacement (or both), that asks questions about the present through social critique, and that is concerned with how science or technology will affect society. This perspective thus links science fiction with utopian literature. Literary critics are divided as to their interrelatedness: some view utopia as a subgenre of science fiction, while others see science fiction as the subgenre of utopia.[8] In either perspective, utopian and dystopian constructs are commonplace across science fiction works.[9]

One association between science fiction and utopia can be found in the depiction of the ideal city, a recurring motif within both genres.[10] The rise of the science fiction novel coincided with several paradigm shifts in the West: the Industrial Revolution in the eighteenth and nineteenth centuries, the rapid technological explosion that followed in the late nineteenth and early twentieth centuries, the rise of modernism as a prevalent philosophical worldview, and a progressive view of human nature that

---

8. Darko Suvin (1974, 114) advocates the former position; Lyman Tower Sargent (1994, 11) has championed the second view.

9. See my discussion of the relationship between these genres and their applicability to biblical texts in Schweitzer 2007b, 14–23, esp. 19–20; and 2007a, 141–56, esp. 144–45.

10. This section draws on the science fiction works identified and discussed in Abbott 2016; Feuerstein 2008; and Gold 2001.

concluded it would transcend its baser instincts toward a "brighter future" of which these technological achievements offered a taste. Nowhere was this technological achievement more striking than the population growth and expansion of urban centers. The ideal city became the focus of utopian speculation.

For example, *The Shape of Things to Come* (1933), by H. G. Wells, and its film adaptation *Things to Come* (1936) present the utopian city as a solution to humanity's ills. The novel is set in a future world after a devastating war and a series of plagues that kill millions. Out of these conditions, a benevolent dictator is able to unite the world, foster science, and restrict religion, which leads over time to a utopian society in the city of Everytown. This society abandons classism and centers on the pursuit of continued technological achievement for the good of all.

Such utopian ideals, however, gave way to dystopian portrayals in the aftermath of World War I. Since the 1920s, the depiction of the ideal city has frequently been used to present what initially appears to be a utopia but is revealed to be a dystopia as the plot unfolds.[11] One of the classic examples depicting the ideal city as "dystopia in disguise" is Fritz Lang's *Metropolis* (1927). In this reimagined New York City approximately one hundred years in the future, the city is defined by skyscrapers, orderliness, precision, and pristine conditions. However, such extravagance and technological achievement is built on the oppression and exploitation of the worker class. Advanced technology seems to come at the cost of restriction of human freedoms.[12]

A similar theme is present in *The Time Machine* (1895), by H. G. Wells. In this novel, a time traveler journeys forward through time to the year 802,701. He encounters the Eloi, who dwell in a simple yet pristine city surrounded by a veritable paradise of lush plants that seem to grow without effort. At first, the time traveler believes the future of humanity is one of peace and harmony with their world, until he learns that these Eloi are uneducated and dispassionate toward the good of others; they are being bred as workers for the Morlocks, who operate an underground, mechanized city. The time traveler surmises that humanity has evolved into two separate races and classes. He is disillusioned that technology will contribute anything positive to this unacceptable future.

---

11. Of course, films such as *Blade Runner* (1982) focus on the dystopian city without any pretense of it being a utopia.

12. For more on *Metropolis*, see the essay by Staples in this volume.

Such dystopias tend to be governed by authoritarian or totalitarian regimes, as illustrated in Ray Bradbury's novel *Fahrenheit 451* (1953) and the film *Logan's Run* (1976). The city provides a ready setting for this approach to creating a dystopia in disguise as the powerful locate themselves in the urban setting and there is functionally no escape, given the wasteland that exists beyond the confines of the urban center(s).[13] The novels by Aldous Huxley, *Brave New World* (1932), and George Orwell, *1984* (1949), both reflect these perceptions of the utopian/dystopian city.

These themes are combined in more recent science fiction works, such as the depiction of the Capitol of Panem and the Districts in The Hunger Game series by Suzanne Collins (2008, 2009, 2010). Following a failed revolution, the urban Capitol exerts control over the rural Districts. Under constant surveillance and threat of force, the Districts provide material goods to the Capitol, whose residents live in luxury, excess, and decadence, without concern for the oppression and exploitation of the workers in the Districts. The Capitol is the ideal city in every way, but it is critiqued as thoroughly reprehensible.[14] In the short-lived series *Firefly* (2002) and its wrap-up film *Serenity* (2005), the future of the earth in the twenty-sixth century concerns the successful Alliance who won the war and control the "central planets," as opposed to those in the terra-formed "outer worlds." The latter have been settled, but with extremely limited resources and concern from the Alliance, unless they can benefit by them in some way. The contrast between the pristine, orderly, stoic Alliance and the dirty, haphaz-

---

13. In a somewhat unexpected way, the contrast between the ideal city and the wasteland surrounding it appears in the first episode of *Buck Rogers in the Twenty-Fifth Century* (1979), in which Buck is accidently frozen for five hundred years and returns to a future earth. There he finds the city of New Chicago controlled by a council made up of various AIs that regulate all necessary conditions for the survival and comfort of the human inhabitants, including food, environment, and security. However, those outside the city exist in the conditions following a nuclear war, with radiation, trauma, food shortages, and a struggle for even minimal survival. The series never returns to address these conditions or those suffering outside the ideal city. The wasteland motif can also be seen in *Blade Runner 2049* (2017), in this case as an even harsher wasteland outside the dystopian city.

14. Compare the visually appealing presentation of Canto Bight, the ideal city in *Star Wars: Episode VIII—The Last Jedi* (2017), with its casino, wealth, and escapism that is built on oppression of people and animals and that is funded by those profiting from war, playing both sides (The First Order and the Resistance) against the other for their own personal gain.

ard, emotional existence of those trying to make their way in outer worlds is further accentuated by the latter's "old West" culture and constructs.[15]

Science fiction employs the motif of the ideal city to offer critique of the present, either through a utopian vision that corrects its errors or through a warning of a dystopia for those not privileged enough to enjoy the utopia that has been created. While the details vary, the utopian city serves its role as both vision of the future and critique of the present.

The Utopian City in *The Matrix* Trilogy

The Matrix trilogy provides a particularly intriguing example of how these various themes play out in science fiction narratives. The plot of the film trilogy takes place centuries in the future following a war between humanity and machines.[16] Created by humanity, the machines achieved artificial intelligence and took over the entire earth. Rather than kill the humans, the machines enslaved humanity so that they could use humans as a power source. In order to suppress and to exploit humanity in (apparently) the most efficient way, the machines designed the Matrix.

The Matrix is a computer-generated virtual reality simulation into which humans are "plugged in." As explained in the second film (*The Matrix Reloaded*), the original Matrix was created by the Architect (one of the machines) to be a true utopia, but humans rejected it, according to the Architect, because of the "imperfection inherent in every human being." Humans could not embrace utopia as reality. Therefore, a new model was created, reflecting the "world as it was in 1999." This model was more believable, and most humans now live their entire lives in it without knowing the true nature of their existence. A small minority of humans, however, sense (subconsciously) that something is wrong with reality, and they reject the imposed system, causing problems for the machines. To counteract this problem, the machines create a code and implant into one particular human ("the One") who is engineered to "self-correct" this prob-

---

15. While not a single city, the Alliance displays many of the characteristics of the utopian city.

16. At the time of writing, the fourth film in *The Matrix* franchise (*The Matrix Resurrections*) had recently finished principal photography in November 2020. It is scheduled to be released in December 2021. How this new installment will change, expand, critique, or possibly retcon any of the themes or plot points within the current trilogy is unknown.

lem. The One establishes a new enclave ("Zion"), where a small number of humans who doubt the validity of the Matrix can withdraw from the simulation. The program is reset, and the computer code for the One is reintegrated into the system ("the Source"), until the anomaly becomes problematic again and another "the One" arises to balance the equation. In other words, the One is designed to save humanity in such a way that the machines always remain in control. This cycle can theoretically repeat itself in perpetuity.

The Matrix trilogy asks questions of epistemology (how we know things) and delves into classic science fiction themes such as the nature of reality, destiny and free will, what it means to be human, the dangers and appropriate roles of technology, and a range of other ethical questions.

Central to *The Matrix*, however, is the theme of the ideal city, which appears in the trilogy as the "last human city" known as Zion. Although it does not appear visually on screen in the first film, Zion is referenced in the dialogue multiple times. The first discussion about Zion comes soon after Neo (the current iteration of the One) is liberated from the Matrix. Neo was plugged into the system through holes in his body, and he notices that another human (Tank) does not have these ports. Tank explains that he is a "genuine child of Zion," born free in the real world. When Neo asks about Zion, Tank replies, "If the war was over tomorrow, Zion's where the party would be ... the last human city."

Of course, Tank and those with him are not aware that this is the sixth iteration of Zion, which has been destroyed and repopulated five times up to this point (as explained to Neo by the Architect in the second film, *The Matrix Reloaded*). From the human view, if Zion is destroyed, then any hope for humanity's independence from the machines perishes with it. In many respects, Zion is *all* that matters. When the inspirational human leader Morpheus is captured by machine agents who seek to extract the codes needed to enter Zion and destroy it, Tank is willing to sacrifice Morpheus to protect Zion, saying, "Zion's more important than me or you or even Morpheus" (*The Matrix*). However, if humans can "win the war" and defeat the machines, then Zion becomes the place of salvation for all of humanity, even those who remain "plugged in" to the Matrix.

In the first film, then, Zion functions in ways similar to Zion/Jerusalem from the biblical tradition: it is the besieged city that is destined to be redeemed and exalted as a result of victory in the final battle. At the end of the first film, Neo threatens the machines, promising to defeat them. One expects, then, that the machines will be defeated, Zion will be saved, and all (or at least almost all) of humanity will be liberated from their enslavement (through the actions of Neo) in the subsequent films.[17] However, while Zion is ultimately saved and some humans are indeed freed, most of humanity remains enslaved at the end of the third film, a fact that will be discussed in more detail below.

The first on-screen visual of Zion comes near the beginning of the second film as the *Nebuchadnezzar* (Morpheus's hovercraft, whose name borrows from a well-known Babylonian king who appears in the biblical book of Daniel) comes to the city to resupply amid rumors that the machine army is moving to attack Zion. The final battle seems to be on the horizon. As the ship contacts Zion's control operators, the image of a pristine control room with sophisticated computer mechanisms intermixes with cuts to the ship in the real world. However, it soon becomes clear that this sanitized and idealized projection of Zion's operations is virtual (similar to the constructs of the Matrix), and the reality of Zion's condition is identical to the roughness, dirt, and harshness of existence for those on the *Nebuchadnezzar*. Zion's physical existence is not presented in idealized or utopian imagery but in rather stark and realistic portrayals. If the viewer expects to see Zion presented in stereotypical depictions of the sterile and sleek future human city common in science fiction, such assumptions are quickly subverted.

The second and third films spend a significant amount of screen time on events within Zion. In contrast to the homogeneous depiction of the agents within the Matrix (who are all white and all male), the humans of Zion exhibit a diverse demographic composition and a more egalitarian society.[18] The inhabitants of Zion come from multiple races and ethnicities. The city is governed by a council, and the military seems to be accountable to that body. Positions of power, including serving on the ruling council and in key military posts, are held by persons of color and by women.[19] While the biblical tradition tends to emphasize "all nations" coming to Jerusalem, with the Jewish people holding prime position, the

---

17. Some of these basic points of connection between the biblical Zion and *The Matrix*'s Zion are briefly outlined in Fontana 2003, 175–76.

18. This is similar to the depiction of those aligned with the Empire and with the Rebellion/Resistance in the *Star Wars* saga, especially in *Episodes IV–VI*.

19. See the nuanced treatments of the topic in Nakamura 2005, 126–37; Nama 2008, 143–47.

racial composition of Zion in *The Matrix* trilogy promotes a multiethnic, if not completely equitable, society.

The city of Zion in *The Matrix* trilogy is a self-contained location. From the films, one infers that all supplies, food, and other necessities for existence originate within the confines of the city. There is, in fact, no other location where such necessities could come, because sentinels (machines designed to hunt down humans) patrol the wasteland that exists across the scorched earth and the ruins of the human civilizations that once inhabited the planet. The city has a system designed to recycle its resources (such as its water supply). However, such resources seem to be limited, as city propaganda and infrastructure focus on necessity, persistence, and survival. No one, not even the council members, seems to have luxuries or surpluses of food, clothing, or other commodities. The crew of the *Nebuchadnezzar* also have limited resources, and their food is "what the body needs" in terms of nutritional components, but not much more beyond the basics. Often, the ideal city in science fiction is depicted as a place of physical abundance or economic prosperity (at least for some or to some extent). The biblical tradition uniformly affirms this perception of the utopian city in the future. However, the city of Zion in *The Matrix* trilogy does not follow this pattern; instead, it presents a human city fighting and struggling for its very survival as it is under constant threat from the machines.

In contrast to the rationalistic logic of the machines bent on their destruction, the humans of Zion are emotional and passionate. One of the most striking examples of this occurs in the second film during a dance scene on the eve of an approaching attack. The inhabitants of Zion are gathered in a large cave (later called the temple).[20] Councilor Hamann has offered an "opening prayer" and invites Morpheus to "close."[21] Rather than offer another prayer, Morpheus exhorts the massive crowd to not be afraid about the rumors of the machine army that is coming to destroy them. They are coming, but Morpheus is confident that the humans will con-

---

20. In *The Matrix Revolutions* (2003), this cave is the site where humanity will make its last stand against the machines during an assault on the city of Zion.

21. It is interesting that no mention is made of the prayer's intended recipient or its content. *The Matrix* trilogy incorporates aspects from various religious traditions, so there is nothing that requires this event to be linked with one particular religious persuasion. See the discussion of religious pluralism in the first film in Bassham 2002, 111–25.

tinue to survive. With defiance, he proclaims, "We are still here!... This is Zion! And we are not afraid!" The crowd then erupts into cheering, dance, and overt sensuality.[22] In this moment, the humans express their passions, emotions, and need for physical touch and release. Within ideal Zion of *The Matrix*, humanity appears most authentically and distinctively human.

This contrast between humans and machines is further extended in the third film, which juxtaposes the city of Zion and the Machine City. In this film, Neo travels with his romantic partner Trinity to the Machine City in order to try to save humanity. As their hovercraft approaches the city, Neo's ability to see the Matrix's code "lights the way" as he sees the energy coming from the system. His illuminated vision is contrasted with what Trinity (and the audience) sees as the Machine City: a technologically orientated and metallic city shrouded in darkness. When Neo walks into the Machine City, he continues to see the light energy, but the viewer sees only darkness with spider-like machines crawling eerily and somewhat menacingly around the cityscape. This representation of the Machine City reflects several common tropes in the depiction of dystopian cities in science fiction and contrasts readily with the realism and grit of Zion noted above. The machines need only energy (no food, shelter, clothing, or other human necessities) and are supplied with these from the fields of humans who exist to provide these resources. However, according to the Architect in *The Matrix Reloaded*, without these humans the machines would cease to function (or they would at least need to accept "levels of survival" that would radically change how they presently exist). This interconnection between humans and the machines points to the solution offered by Neo—namely, that if the machines spare Zion, he will sacrifice himself and allow the machines to eliminate the threat of the rogue agent Smith (see the next paragraph)—that results in the salvation of Zion and a new chance for peace at the conclusion of *The Matrix Revolutions*.

While the biblical tradition presents a future in which the righteous are victorious over the wicked or at least that the wicked are subjugated under the rule of the righteous who dwell in the utopian city, *The Matrix* trilogy resolves the outcome of the final battle in an unexpected way. Peace between

---

22. The dance scene in *The Matrix Reloaded* (2003) celebrates human sensuality. This is intensified by the series of spliced cut-aways to the only sex scene in the trilogy, as Neo and Trinity passionately engage in sexual intercourse, happening elsewhere in Zion at the same time as the dance.

humans and machines and the continued existence of Zion is brokered by Neo's bargain. Neo allows himself to be used to capture Smith, a rogue machine agent who has become able to corrupt and manipulate the virtual and real worlds with the goal of ending all life; he thus poses a serious threat to both the Matrix and to the real world. The machines are unable to control and deal with Smith, but Neo tricks Smith into being reconnected with the Matrix and directly to the Source. This also results in Neo's death and the reintegration of his code as the One into the Source. In this scenario, Zion is saved (i.e., not destroyed), but the machines continue to harvest humans for their energy. Those humans who reject the nature of reality are promised to be released into Zion, but the "bad guys" are not defeated.

Not all fans of *The Matrix* trilogy found this resolution satisfying. Several reasons can be offered for this response. First, as with the biblical tradition and most science fiction (and perhaps storytelling in general), audiences—especially in the West and particularly in North American culture—have come to expect that "good will always win in the end" and that "freedom is the highest good." Second, the end of the first film sets up the narrative for a sequel in which Neo will fulfill his role as messianic deliverer and save humanity. Instead, Neo's messianic role takes an unexpected form: death and reincorporation into the Matrix. This resolution parallels the tension found in the gospels between the expectations many in first-century Palestine had concerning Jesus and the way his story concludes. Rather than a messiah who would defeat the Romans and liberate the people of Israel through a military victory, as many expected, Jesus dies on the cross, executed as a common criminal by the Romans. His death and resurrection are understood theologically in the New Testament as victory over sin and death itself, but the Roman Empire was not defeated. Similarly, the citizens of Zion and audiences expect Neo to achieve permanent victory over the machines, but the machine empire is not defeated. Finally, at the end of the third film, when the Oracle and the Architect discuss this new state of affairs, they note that such a change in the cycle is "dangerous." Peace between humans and machines cannot be permanent; it is tenuous at best (*The Matrix Revolutions*). This is hardly the promised utopian future of unending peace and prosperity that is envisioned in the biblical tradition.

While it is understandable that fans might have wanted a more stereotypically hopeful resolution, the power of *The Matrix* trilogy rests precisely in how it breaks with such cultural expectations. *The Matrix* trilogy is a series that has glorified violence from the start (e.g., the numerous and lengthy fight sequences and especially the line "We need guns, lots of guns" as the solution to saving Morpheus in the first film). This incomplete conclusion—in which Neo loses, Zion is free but humanity is still enslaved, and the future of a brokered peace is unknown—should cause the audience to reconsider what it has seen and question its own expectations. *The Matrix* trilogy seems to critique stereotypical depictions of humanity's ability to save itself and possibly its dependence on such a traditional messianic intervention as part of that construct.

In the second film (*The Matrix Reloaded*), there is a conversation between Councilor Hamann and Neo that foreshadows this resolution. While discussing the necessity of technology for human existence in their utopian city of Zion, Hamann reflects on the irony of using Zion's machinery to keep the humans alive while other machines are trying to kill them. Neo suggests that the difference is one of human control over the machinery, but Hamann counters that the sense of control is an illusion. If humans turned off their machines, people would die, and if the machines freed all the humans, then they would also come to their end. Neo muses, "So we need machines, and they need us." Ultimately, this is precisely how the war comes to an end and a peace is forged, but not in terms that either side would have accepted at the outset.[23] Instead of a "final battle" between human and machine or between Neo and the Source, the fight sequence between Neo and Smith is understood as only a ruse, and the deliverance of Zion comes as a concession by the machines in exchange for Neo's self-sacrifice. The biblical tradition of the salvation of the utopian city after the rout of the enemy is subverted by the trilogy's conclusion.

While the depiction of the ideal city in *The Matrix* trilogy invokes elements found in the biblical tradition of the utopian city, the films rework these expectations and use these new constructs to critique simplistic descriptions of the future. Utopias, according to the film, must be dynamic

---

23. The *Battlestar Galactica* episode "Epiphanies" (2006, season 2, episode 13) contains a similar foreshadowing of the final resolution between humans and the mechanical (but sentient and self-aware) Cylons who are trying to eliminate all of humanity. The activist group Demand Peace contends that the only way to end the conflict between the two groups is for human and Cylon to come together and create a peaceful coexistence. The Cylons want their human oppressors destroyed, and the humans want revenge for the Cylons' act of attempted genocide. But in the fourth season, it becomes clear that "the way out of here" (to quote the lyrics of the song that plays an important role in the plot) is for Cylons and humans to work together for the survival of both species, as was argued by Demand Peace.

and open to change. *The Matrix* trilogy uses the city of Zion motif to challenge the nature of our present reality and offer new answers to the questions posed by the changing nature of our complex world.

Representative Examples in Science Fiction

Blade Runner. 1982. Directed by Ridley Scott. Written by Hampton Fancher and David Peoples. Warner Bros.

Blade Runner 2049. 2017. Directed by Denis Villeneuve. Written by Hampton Fancher and Michael Green. Warner Bros.

Bradbury, Ray. 1953. *Fahrenheit 451*. New York: Ballantine Books.

Buck Rogers in the Twenty-Fifth Century. 1979–1981. Created by Glen A Larson. NBC.

Collins, Suzanne. 2008. *The Hunger Games*. New York: Scholastic.

———. 2009. *Catching Fire*. New York: Scholastic.

———. 2010. *Mockingjay*. New York: Scholastic.

"Epiphanies." 2006. *Battlestar Galactica*. Directed by Rod Hardy. Written by Joel Anderson Thompson. Sci-Fi Channel.

Firefly. 2002. Created by Joss Whedon. Fox.

Huxley, Aldous. 1932. *Brave New World*. London: Chatto & Windus.

Logan's Run. 1976. Directed by Michael Anderson. Written by David Zelag Goodman. MGM.

The Matrix. 1999. Directed by The Wachowskis. Written by The Wachowskis. Warner Bros.

The Matrix Reloaded. 2003. Directed by The Wachowskis. Written by The Wachowskis. Warner Bros.

The Matrix Revolutions. 2003. Directed by The Wachowskis. Written by The Wachowskis. Warner Bros.

Metropolis. 1927. Directed by Fritz Lang. Written by Thea von Harbou. Universum Film.

Orwell, George. 1949. *1984*. London: Secker & Warburg.

Serenity. 2005. Directed by Joss Whedon. Written by Joss Whedon. Universal Pictures.

Star Wars: Episode IV—A New Hope. 1977. Directed by George Lucas. Written by George Lucas. Twentieth Century Fox.

Star Wars: Episode V—The Empire Strikes Back. 1980. Directed by Irvin Kershner. Written by George Lucas. Twentieth Century Fox.

Star Wars: Episode VI—Return of the Jedi. 1983. Directed by Richard Marquand. Written by Lawrence Kasdan and George Lucas. Twentieth Century Fox.

Star Wars: Episode VIII—The Last Jedi. 2017. Directed by Rian Johnson. Written by Rian Johnson. Walt Disney Studios.

Things to Come. 1936. Directed by William Cameron Menzies. Written by H. G. Wells. London Film Productions.

Wells, H. G. 1895. *The Time Machine.* London: Heinemann.

———. 1933. *The Shape of Things to Come.* London: Hutchinson.

Works Cited

Abbott, Carl. 2016. *Imagining Urban Futures: Cities in Science Fiction and What We Might Learn from Them.* Middleton, CT: Wesleyan University Press.

Bassham, Gregory. 2002. "The Religion of *The Matrix* and the Problems of Pluralism." Pages 111–25 in The Matrix *and Philosophy: Welcome to the Desert of the Real.* Popular Culture and Philosophy 3. Edited by William Irwin. Chicago: Open Court.

Feuerstein, Günther. 2008. *Urban Fiction: Strolling through Ideal Cities from Antiquity to the Present Day.* Stuttgart: Edition Axel Menges.

Fontana, Paul. 2003. "Finding God in *The Matrix.*" Pages 159–84 in *Taking the Red Pill: Science, Philosophy and Religion in* The Matrix. Edited by Glenn Yeffeth. Dallas: BenBella Books.

Gold, John R. 2001. "Under Darkened Skies: The City in Science-Fiction Film." *Geography* 86:337–45.

Gunn, James. 2005. "Toward a Definition of Science Fiction." Pages 5–12 in *Speculations on Speculation: Theories of Science Fiction.* Edited by James Gunn and Matthew Candelaria. Lanham, MD: Scarecrow.

Koester, Craig R. 2020. "Revelation's Vision of New Jerusalem: God's Life-Giving Reign for the World." *WW* 40:112–19.

Nakamura, Lisa. 2005. "The Multiplication of Difference in Post-millennial Cyberpunk Film: The Visual Culture of Race in the *Matrix* Trilogy." Pages 126–37 in The Matrix *Trilogy: Cyberpunk Reloaded.* Edited by Stacy Gillis. London: Wallflower Press.

Nama, Adilifu. 2008. *Black Space: Imagining Race in Science Fiction Film.* Austin: University of Texas Press.

Sargent, Lyman Tower. 1994. "The Three Faces of Utopianism Revisited." *Utopian Studies* 5.1:1–37.

Schweitzer, Steven. 2006. "Visions of the Future as Critique of the Present: Utopian and Dystopian Images of the Future in Second Zechariah." Pages 249–67 in *Utopia and Dystopia in Prophetic Texts*. Edited by Ehud Ben Zvi. Publications of the Finnish Exegetical Society 92. Helsinki: Finnish Exegetical Society.

———. 2007a. "Exploring the Utopian Space of Chronicles: Some Spatial Anomalies." Pages 141–56 in *Constructions of Space I: Theory, Geography, and Narrative*. Edited by Jon Berquist and Claudia Camp. LHBOTS 481. London: T&T Clark.

———. 2007b. *Reading Utopia in Chronicles*. LHBOTS 442. London: T&T Clark.

Suvin, Darko. 1974. "The River-Side Trees, or SF and Utopia." *Minnesota Review* 2–3:108–15.

———. 1976. "On the Poetics of the Science Fiction Genre." Pages 57–71 in *Science Fiction: A Collection of Critical Essays*. Twentieth Century Views. Edited by Mark Rose. Englewood Cliffs, NJ: Prentice-Hall.

The Land

JACKIE WYSE-RHODES

Is nature a possession? Can the earth be owned? In her 1995 poem "The Moment," Margaret Atwood answers no. Even when humans plant their flags in soil, they have not discovered anything. As the voice of nature states in her poem, "We never belonged to you.... It was always the other way around" (Atwood 2011, 109). Similar themes recur in many of Atwood's novels, where nature is considered vast, enduring, and ultimately independent. But it is also threatened, specifically by human meddling. Many science fiction writers address pressing questions about land and the natural world in their work, too, exploring topics such as the human desire to cultivate land, the danger inherent in landscapes that cannot be domesticated, and the frequent human experience of living in exile.

Related questions permeate the stories and poems left behind by biblical writers as well. Although thousands of years have passed since these texts were first written down, the Bible preserves conversations that can sound surprisingly contemporary: Who is the earth for? Do humans have a unique right to its resources? Is there space in the land for me and my loved ones? Will we survive this war or that catastrophe? Is there hope for the future—for us and for the land we call home? Such questions recur throughout the Bible, with varying answers, from Genesis to Revelation and in many books in between. By reading science fiction alongside the Bible, we can enter into conversations spanning centuries about the earth and our place within it.

Land in the Bible and Beyond

As a diverse anthology with wide-ranging contents, the Bible does not speak with one voice on any given topic. However, across genres and eras, land persists as an ongoing category for reflection. The Bible portrays land in a variety of ways, including land as a garden full of nourishment and beauty, land as a wilderness posing challenges to survival, and land as something lost when a community experiences exile. Sometimes the Bible addresses actual gardens and actual wilderness locales. At other times, biblical writers use such concepts as metaphors for understanding their own experiences. Depictions of land shift from category to category depending on whether biblical writers are analyzing their own historical circumstances, imagining a potential future for their people, or portraying an idealized past.

Biblical gardens are cultivated spaces, designed and domesticated, in need of continual management, with defined boundaries. The Bible's first garden, Eden, is its most famous. In several biblical texts (Gen 13:10; Isa 51:3; Ezek 28:13–19; 31:8–9), Eden is referred to as "the garden of the LORD" or "the garden of God" (Fretheim 1994, 1:349). Indeed, the deity is the Bible's first gardener (Gen 2:8–9; Fretheim 1994, 1:350), and humans are created for the express purpose of tending God's garden (2:15). Though it requires human attention, gardening in Eden does not seem labor-intensive; only after the land is cursed in Gen 3 do gardens require "toil" (3:17) and "sweat" (3:19) on the part of their caretakers. Biblical images of the world's first garden are idealized, the template of a longed-for, perfect past. Other biblical gardens reflect idealized spaces, too. The Song of Songs is a collection of love poetry that takes place in a palace garden inhabited by lovers who are part of the wealthy elite. Their love is nestled in a verdant landscape maintained "off-screen" by workers whose livelihoods and well-being are outside the lovers' purview yet dependent on the lovers' wealth. The garden in Song of Songs, though idealized, is private and exclusive. Like Eden, in the world of the garden, there is room only for two humans. Isaiah depicts a much more accessible garden; indeed, the whole land of Israel is God's garden, and God is its gardener (Isa 5:1–7). However, just as in Gen 3, access to the garden can be revoked. In this poem, God is fed up with the behavior of those who dwell in the garden and threatens to uproot the garden and abandon it—functionally allowing it to revert to wilderness, at least for a time. In the Bible, the categories of garden and wilderness are somewhat slippery. Without tending, a garden can become a wilderness or at least wild; likewise, a wilderness might partially unwild itself with enough care and attention.

In biblical texts, a geographic area is considered wilderness if it is hostile to the flourishing of humans and domesticated plant and animal life. It is likely that the Bible's portrayals of wilderness are influenced by communal experiences with actual wilderness landscapes in the region where the Israelites settled. Geographically, wilderness is present in a variety of locales, such as

> poor steppe land (e.g., the area surrounding the oasis of Damascus, 1 Kgs 19:15), the marginally cultivated land on the Transjordan plateau (Num 21:13; Deut 4:43), and the pastureland east of Bethlehem.... Wilderness could also comprise tangled thickets and scrub, such as the area near Succoth in the Jordan Valley (Judg 8:7, 16). Wilderness (*midbar*) in fact merged into wooded areas ... since both were perceived by the settled Israelites as dangerous trackless country where one could rapidly become lost or be attacked by wild beasts. (Baly and Achtemeier 2011, 1104–5)

The wilderness was a real and terrifying location, and it is usually portrayed negatively in the Bible, "held in awe as a place of danger and terror, its mysterious vastness to be entered only at great risk" (Hillel 2006, 118; see, e.g., Hagar's harrowing exile to the wilderness in Gen 21). Several times the prophet Isaiah envisions the cities of Israel's enemies as empty and laid waste, given over to wild animals and overtaken by plant life (13:19–22; 18:6). Isaiah's original audience must have felt glee in imagining the once-powerful towns of their enemies reverting to a wilder, more natural state. In most cases, for a landscape to become a wilderness was considered a curse.

The book of Job offers a more positive assessment of wilderness. Job is uninterested in exclusive human claims on land. At the end of the book, the divine speeches (38:1–42:6) remind the reader of the inherent goodness of wild places, inhospitable for human habitation but perfectly suited for animal and plant life. Carol Newsom (2003, 241) writes of these chapters, "In the social map of the cosmos as God describes it, what is celebrated is the refusal of the social bond between wild animals and humans." God is depicted as intimately concerned with the well-being of wilderness landscapes that are indifferent or even hostile to human concerns. The book of Job never highlights one parcel of land as evidence of Israel's particular covenant with God. Rather, land is considered in its universal form as earth—created with room enough for wild animals and domesticated animals alike (Gen 1:24). Job makes it especially clear that some spaces on earth were never intended for humans to occupy at all (e.g., Job 38:25–26).

Images of garden and wilderness are present in the stories the Bible tells about Canaan, often called the promised land. Canaan has identical geographical boundaries as the later kingdoms of Israel and Judah combined (Schmitz 1992, 1:830). In the Bible, the promised land sometimes refers to this particular geographical location; at other times, it takes on the character of an imagined paradise, especially in texts written while the biblical writers were experiencing exile. By the end of Genesis, Abraham and Sarah's numerous descendants are settled in this divinely gifted homeland, whose bounty at first sustains them, much like a garden. But a subsequent famine forces the family to migrate to Egypt, where they remain in exile for generations. The book of Genesis as a whole thus portrays land as a garden, land as a wilderness, and land loss as fundamental to a family's identity. The rest of the Torah narrates the people's journey through a literal wilderness back to Canaan, once again portrayed as a place of provision and plenty—a garden of grapes, pomegranates, and figs (Num 13:21–29).

Eventually, so the books of Samuel through Kings narrate, two kingdoms are formed in the land of Canaan: the northern kingdom of Israel and the southern kingdom of Judah. After a brief period of unity, a civil war rends the land into two kingdoms with distinct royal lines. These two kingdoms are subsequently conquered by foreign empires, and many of their residents are forcibly deported, leading to two collective experiences of exile.[1] Exile is another name for land loss. Much of the Bible was written by those making sense of the trauma related to this displacement. However, the experience of exile, though poignant, is not the only story the Bible tells. Hopes for a restored future "back home" in the promised land—whether as an actual political nation or an idealized heavenly kingdom—crop up repeatedly.

For some of the Hebrew prophets, exile was a clear sign that the covenants with God had been broken by Israel's bad behavior (e.g., Amos 2:6–16; Jer 31:32). Most prophetic books, however, also anticipate a future day when the relationship between the people and their land might be restored (e.g., Isa 9:1–7; 11:1–9; Jer 23:5–6; Ezek 37:24–28; Amos 9:11–15). Sometimes the land itself personifies restoration: flourishing plant life and bountiful harvests signal a less-troubled future when all will again be well (e.g., Isa 40:3–5; 51:3). The prophet Isaiah includes nations beyond Israel in an idealized vision of peaceful coexistence at God's mountain in future

---

1. The northern kingdom of Israel was conquered by the Assyrian Empire in 722 BCE. The southern kingdom of Judah endured until 586 BCE, when the Babylonian Empire took over, razing the temple in Jerusalem.

days (2:1–4). In many apocalypses, however, future hope is displaced more completely to the heavenly realm, which is sometimes imagined as an idealized earth. In the New Testament book of Revelation, a new Jerusalem descends from the heavens and takes root in the exact spot of the old city and temple, recently destroyed by the Roman government, and in this way the book envisions an ultimate return from exile. The revived and restored city even has a garden reminiscent of Eden within its walls (Koester 2001, 199). The noncanonical apocalyptic book of 1 Enoch imagines a more expansive heavenly realm that looks a lot like earth (but more spectacular), featuring divine versions of gardens, forests, and mountains (see 1 En. 17.2–3; 24.2–6; 26.1–5; 31–32), as well as inhospitable wilderness spaces where disobedient angels are imprisoned (1 En. 18.12–13; 21.1–3). In both books, land is key to a hopeful future, but only Revelation is interested in retaining something of the geography of the traditional promised land and its capital city.

Gardens, wilderness, loss of land—the Bible gives testimony to the human experience of all three. For much of the Bible and related literature, land also occupies a space in the imagination: an idealized future dwelling place, a container for a people's hopes. Land security is correlated with an unbroken covenant relationship with the deity. In exile, the biblical writers struggled to make sense of their current circumstances. As a result, the Bible gives voice to a tension that its first writers and readers must have felt in their very bones: the land is for us! Still, the land is for all—not only for other humans, like those who assemble at God's mountain (Isa 2:2–4), but also for wild animals whose well-being neither benefits from nor contributes to human flourishing (see Newsom 2003, 241–43). Although primarily focused on human experience, the Bible preserves voices that challenge anthropocentrism, asking: What if humankind does not—or should not—have the last word about land?

Thousands of years later, the Bible's multiple perspectives on land still matter. Conflicts about land animate political and cultural discourse in the modern era. Countless humans today experience forced migration. In North America, the vast majority of land bears witness to the suffering of displaced indigenous communities, and land ownership conveys social standing that marginalizes those in precarious housing situations. On top of regional and national conflicts, the global community is facing climate change and environmental degradation on a massive scale. How do we make sense of it? Where do we find hope? Such questions are often taken up by contemporary science fiction, especially of the apocalyptic variety.

Land in Science Fiction

In biblical apocalypses, hope is often delayed to a future time or displaced to the heavenly realm or afterlife.[2] Modern science fiction sometimes makes the same move, displacing contemporary human hopes to an idealized future or a far-flung world among the stars. An obvious example is the *Star Trek* franchise, in which societal ills such as systemic racism, global poverty, and environmental catastrophe have been solved on earth, and the crew of each iteration of the Enterprise faces new challenges on an intergalactic landscape. Potentially apocalyptic catastrophes are averted by common sense and good old-fashioned human ingenuity. Other works of science fiction are less optimistic about humanity's innate potential for upward evolution, positing instead that the earth is too far gone for apocalypse to be averted. This might mean that everything really does come to an end (e.g., *Seeking a Friend for the End of the World* [2012]; *Melancholia* [2011]; *The Age of Miracles* [Walker 2012]), or the apocalypse could result in a desolate postapocalyptic landscape in which those who remain struggle for mere survival (e.g., *Parable of the Sower* [Butler 1993]; *The Road* [McCarthy 2006]). Science fiction frequently explores the tension between individual human self-interest and a way of life that is the most beneficial for the most life, and land plays a crucial role in these explorations. Usually, human arrogance or greed has brought infertility and desolation to the earth. When coping with these scenarios, science fiction raises questions such as: Can the earth persist, or will it be destroyed? If it does persist, will it still be for humans? If the earth is destroyed or lost, how will it be remembered? If we find ourselves in exile, will we find our way back home?

Remarkably often, science fiction uses the biblical themes concerning land outlined above to answer these questions. For instance, land is often imagined as a garden or a paradise, especially when compared with the claustrophobic conditions of space travel (e.g., *Gravity* [2013]). In two episodes of *Star Trek: The Original Series*, the myth of Eden is referred to directly. In both cases, planets that appear to be paradise actually harbor hidden dangers, much like the biblical Eden ("The Apple" [1967]; "The Way to Eden" [1969]). When Eden is not directly named in science fiction, the idea of a garden still can represent paradise, a kind of genetically

---

2. See Kelly Murphy's essay on "Apocalypse" in this volume.

engineered utopia created by and for humans. For example, in the *Battlestar Galactica* (2004–2009) reboot, "botanical cruisers" are miniparadises on which space-dwellers vacation. Tellingly, one of the largest of these cruisers is destroyed right as the exile of the people begins ("The Miniseries" [2003]).

Yet gardens have boundaries; their very existence implies uncultivated, wild spaces outside their gates, and we can see the biblical theme of a sometimes hostile and dangerous wilderness landscape running throughout science fiction narratives, too. In such cases, the earth is often depicted as a wilderness, bereft of what is needed for life to flourish, usually as the result of ecological catastrophe, natural disaster, or warfare.[3] A chilling example is *The Road* by Cormac McCarthy (2006), which portrays a man and his child's journey by foot after the earth has been made desolate by climate change. In *The Road*, the whole earth has become wilderness, and humans who choose to survive do so in the face of continual hunger, depleted resources, and a horrific turn to cannibalism. In Isaac Asimov's *Robot* series, humans who inhabit outer space break away from humans on earth. Later, earth is overcrowded and then made uninhabitable by radiation (Asimov 1985). *The Road* depicts a dying earth, with little hope for renovation; in Asimov's writing, the earth has already died—also revealed to be the case in the *Battlestar Galactica* reboot.

Faced with wilderness, science fiction characters, like the ancient Israelites, often search for a promised land, a place where they can make a new home. Sometimes this involves finding a small pocket of safety on an otherwise-wild earth. In Octavia Butler's *Parable of the Sower* (1993), the main character Lauren and her community start over again at the novel's end in a kind of protected promised land in Northern California, which Lauren dubs Acorn, the first community that follows the tenets of the Earthseed movement she founded. Eventually, Lauren's movement will leave earth and head to space (e.g., *Parable of the Talents* [Butler 1998]). Spaceships may even serve as surrogate Edens while characters journey through the wilderness of space to find their promised land. The Battlestar Galactica (the ship itself) plays this role for its crew, especially considering the waning number of humans left who live aboard it, together searching

---

3. See the representative list in Nicole Tilford's chapter on "Noah's Ark" in this volume.

for a new planet to inhabit. The same could be said for the Enterprise and especially for the Voyager crew on its long journey home (see below).

In science fiction, as in the Bible, exile sometimes seems permanent. When enough time has passed, dreams of returning home are often replaced by determination to make the best life you can on the land (or spaceship) you currently occupy. If the promised land cannot be found, if Eden cannot be reclaimed, then perhaps the best possible homeland is the one already under your feet. Space itself thus becomes the final frontier for human exploration and colonization. Such a conclusion can lead to whimsical stories of adventure for its own sake. For example, in the short-lived television series *Firefly* (2002–2003), the characters dress in cowboy attire, and some speak with a southern drawl, a nod toward the settling of the American West—yet, the crew members of *Firefly* have no desire to inhabit land. Space is their chosen homeland. In one exchange, the captain explains that the *Serenity*, the name given to the spaceship that serves as their home, might be old and ugly, but the first mate Zoe must "try to see past what [the ship] is and on to what she can be." When Zoe asks what that is, Mal responds, "Freedom is what" ("Out of Gas" [2002]). The ship, with its ability to go anywhere, is the promised land for its crew. Land as such is no longer important. As the theme song says, "Take my land ... but you can't take the sky from me" (Rhodes 2017).

Much of the time, however, land remains important in science fiction, especially as a hoped-for promised land during times when the protagonists are exiled from their homes. In *Star Trek: Voyager* (1995–2001), a starship is stranded seventy thousand light-years from Earth in the Delta Quadrant, and the displaced crew embarks on a journey home that will take seventy-five years. They encounter many difficulties on their journey, but Earth remains forefront in their minds as the promised land. Their particular journey is, in the end, successful, but success is not guaranteed. For instance, in both *Battlestar Galactica* series (1978–1979, 2004–2009), the displaced crew of Galactica debate whether they can find their way home to Earth, a lost colony that has taken on mythic characteristics, so much so that many doubt it ever existed. Those aboard the Galactica are on their way to what they hope is a rediscovered Eden—or it might be a ruse. In the end, the crew does find Earth, but it is uninhabitable. Old Eden is no more. Humankind makes its new start on another planet, which they name Earth even though it is not their ancestral homeland. Their time of exile from earth has culminated in a new Eden, a new promised land.

Especially in twentieth-century American science fiction, space is sometimes uncritically presented as the next logical step for human expansion, with the earth serving as an ever-present fail-safe in case the journey goes wrong (e.g., *Star Trek*). But when the earth is no longer viable—when it has been destroyed by war, time, or human neglect—the stakes for finding a new home for humans are raised higher. Technologies are then developed for terraforming other planets to make them habitable for humans, often with disastrous consequences for other life forms and for the land itself. In the *Star Trek* original movies, *The Wrath of Khan* (1982) and *The Search for Spock* (1984), the Genesis project is a terraforming technology originally intended to aid human flourishing, but it is stolen and used as a military technology, to disastrous consequences. *Battle for Terra* (2007) narrates how Earth's terraforming of Mars and Venus leads to war and ecological disaster. As a result, an ark of humans arrives on the inhabited planet Terra with hopes to terraform it as their new Eden—which would kill the Terrians who live there. In the end, the Terrians create a hospitable space on their planet's surface where the human race can thrive.[4] In *Avatar* (2009), humans seek to mine the mineral unobtanium from Pandora, a verdant, paradisical planet in the Alpha Centauri system, all because humans have depleted earth's natural resources. Human greed almost leads to the destruction of Pandora's ecosystem, which supports abundant lifeforms, including the humanoid Na'vi. These relatively recent science fiction films acknowledge the complexity of viewing space as a natural frontier for human expansion. Like the Israelites upon arrival in their promised land, humans in science fiction often have to contend with the fact that their promised land is already someone else's ancestral home.

Environmental concerns heighten in urgency if space travel is removed from the equation altogether. Absent an escape hatch to another planet, what would humankind do in the face of global catastrophe? If earth is all we have, do humans even deserve to keep it? Sometimes, science fiction says no. Apocalyptically oriented science fiction often raises such questions by assuming the inevitability of disaster. Postapocalyptic science fiction explores the world after the end has failed to be averted. In these works, hope is, at best, displaced or realigned; at worst, hope is absent. In postapocalyptic earth-bound science fiction, the earth is all we have, so any hope

---

4. Similarly, in the *Stargate* episode "Scorched Earth" (2000), an alien species arrives to terraform a planet but discovers that another species already lives there. The aliens compromise with the native population by leaving a small pocket unterraformed.

humans have for the future is geographically bound to the present time and place. *The Age of Miracles* by Karen Thompson Walker (2012) explores hope in the wake of a slowing of the earth's rotation that will inevitably make human life untenable. Similarly, in the face of mass human extinction, Margaret Atwood's MaddAddam trilogy (2003, 2009, 2013; explored in detail below) plays with the idea of human hope when humans themselves are the enemy of the earth and its nonhuman inhabitants.

Science fiction sometimes turns the tables on human desire to explore space, this time playing with the possibility of alien colonialist expansion. What if our earth is someone else's promised land? What if our land is the destination toward which another species has journeyed? In Ursula Le Guin's collection of works sometimes called the Hainish Cycle, she posits a reality in which humans did not originate on earth but are themselves the products of colonization by the planet Hain (e.g., *Rocannon's World* [1966], *The Left Hand of Darkness* [1969], *The Dispossessed* [1974]). Le Guin asks: What if humans are not as human as we think? In other stories that flip the colonialist script, humans currently occupy land that other life forms wish to settle. Sometimes these settlers are hostile and do not seem to care for human survival (e.g., *Planet of the Apes* [1968]); at other times, they are more benevolent, and compromises are reached. In Octavia Butler's Xenogenesis series, collectively called *Lilith's Brood* (1987, 1988, 1989), Earth has been devasted by nuclear war and few humans are left. An alien species named Oankali rescues the survivors, healing them with advanced technology—but the price of survival is biological change. Humankind can persist only if they consent to join with Oankali genetically, resulting in a new species. Although this feels like a loss to many of the human characters in Butler's novels, for the Oankali it is their way of being in the cosmos; combining with other species is the way they evolve and survive. If humans are to remain on Earth or persist as a species, they must change, down to their very DNA. Octavia Butler asks: What if humans must dilute their humanity in order to survive? In the Bible, the Israelites who made their home in a foreign land, intermarrying with people from other cultures and religions, may have experienced themselves as making similar compromises—yet they chose a future that embraced change rather than choosing stagnation and possibly extinction.

When we read the biblical story of land alongside modern science fiction, we can see distinctions in the way land is handled by each collection. The Hebrew Bible is concerned with stories of both human origins (Gen 1–11) and national origins, with emphasis on the stories of Israel's particular ancestors (Gen 12–50). Science fiction is mostly concerned with the origins of humankind as a species, rather than any one nationality, ethnicity, or subculture. It is the particularity of humankind in the cosmic ecosystem that is at stake. In the mid- to late twentieth century, the popularity of space travel in science fiction (especially in *Star Trek*) served to challenge implicit anthropocentrism, depicting humankind as merely one sentient life form among many, and science fiction has continued in that vein. For example, in "The End of the World" (2005), the second episode in the reboot of *Doctor Who*, the characters witness the literal end of the world, but earth's species have moved on (even trees, who have gained sentience), mingling with other species and colonizing the universe. Earth is no longer the defining feature of those species; even without the land that united them originally, they are thriving in their new habitats and networks of relationships. In both the Bible and in science fiction, living in exile from one's original homeland can lead to moments of exceptional creativity as humans renegotiate their relationships with one another and their environment. Such an experience of intense change can have drastic implications for the relationship between humans and the land that sustains them.

Land in *The Year of the Flood*

Themes related to land are ubiquitous in Margaret Atwood's award-winning MaddAddam trilogy: *Oryx and Crake* (2003), *The Year of the Flood* (2009), and *MaddAddam* (2013).[5] This trilogy is sometimes called an ecoapocalypse due to the way it weaves together environmental concerns with traditional apocalyptic tropes such as a global pandemic and the potential extinction of the human race.[6] All three novels begin in the same postapocalyptic reality but, via flashbacks, also tell the story of what came before. Thus, literary scholar Gerry Canavan (2012, 143) argues that

---

5. In 2003, *Oryx and Crake* was short-listed for the Man Booker Prize, the Giller Prize, the Governor General's Award for Fiction, and the Orange Prize. *The Year of the Flood* was short-listed for the 2010 Trillium Book Award and long-listed for the 2011 International Dublin Literary Award. *MaddAddam* won the 2014 Orion Book Award. An extensive list of Margaret Atwood's awards and honors is available at http://margaretatwood.ca/awards-recognitions/.

6. Atwood (2012, 6–7) herself eschews the label *science fiction*, arguing that her work is better considered *speculative fiction*, since she depicts events that could reasonably take place in the present or near future, given the current state of technology.

Atwood presents the reader with two dystopias simultaneously: one that is "post-apocalyptic, representing the fear that things might change," and the other "pre-apocalyptic, representing the fear that things might not." In both dystopias, characters experience land as garden and wilderness in turn, while also enduring various kinds of exile.

As a whole, the trilogy tells the story of the following key figures:

- Jimmy ("Snowman"): An "everyman" who is inoculated against the apocalyptic pandemic by his best friend Crake.
- Crake: A scientist who engineers a virus with the power to wipe out humankind.
- Children of Crake (Crakers): A new species genetically engineered by Crake to take humanity's place after the pandemic wanes.
- Oryx: A former sex worker who befriends Crake and Jimmy. She serves as teacher and guide to the Crakers. Neither Crake nor Oryx survives the apocalypse.
- God's Gardeners: An ecoreligious and pacifist communitarian sect. The Gardeners grow their own food on urban rooftops. They live in expectation of an imminent apocalypse, which they call the Waterless Flood.
- Toby: A member of God's Gardeners, also called Eve Six, who survives the apocalypse at her workplace, the AnooYoo Spa.
- Ren: A former God's Gardener who survives the apocalypse in a safe room at her workplace, the Scales & Tales sex club.
- Zeb: A cofounder of God's Gardeners who works underground as an ecoterrorist. MaddAddam is his screen name. Zeb survives the apocalypse and is in a relationship with Toby. Adam One's half-brother.
- Adam One: A cofounder of God's Gardeners and its leader. Adam One is the author of all sermons and hymns that appear in *The Year of the Flood*. He does not survive the apocalypse. Zeb's half-brother.

In *Oryx and Crake*, we witness the postapocalyptic earth through the eyes of Jimmy, who has survived a global pandemic caused by a human-engineered virus hidden inside BlyssPlus, a sex pill that also functions as birth control. The novel plays with the boundaries that separate garden from wilderness, both within Jimmy's memories of his former life and in

Jimmy's experience of the postapocalyptic landscape. Jimmy's mind often wanders to his past, when human civilization was divided between the Compounds and the pleeblands. The Compounds were gated communities owned by corporations—the same corporations who ran all aspects of society, including police and government, before the collapse of society. The pleeblands, on the other hand, were urban wilderness areas, unregulated environments where the poor and working class made their homes. At first glance, the Compounds seemed idyllic. Every plant, animal, and blade of grass had been genetically engineered to perfection. Only those employed by corporations were permitted to live within the confines of the Compounds, and everything they needed was manufactured or genetically engineered within those walls. Jimmy grew up as a Compound kid. His family was not excessively wealthy, and he did not get into the best schools, but his life was privileged compared with pleebland dwellers. As protected enclaves with gates and identification required for entry, the Compounds were a kind of artificial Eden. Yet their inhabitants were not naïve innocents like Eve and Adam in Gen 2. Rather, the sterile safety of the Compounds was dependent on the chaos beyond its walls. From the perspective of those living in the Compounds, the pleeblands were a wilderness—a hostile and dangerous environment where violence and corruption ruled the day and disease ran rampant. For rebellious Compounders, the pleeblands, with their bars and sex clubs, also served as a place to let off steam.

The Compounds were not the only Eden in Atwood's preapocalyptic world. Paradice, the aptly named laboratory where the Crakers were incubated, was a garden-like environment bioengineered to mimic the outdoors. The Crakers, like Adam and Eve, were innocent. Though confined, they had no idea there was anywhere else to go. Unlike the story in Genesis, however, it was not the Crakers' disobedience that precipitated their eviction. Rather, they left because their habitat failed in the wake of Crake's apocalypse. After the apocalypse, Jimmy led the Crakers forth to make their home outdoors amid the postapocalyptic landscape. Was Jimmy like Moses, liberating the people from captivity? Or was he like the serpent of Eden, providing knowledge of the outside world that would eventually corrupt the Crakers? Perhaps both. From Jimmy's perspective, he led the Crakers from a protected garden to a hostile wilderness; however, the Crakers experienced it as a gentle exile. They were designed for this, after all! Immune to sunburn and biting insects, the Crakers were vegetarians who digested grass, lived outdoors, wore no clothes, and mated seasonally. The children of Crake exhibit "queer animalities," a term used by Ken Stone (2020, 261) to indicate the blurring of "species boundaries" between humans and nonhuman animals. The Crakers unsettle Jimmy. "These new women ... they're placid, like animated statues. They leave him chilled" (Atwood 2003, 100). Jimmy finds Craker hybridity equal parts alienating and intriguing—alienating because it calls into question human uniqueness, intriguing because of the survival advantages hybridity conveys. The postapocalyptic natural world, experienced by Jimmy as a harsh and unforgiving wilderness, functioned for the Crakers as a kind of promised land.

Like its predecessor, *The Year of the Flood* alternates between pre- and postapocalyptic settings, and in both, land emerges as a prominent theme. All three narrators—Toby, Ren, and Adam One—were members of God's Gardeners, an ecoreligious movement active in the pleeblands. The Gardeners lived a separatist life, squatting in abandoned buildings, cultivating rooftop gardens, producing their own food, wearing handmade clothing, and eschewing private property. Inspired by Gen 2–3, their leaders were called Adam or Eve, numbered according to their level of authority in the group. Literally and metaphorically, the Gardeners gardened. Living in the pleeblands, they engaged in the actual work of food production and environmental conservation, seeking to live sustainably in a world that had mostly given up trying. The Gardeners saw their labor as a reflection of God's work: God was the primary gardener of the earth, the earth was a "shared garden" (Atwood 2009, 423; Grimbeek 2017, 170), and they were God's fellow gardeners. The Gardeners had an "earth first mentality" (Bouson 2016, 346) and saw themselves as merely one part of a greater whole.

The Gardeners anticipated that their gardening days would come to an end, but they believed the vitality of the land would sustain them even if the worst came to pass. Continuing to draw inspiration from Genesis, they awaited the Waterless Flood, an apocalyptic event that would usher in a new era, after which they hoped to occupy a New Eden. Like other writers, both ancient (e.g., 1 Enoch) and modern, the Gardeners used the biblical flood story as a template for the apocalypse they anticipated.[7] The Gardeners had what some call a "tragic" view of the apocalypse: they did not believe it could be averted (Jennings 2010, 13). They shared this view with Noah and family in Gen 6–9, along with a sense of being chosen for

---

7. See "Noah's Ark," by Nicole L. Tilford, in this volume.

a greater purpose (Bouson 2016, 347): they were to care for God's Garden now and continue to cultivate it after the flood. Finally, like the biblical narrative, they had hope that a new world order would be instituted in the flood's wake. Throughout the pleeblands, the community established Ararats, stores of food and supplies to help them survive the Waterless Flood. These were named after the biblical mountain upon which Noah's ark landed and where Noah and his family awaited the draining of the floodwaters so they could start again (Gen 8:4). Even though the Gardeners thought the end was unavoidable, their hopes for the future included a return to Eden in which the earth itself would be restored to the verdant garden God intended. In the Bible, land is a garden when it functions hospitably toward its human inhabitants, but humans are not called upon to remake wilderness into a garden, as the Gardeners are in *The Year of the Flood*. The Gardeners emphasized human responsibility for land in a way that extends and exceeds biblical portrayals.

The Gardeners' ecotheology lead them to read their scriptures with an eye to the impending apocalypse. Just as human evil ushered in the first flood, Adam One preached that human irresponsibility was going to bring about the Waterless Flood. Although God promised never to curse the ground again (Gen 8:21), humans made no such oath: "Yes, my friends—any further cursing of the ground would be done not by God but by Man himself" (Atwood 2009, 90). As biblical scholar Shayna Sheinfeld (2020, 211) explores, Adam One interpreted Gen 9:2 ("The dread of [humans] shall be upon every beast") as a warning to animals (Atwood 2009, 90), and the Gardeners expected the Waterless Flood to undo and redo creation in the same manner as the biblical flood. In other words, "the majority of humankind is wiped out, animals survive, and a small remnant of humans also survive, based mainly on their foresight" (Sheinfeld 2020, 214). Adam One's use of the flood story made it clear that he regarded his congregation as a faithful remnant who were appointed to be caretakers of God's creatures and the land that nourished them.

Though fervent in their religious devotion, the Gardeners were not biblical literalists. Instead, they interpreted Jewish and Christian scripture symbolically and allegorically so that it might cohere with their high view of science. Their interpretations—available to the reader in the form of song lyrics and sermons included at regular intervals throughout *The Year of the Flood* as a structuring device—reinforced their identity as a community of resistance. The novel's first sermon focused on the group's own rooftop garden, called Edencliff. Adam One called Edencliff their "redemption"

(Atwood 2009, 12), arguing that the human act of gardening was participation in the divine act of creation. Put simply, creation was not a singular event that occurred at the Big Bang; rather, creation is ongoing.[8] Adam One interpreted the seven days of Gen 1 metaphorically, insisting that the Gardeners were still living in day six—the day when animals and humans were both created—and, as such, were cocreators. Adam One claimed that the first human words ever spoken aloud were the names of the animals (Gen 2), and this act of naming gave the first human a soul (Atwood 2009, 12). Adam One called his congregants to continue to bear witness to earth's animal life, once abundant but now largely extinct or genetically engineered into obscurity. The sermon closes with the simple command: "Say their names" (13). Later, Toby remembered Adam One saying that such acts of remembrance for extinct animals are "a way of keeping them alive" (315). As Richard Walsh (2020, 121) writes, "This naming does not assert mastery over the animals, but, in a Levinas fashion, evokes trust and community," even as it acknowledges human complicity in the species' downfall. Literary scholar Mariette Grimbeek (2017, 175) finds the Gardeners' emphasis on bearing witness and naming to be "a peculiarly passive element in their action-based faith," but Jennifer Koosed (2020, 136–37) writes that "words matter" in the MaddAddam trilogy, "not as fixed and authoritative canon but as fluid and flexible threads that can be woven and re-woven to bind and sustain communities." For the Gardeners, words have creative power, much like divine speech in Gen 1. The Gardeners' "emphasis on naming that appears throughout the new community … underscores the utter irreducibility of the individual whether it be human, humanoid, or other animal and contrasts with the 'macro-politics of globalization' and commodification that was the reigning ethic of the world before the flood" (Koosed 2020, 154). By naming each individual life form with attention and gratitude, the Gardeners forged an inclusive earth com-

---

8. Not only is creation ongoing, preaches Adam One; the "fall" of humankind is, too. In Gardener theology, humans fell in multiple ways: "The ancestral primates fell out of the trees; then they fell from vegetarianism into meat-eating. Then they fell from instinct into reason, and thus into technology; from simple signals into complex grammar, and thus into humanity; from firelessness into fire, and thence into weaponry; and from seasonal mating into an incessant sexual twitching" (Atwood 2009, 188). All of these falls serve to separate humans from their original primate identity (52). Though Adam One does not use these words, one could extrapolate that an overemphasis on human uniqueness is thus the original sin.

munity, including extinct species, living animals, plants, trees, insects, and bacteria. The community the Gardeners sought to sustain with their words is that of the earth itself.

The Gardeners viewed the whole earth as God's garden, but they were realists, too, who would not deny that the current earth was more like wilderness than the garden it was meant to be. Twice in his sermons, Adam One quoted directly from Isaiah, one of the prophetic books in the Hebrew Bible that envisions the natural world taking back uninhabited spaces abandoned by humans. After the Gardeners were forced out of Edencliff and into hiding, but prior to the outbreak of the pandemic wrought by Crake, Adam One quoted Isa 18:6: "They shall be left together unto the Fowls of the mountains, and to the Beasts of the Earth; and the Fowls shall summer upon them, and all the beasts of the Earth shall winter upon them" (Atwood 2009, 312). In Isaiah, these words are part of an oracle against an enemy nation emphasizing how quickly human civilizations crumble when given over to the natural processes set into motion by God at creation. Adam One interpreted these words as signifying what would happen to human habitation after the Waterless Flood. Both in its original prophetic context and in the novel, the words were intended to engender hope in the audience by offering a picture of the downfall and impermanence of human evil. Adam One continued: "For all works of Man will be as words written on water" (312). Later, after many Gardeners had already succumbed to the virus, Adam One quoted from Isa 34:10b–11: "'From generation to generation it shall lie waste.... But the Cormorant and the Bittern shall possess it.... There shall the great Owl make her nest, and lay, and hatch, and gather under her shadow; there shall the Vultures also be gathered, every one with her mate.' And so it has come to pass" (Atwood 2009, 372). Once again, Adam One highlighted a biblical oracle about divine punishment that results in land returning to the control of the natural world. Adam One hoped for a new Eden but also acknowledged that the future of the earth might look more like wilderness than garden—and that was as it should be.

In *The Year of the Flood*, land was a text that the gardeners read alongside the Bible. The Gardeners made meaning from their lives by intertwining their well-being with that of the earth. A meaningful life, in their view, would bear witness to land and nature with respect and care. In fact, the anthropology of the Gardeners was mostly land-based, drawing on gardening and wilderness metaphors alike. According to the Gardeners' ecotheology, humans are themselves gardens. Each Gardener's body was "a garden for sub-visual life forms" (Atwood 2009, 160), a host for microscopic life. Human imagination was a garden, too: Adam One spoke of the "inner Gardens of our Minds" (345) through which one's kinship with the earth can be strengthened. The Gardeners also recognized that humans could enter a "fallow state" of severe depression; like overworked land, humans in this state can be renewed and restored given time and care. Gardener anthropology also spoke of humans as arks that will bring knowledge of the many extinct species forward into the postflood era (93). In his sermons, Adam One addressed his congregants as "Fellow Mammals" and "Fellow Mortals," reminding humans of their kinship with animals and their inevitable deaths.[9] When a Gardener died, the body was lovingly referred to as Compost; it was returned to the earth so it may continue "God's great dance of proteins" (404) in which "no atom is lost" (423).

Over the course of the trilogy, the Gardeners' relationship with earth demonstrates a significant interplay, even a tension, between staying put (gardening) and going out (living in exile). At first, the Gardeners' story is one of rootedness, as they dwell together in the pleeblands, equally committed to radical environmentalism in the present and apocalyptic expectation for the future. In another sense, though, they were already living in exile at Edencliff, as they considered their dwelling temporary in comparison with the new and lasting Eden to come. When disaster struck, and the Corporations outlawed their way of life, the community journeyed out, now living in a double exile from both their past pleebland garden home and from the new Eden that had failed to materialize (Walsh 2020, 121–22). Adam One's final sermon emphasized the gift of the journey. Although there was "disappointment" (Atwood 2009, 371) that the Gardeners were not destined, after all, to be the meek who shall inherit the earth, Adam One reinterpreted their mission. On the feast day dedicated to Saint Terry[10] and All the Wayfarers, Adam One said: "The Saints of this day are all Wayfarers. They knew so well that it is better to journey than to arrive, as long as we journey in firm faith and for selfless ends.

---

9. Throughout his sermons, Adam One struggled with the extent to which humans were distinct from other species. Although he insisted that humans should not act like simple chimpanzees (Atwood 2009, 159), he also lamented that humans could not simply "believe as other creatures do" (235).

10. Each feast day was dedicated to a saint, some well-known and others obscure. This particular day was in honor of Terry Fox, a distance runner with a prosthetic leg who raised money for cancer research.

Let us hold that thought in our hearts, my Friends and fellow Voyagers" (404). By emphasizing journey rather than arrival, Adam One translated the community's former personal hopes into a global hope for the land itself, whether or not they would be present to occupy it.

The biblical narratives explored above were usually clear when portraying land as garden, wilderness, or that which has been lost. In the Bible, land frequently shifts from one category to another over time, but its identity is generally stable within any given text. In modern science fiction, and in Atwood's MaddAddam trilogy in particular, these categories are less distinct. Land can be simultaneously garden and wilderness depending on whose perspective one considers, and, as identities shift, characters can feel both at home and in exile in the same location.

Conclusion

Adam One and his flock did not inherit the earth. But as the novel *MaddAddam* reveals, another diaspora community does. This apocalyptic community includes pigoons, pigs genetically engineered with human brain tissue, who exhibit their own "queer animalities" (Stone 2020, 267–69), including language and individual names. The pigoons ally themselves with the human remnant and the Children of Crake, and this rag-tag community works together to ensure the survival of all. The next generation of earth-dwellers also includes children, some of whom are human-Craker hybrids. In Atwood's trilogy, hope for humanity and the land itself is found in hybridity. Although Crake's rebooted earth has not eradicated evil, those who remain have been given the chance to choose a different path than their predecessors. Preflood hybridity was forced, profit-driven, corporate-sponsored, and anthropocentric, but postflood hybridity respects the choice of the subject and gives the land and all its inhabitants an equal voice. The choice to survive by way of hybridity is, in the *MaddAddam* universe, an example of what Atwood (1972, 36–39) elsewhere calls "creative nonvictimhood," the claiming of one's agency to resist victimization. In this way, the Trilogy's postapocalyptic landscape offers far greater hope than one might expect from a traditional dystopia.

After the end of the world, where can hope for the land be found? Similar to the biblical flood story, hope is found in renovating the earth, but in Atwood's novels, humankind needs renovation far more. In *MaddAddam*, the earth might still be for us—but not only us and not unless we are willing to change. If any flags are planted in the postflood *MaddAddam* world, they belong to nature, who plants them within us: our bodies, earth's garden.

Representative Examples in Science Fiction

Novels

Asimov, Isaac. 1985. *Robots and Empire.* New York: Doubleday.
Atwood, Margaret. 2003. *Oryx and Crake.* New York: Doubleday.
———. 2009. *The Year of the Flood.* New York: Doubleday.
———. 2013. *MaddAddam.* New York: Doubleday.
Butler, Octavia. 1989. *Lilith's Brood: Dawn–Adulthood Rites–Imago.* New York: Warner.
———. 1993. *Parable of the Sower.* New York: Four Walls Eight Windows.
———. 1998. *Parable of the Talents.* New York: Seven Stories Press.
Le Guin, Ursula K. 1966. *Rocannon's World.* New York: Ace.
———. 1969. *The Left Hand of Darkness.* New York: Ace.
———. 1974. *The Dispossessed.* New York: Harper & Row.
McCarthy, Cormac. 2006. *The Road.* New York: Knopf.
Walker, Karen Thompson. 2012. *The Age of Miracles.* New York: Random House.

Films

Avatar. 2009. Directed and written by James Cameron. Twentieth Century Fox.
Battle for Terra. 2007. Directed by Aristomenis Tsirbas. Written by Evan Spiliotopoulos and Aristomenis Tsirbas. Menithings Production.
Gravity. 2013. Directed and written by Alfonso Cuarón. Warner Bros. Pictures.
Melancholia. 2011. Directed and written by Lars von Trier. Zentropa Entertainments.
Planet of the Apes. 1968. Directed by Franklin J. Schaffner. Written by Michael Wilson and Rod Serling. APJAC Productions.
Seeking a Friend for the End of the World. 2012. Written and directed by Lorene Scafaria. Mandate Pictures.
Star Trek II: The Wrath of Khan. 1982. Directed by Nicholas Meyer. Written by Harve Bennett and Jack B. Sowards. Paramount Pictures.

Star Trek III: The Search for Spock. 1984. Directed by Leonard Nimoy. Written by Harve Bennett. Paramount Pictures.

TV Series/Episodes

"The Apple." 1967. *Star Trek: The Original Series.* Directed by Joseph Pevney. Written by Gene Roddenberry, Max Ehrlich, and Gene L. Coon. Paramount Television.
Battlestar Galactica. 1978–1979. Produced by Glen Larson. Larson Productions.
Battlestar Galactica. 2004–2009. Produced by Ronald D. Moore et al. R&D TV et al.
"The End of the World." 2005. *Doctor Who.* Directed by Euros Lyn. Written by Russell T. Davies. BBC One.
Firefly. 2002–2003. Produced by Joss Whedon and Tim Minear. Mutant Enemy Productions and Twentieth Century Fox Television.
"Miniseries." 2003. *Battlestar Galactica.* Produced by David Eick and Ronald D. Moore. R&D TV et al.
"Out of Gas." 2002. *Firefly.* Directed by David Solomon. Written by Tim Minear. Mutant Enemy Productions and Twentieth Century Fox Television.
"Scorched Earth." 2000. *Stargate.* Directed by Martin Wood. Written by Joseph Mallozzi and Paul Mullie. MGM Television and Double Secret Productions.
Star Trek: Voyager. 1995–2001. Produced by Rick Berman et al. Paramount Pictures.
"The Way to Eden." 1969. *Star Trek: The Original Series.* Directed by David Alexander. Written by Gene Roddenberry, Arthur Heinemann, and D. C. Fontana. Paramount Television.

Works Cited

Atwood, Margaret. 1972. *Survival: A Thematic Guide to Canadian Literature.* Toronto: Anansi.
———. (1995) 2011. "The Moment." Page 109 in *Morning in the Burned House.* Boston: Houghton Mifflin.
———. 2012. *In Other Worlds: SF and the Human Imagination.* New York: Anchor.

Baly, Denis, and Paul J. Achtemeier. 2011. "Wilderness." Pages 1104–5 in *The HarperCollins Bible Dictionary*. Edited by Mark Allan Powell. New York: HarperCollins.

Bouson, J. Brooks. 2016. "A 'Joke-Filled Romp' through End Times: Radical Environmentalism, Deep Ecology, and Human Extinction in Margaret Atwood's Eco-Apocalyptic MaddAddam Trilogy." *Journal of Commonwealth Literature* 51:341–57.

Canavan, Gerry. 2012. "Hope, but Not For Us: Ecological Science Fiction and the End of the World in Margaret Atwood's *Oryx and Crake* and *The Year of the Flood*." *Lit* 23:138–59.

Fretheim, Terence E. 1994. "Genesis." *NIB* 1:321–674.

Grimbeek, Marinette. 2017. "Margaret Atwood's Environmentalism: Apocalypse and Satire in the MaddAddam Trilogy." PhD diss., Karlstads Universitet.

Hillel, Daniel. 2006. *The Natural History of the Bible*. New York: Columbia.

Jennings, Hope. 2010. "The Comic Apocalypse of The Year of the Flood." *Margaret Atwood Studies* 3.2:11–18.

Koester, Craig R. 2001. *Revelation and the End of All Things*. Grand Rapids: Eerdmans.

Koosed, Jennifer. 2020. "Margaret Atwood's Primordial Myth." Pages 135–56 in *"Who Knows What We'd Make of It, If We Ever Got Our Hands on It?": The Bible and Margaret Atwood*. Edited by Rhiannon Graybill and Peter J. Sabo. Biblical Intersections 18. Piscataway, NJ: Gorgias.

Newsom, Carol. 2003. *The Book of Job: A Contest of Moral Imaginations*. Oxford: Oxford University Press.

Rhodes, Sonny. 2017. "Ballad of Serenity." *The Essential Sonny Rhodes: Songs and Stories*. Santa Cruz, CA: Need to Know Handmade Music.

Schmitz, Philip C. 1992. "Canaan." *ABD* 1:828–31.

Sheinfeld, Shayna. 2020. "Scenes from the End of the World in American Popular Culture." Pages 201–18 in *The Oxford Handbook of the Bible and American Popular Culture*. Edited by Dan W. Clanton Jr. and Terry R. Clark. Oxford: Oxford University Press.

Stone, Ken. 2020. "Queer Animalities in Margaret Atwood's *MaddAddam* Trilogy and the Hebrew Bible." Pages 259–83 in *"Who Knows What We'd Make of It, If We Ever Got Our Hands on It?": The Bible and Margaret Atwood*. Edited by Rhiannon Graybill and Peter J. Sabo. Biblical Intersections 18. Piscataway, NJ: Gorgias.

Walsh, Richard. 2020. "Margaret Atwood's Speculative Bibles: 'First the Bad Things, Then the Story.'" Pages 111–33 in *"Who Knows What We'd Make of It, If We Ever Got Our Hands on It?": The Bible and Margaret Atwood*. Edited by Rhiannon Graybill and Peter J. Sabo. Biblical Intersections 18. Piscataway, NJ: Gorgias.

Babylon

JASON A. STAPLES

A group of protagonists face seemingly impossible odds: a technologically advanced conglomeration of nameless, faceless troops serving a despotic ruling class; a decadent metropolis that presents itself as a bringer of civilization while imposing totalitarian rule on the diverse groups who dare oppose it. This "evil empire" scenario could describe innumerable works of science fiction, but it applies equally well to the original evil empire: Babylon, the greatest city of the ancient world, legendary for its power, wisdom, wealth, and cruelty.

The biblical authors were familiar with imperial domination—in contrast to the cliché that history is written by the victors, the story of ancient Israel and Judah is one of frequent subjugation by powerful empires: Egypt, the Assyrians, the Persians. But it was the Babylonians who ultimately sacked Jerusalem, destroyed the temple of Israel's God, and took the royals, priests, and upper classes into exile. These tragic events deeply impacted the biblical authors and were central to the formation of biblical literature. Babylon consequently came to be portrayed as the archetypal evil empire in early Jewish and Christian literature, the megacity representing imperial power and culture in all its oppressive splendor, the image of hubristic ambition and (ultimately doomed) human attempts to gain godlike power.

Babylon in the Bible and Beyond

A Brief History of Babylon

Babylon was situated along the Euphrates River about 50 miles (80 km) southwest of modern Baghdad in Iraq. It was one of the oldest cities in the region, having been founded sometime before 2300 BCE. The city became a regional power in the time of Hammurabi (ca. 1792–1750 BCE), who declared himself king and controlled all of southern Mesopotamia. Hammurabi is best known for his legal code, which contains many parallels to legislation appearing in the Torah (Radner 2020, 35–54).

The Old Babylonian Empire fragmented soon after Hammurabi's death, and the region of Babylonia was too internally divided throughout most of antiquity to maintain a unified standing army or project political dominance outside the region. The old native Babylonian population (itself an amalgam of ancient ethnic groups) was centered in cities, while three Chaldean tribes dominated most of the southern land and various Aramean tribes were scattered about the periphery. Consequently, the city of Babylon fell to the Hittites around 1595 BCE and was controlled by the Kassites until about 1250 BCE and then the Assyrians until the late 600s BCE (Leick 2003, 43–60). Nevertheless, throughout this time Babylon, which had become the new home for gods displaced by migration from abandoned cities in southern territories (Radner 2020, 51–52), came to be venerated as a holy city. The Assyrians borrowed Babylonian divination practices (Radner 2020, 90–92) and showed great respect to the Babylonian gods—Babylon's reputation as a center of magic and spiritual power long outlasted the city itself—regarding Babylon as the cultural capital of Mesopotamia (Brinkman 1973, 89–90). Nevertheless, after half a century of repeated Babylonian rebellions, Sennacherib (705–681) sacked Babylon in 689, razing its walls, temples, and palaces and smashing the images of the Babylonian deities other than Marduk, whose image was taken to Assyria. Sennacherib's successor, Esarhaddon (680–669), attempted to atone for his father's desecration of Babylon by releasing Babylonian exiles and rebuilding the city and its temples, even choosing to live part of each year in Babylon (Radner 2020, 103–6).

Babylon gained its independence and supremacy over Assyria between 612 and 605 BCE, and the city became the capital of the Neo-Babylonian Empire. Nebuchadnezzar II (605–562) then greatly expanded Babylonian power and enlarged Babylon to an area of six square miles (1,554 hectares), building up the city with beautiful buildings and massive fortifications (Radner 2020, 111–38; George 2009). The center of the city prominently featured a large temple complex that housed the main statue of the god Marduk (Bel) and a 300 foot (91 m) tall central ziggurat (temple tower) called Etemenanki ("temple of the foundation of heaven and earth"). Babylon became especially famous for its hanging gardens, a terraced garden complex designated one of the Seven Wonders of the ancient world (Finkel and Seymour 2009, 104–23).

Babylon's rule was short-lived, however, as Cyrus the Great and the Persians took the city with little resistance in 539 BCE (Radner 2020, 139–41). Still, even a century later, the Greek historian Herodotus describes Babylon as the world's largest and most spectacular city (*Hist.* 1.178–187), and later classical authors frequently used Babylon as a symbol for impressive human works and decadent imperial ambition (Scheil 2016, 21–28). After two centuries of Persian rule, the city surrendered to Alexander the Great without resistance in 331 BCE. Alexander's regional successor chose to build a new capital, Seleucia, on the Tigris River, after which Babylon eventually fell into ruin. The city continued to cast a long historical shadow even as a ruin thanks to its imposing structures, which still received attention even from Roman historians, and it remains the largest archaeological site in the Near East.

Babylon in Early Biblical Literature

The various books of the Bible contain over 260 references to Babylon (Hebrew *babel*) and its people, along with eighty-nine references to Chaldea/Chaldeans. The first biblical appearances of Babylon are in the primordial history, setting the stage for later expectations. Genesis 10 tells of the imperial king Nimrod, who began his kingdom with "Babel, Erech, Akkad, and Calneh in the land of Shinar" (10:10).[1] Nimrod is described as a "mighty hunter," understood by many later interpreters as referring to hunting humans rather than animals, and his name is a play on the similarity between the Hebrew word *marad* ("to rebel") and the Akkadian *namru* or *nimru* ("shining"), which was used as an epithet of various Mesopotamian gods, including Marduk, whom tradition held as the original builder of Babylon.

The next chapter in Genesis tells of the tower of Babylon, a legendary tale that alludes to the famous Etemenanki ziggurat. By playing on the similarities between the word Babel (= Babylon) and the Hebrew word *balal*, which means "to confuse" or "mix up," this story challenges Babylonian propaganda that sees the city as the "gate of God" and the center of a unified empire. Instead, according to Genesis, from its very inception

---

[1]. Unless otherwise indicated, biblical translations are my own.

Babylon has been the epicenter of human rebellion against God and the source of confusion and dispersion of peoples (Arnold 2009).[2]

Notably, we are then told that Abraham came from "Ur of the Chaldeans" (11:28, 31; 15:7), identifying Israel's ancestor with the region of Babylonia dominated by the Chaldean ethnic group that ruled the Neo-Babylonian Empire. Abraham's migration from Babylonia and rejection of Babylonian deities—the latter made more explicit in postbiblical literature—therefore establishes an early contrast between Babylon and the children of Abraham, who have rejected the ways—and the gods—of Babylon. The pastoral wanderings of Abraham and his descendants also stand against the urban decadence represented by Babylon.

These stories in Genesis establish a foundation for the later symbolic functions of Babylon across a wide range of literature, including many of the other biblical books. The remaining appearances of Babylon in the Bible can be divided into two categories: (1) historical and prophetic references to the city of Babylon and the Neo-Babylonian Empire and (2) Babylon as a paradigmatic image of human arrogance, debauchery, and violence.

Babylon in Historical Narrative

In 722 BCE, Assyrian king Sargon II sacked the northern kingdom of Samaria. According to 2 Kgs 17, the Assyrians then replaced much of the population of Samaria with persons from Babylon and several other Mesopotamian cities. The report in 2 Kings served as anti-Samaritan propaganda well into the Common Era, as many Jews regarded the neighboring Samaritans as descendants of the intermarriage between the remaining Israelites and the Babylonian peoples resettled into the area by the Assyrians.

Later 2 Kings reports how the Babylonian king Merodach-baladan (Marduk-apla-iddina II) sent emissaries and a gift to Hezekiah, the king of Judah, in an effort to incite a mutual rebellion against Assyria (2 Kgs 20:12–13; Isa 39:1–2). This most likely occurred immediately before Sennacherib's invasion and the siege of Jerusalem in the late eighth century BCE. Hezekiah eagerly showed his wealth and resources to the Babylonian emissaries, much to the displeasure of the prophet Isaiah, who predicted

---

2. For more on the tower of Babel/Babylon in the Bible and science fiction, see the essay by Tom de Bruin in this volume.

that the Babylonians would eventually come to claim that wealth for themselves (2 Kgs 20:14–18; Isa 39:3–7). The rebellions of both Hezekiah and Merodach-baladan failed.

Isaiah's prediction of the Babylonian sack of Jerusalem was fulfilled two generations later. By then Judah had become a vassal kingdom under the Neo-Babylonian Empire. The prophet Jeremiah was active in Jerusalem throughout this period and repeatedly advised Judah and Jerusalem to submit to the Babylonians, arguing that God had in fact put Nebuchadnezzar II in power (Jer 27:6; 28:14) and that those who resisted would be punished and ultimately destroyed by God himself (27:8). Jeremiah's counsel of submission to Babylon was grounded in the conviction that God was using Babylon as a temporary agent of discipline. According to Jeremiah, Babylon would itself later be punished for idolatry, violence, and injustice (Jer 50–51). But the exiles from Judah would return to their own land after seventy years, as long as they submitted and obeyed (29:10). Nevertheless, the Judahite king Zedekiah went against Jeremiah's counsel and rebelled against Babylon. In response, Nebuchadnezzar besieged Jerusalem, destroying the city and its temple in 587/586 BCE and taking a large number of captives to Babylon. As punishment for breaking his oath, Zedekiah was forced to watch his sons slaughtered before being blinded and deported to Babylon (2 Kgs 25:6–7).

The Babylonians systematically dismantled the Jerusalem temple and took everything of value back to Babylon, breaking apart anything too large to be taken as a whole (2 Kgs 25:13–17). The temple was then burned along with all the other large buildings in Jerusalem (25:9), and the walls of Jerusalem were razed (25:10). The devastation of Jerusalem is mourned in the book of Lamentations and Ps 137, the latter of which begins, "By the rivers of Babylon, there we sat and wept when we remembered Zion" (137:1), and concludes with a blessing upon the one who "pays you [Babylon] back what you have done to us" (137:8).

After the fall of the Neo-Babylonian Empire to the unified Medes and Persians under Cyrus the Great, the exiled Jews were permitted to return to Judah—effectively replicating the migration of Abraham—and build a new temple in Jerusalem (Ezra 1–6). The second part of Isaiah rejoices in the Persian overthrow of Babylon, even calling Cyrus the messiah (45:1). The prophet calls to the exiles to "go forth from Babylon! Flee from the Chaldeans!," while joyfully proclaiming that Israel's God has redeemed his people (48:20). The conditions of the return, however, fell far short of the prophecies of Israel's restoration, and the Persians (and later Greeks and

Romans) were often portrayed as continuations of Babylon's rule, as in the visions of Daniel and in Nehemiah's reference to the Persian king Artaxerxes as "the king of Babylon" (Neh 13:6).

Babylon as Metaphorical Image

The centrality of these events in the biblical narratives of Israel and Judah led to the second category of biblical references to Babylon: the poetically heightened, metaphorical use of Babylon as a symbol and paradigm. In the prophets, Babylon is depicted as a manifestation of arrogance (Jer 50:31), a false holy city opposing the true holy city of Jerusalem (50:2), and a fearsome sea monster that consumes peoples and nations (51:34–37). Babylon is "the beauty of [earthly] kingdoms" (Isa 13:19), opposing and inferior to the heavenly kingdom of God. Babylon is an accursed city, doomed to be forever a desolate ruin (Jer 51:26, 37, 62). In Isa 14, the prophet declares that Israel will be restored from captivity, at which time the people will sing a taunting lament for the defeated king of Babylon. Whereas this king had imagined himself divine and had imagined he could "ascend to heaven" and even "raise [his] throne above the stars of God" to "make [himself] like the Most High" (Isa 14:13–14), he suffered the same fate as the poorest humans, with no burial or posthumous honors (14:15–19). Likewise, the city of Babylon—the place of such arrogant ambitions—would itself be utterly destroyed, with no remaining inhabitants (14:22–23; Williamson 2022).

Later Jewish literature frequently uses Babylon or its kings as a coded reference to contemporary evil imperial forces oppressing the Jews. The book of Daniel, for example, though written in the second century BCE, is set among the first exiles to Babylon, who become part of the Babylonian administrative system. Daniel and his friends are a paradigm for faithfulness in the diaspora. The book lampoons Babylon's reputation as the home of powerful magicians and priests, repeatedly contrasting the lifeless gods of Babylon served by ignorant and impotent attendants and the living God of Israel served by humble and wise Jews such as Daniel. For example, when Nebuchadnezzar has a revelatory dream, the Babylonian magicians and sages—famed for their closeness to the gods—are unable to interpret it, while Daniel shows the superiority of Israel's God by successfully interpreting the dream (Dan 2). The famous story of the fiery furnace (Dan 3) emphasizes the supremacy of Israel's God over the lifeless images—and political power—of Babylon. "Bel and the Dragon," a story appearing in Greek versions of Daniel (Dan 14), further lampoons the lifelessness and impotence of Marduk and the dragon associated with him. Babylon's rulers are also portrayed as ignorant, arrogant, and capricious, as they do not understand that their power has been granted to them by God, a theme most clearly illustrated in a pair of stories toward the middle of the book. In the first, Nebuchadnezzar learns this lesson by being driven temporarily insane before properly giving glory to God (Dan 4; Davis Bledsoe 2012). In the next chapter, the later king Belshazzar throws a feast during which he arrogantly drinks from the vessels taken from the Jerusalem temple, at which point a hand appears and writes a decree of divine judgment against him on the wall, namely, that his kingdom had been given to the Medes and Persians (Dan 5; Finkel and Seymour 2009, 170–78).

Apocalyptic Jewish works written around the time of the fall of Jerusalem in 70 CE carry this forward by symbolically representing Rome as Babylon, and similar symbolic uses appear in the New Testament (e.g., 1 Pet 5:13). Famously, the book of Revelation portrays Babylon as a prostitute riding on a seven-headed beast. The city is identified as "the mother of prostitutes and of the abominations of the earth" (Rev 17:5) and as having made the nations drunk with "the wine of the wrath of her immorality" (14:8). This woman is most commonly identified with Rome, though it is perhaps more probable that she represents Jerusalem in union *with* Rome, represented by the seven-headed beast on which she rides (Moloney 2020, 255–83). Jerusalem has essentially become adulterous Babylon by opposing Jesus and his followers. Babylon is then utterly destroyed in catastrophic fashion in Rev 18, an event the book uses to symbolically represent the ultimate victory of God over the wicked forces of darkness.

Conclusion: Babylon in the Bible

In summary, the Bible presents both a nuanced historical picture of Babylon and a more metaphorical and symbolic image of Babylon, each of which provides fertile ground for later literary uses. Babylon emerges from the biblical pages as an image of beauty and power as well as ruin and desolation (Scheil 2016, 35, 197–205), the paradigmatic decadent metropolis ruled by a merciless tyrant, the empire whose expansion brings exile, slavery, and homogenization to the diverse, rustic, freedom-loving people on the periphery. As such, Babylon—the violent, oppressive city ruled by powerful human rulers unrestrained by morality—stands as the dyadic opposite of Jerusalem, the city of peace ruled by the living God.

Nevertheless, the might of Babylon is also relegated to the past, and the city's great ruins attest to the ephemerality of human power and glory. The rise and fall of Babylon thus serves as a paradigmatic story of the limitations of human designs (Scheil 2016, 42). Babylon is "both an agent of destruction and a figure for self-destruction" (198); its cruelty and arrogance sowed the seeds of its own destruction, and it now stands as a dead, accursed city haunted by the ghosts of its awesome past (222–29). Those who are oppressed by the reimagined Babylons need only look at the ruins of the original to know that redemption awaits.

Babylon in Science Fiction

Babylon retained a special place in the Western imagination as later Christian authors continued to borrow from the rich biblical and classical imagery of the ancient city. In general, such interpreters conceptualized Babylon as the essence of pagan falsehood and degeneracy in contrast to Christian truth and virtue (Akbari 2018). Augustine's highly influential *City of God*, for example, represents Babylon as the paradigmatic "city of man" that has stood against the "city of God" throughout history. Early Christian representations of Rome as a new Babylon faded as the empire was Christianized, but the Protestant Reformation brought a resurgence of the Rome-as-Babylon trope, this time representing Babylon/Rome as the seat of false religion, wealth, and decadence (e.g., Hislop 1862), an image that has persisted in many evangelical forms of Christianity especially popular in the United States (e.g., Hunt 1994; LaHaye and Jenkins 2011, 172–77). This continued cultural currency has led to various portrayals of Babylon appearing throughout science fiction literature, cinema, and television.

The first and most obvious connection is the seemingly ubiquitous trope of the evil empire, an authoritarian organization or alliance dedicated to the consolidation of power and the homogenization of culture throughout the world or cosmos. Based in a decadent metropolis, the empire typically presents itself as the guardian of law and order against the forces of chaos, while the protagonists in such stories are often those from the hinterlands. Examples include the Galactic Empire in *Star Wars*, the Alliance in *Firefly/Serenity*, The Capitol in *The Hunger Games*, the

Necromonger Empire in *The Chronicles of Riddick*, the Imperium of *Dune*, and numerous examples from *Star Trek* and *Doctor Who*. Many of these fictional depictions borrow from later historical empires, such as Rome (e.g., *The Hunger Games*) or Nazi Germany (*Star Wars*), but the portrayal of these empires is ultimately derived from the biblical image of Babylon, which provides the original template for such critiques. This is especially true when the empire is also associated with a distinctly evil religion set against the pure religion of the noble protagonists (e.g., the Sith versus the Jedi in *Star Wars*).

Like the historical Babylonian Empire, these fictional empires are typically based in enormous megacities characterized by massive skyscrapers (alluding to the tower of Babel) and a combination of decadent excess and oppressive poverty (Scheil 2016, 229–31). In addition to the examples of empire above (all of which include such megacity capitals), other notable examples include Trantor in Isaac Asimov's *Foundation* series (1951–1953), Mega City-1 in the comic series *Judge Dredd* (1977–) and the subsequent movies *Judge Dredd* (1995) and *Dredd* (2012), Los Angeles in Ridley Scott's *Blade Runner* (1982), and Mega City in *The Matrix* (1999).

On the flip side, some science fiction narratives are told from the perspective of those working on behalf of a centralized state or a megalopolis that is beneficent and brings knowledge, wealth, and civilization to those on the periphery. These could be considered as told from the Babylonian perspective. Examples include the Federation from *Star Trek*, the United Citizens Federation from *Starship Troopers* (subversively satirized in the 1997 film version), the United Systems of the *Alien* films, and the United Nations Space Command from the *Halo* series. In the last, it is the imperialistic alien Covenant that borrows from the Babylon/evil empire trope.

Sometimes these tropes are metaphorized such that the evil empire is not (or at least not yet) political but rather ideological. In C. S. Lewis's *That Hideous Strength* (1945), named after a line from a sixteenth-century poem referring to the tower of Babel, the "two cities" topos is reframed as a battle for the soul of England. The technocratic National Institute for Coordinated Experiments (N.I.C.E) stands for Babylon. Earthly, power-seeking, bellicose, empire-building N.I.C.E. aims for scientific progress without truth or morality. Space travel stands in place of the tower.[3] Logres

---

3. Stanley Kubrick similarly paralleled Babylonian ambition to invade the heavens with the tower of Babel with space travel, observing, "The Tower of Babel was the

stands in the place of Jerusalem. It is the heavenly, peaceful, poetic society that stands opposed to such oppressive progress. It is no coincidence that the book culminates with a recapitulation of the curse of Babel, with those involved in N.I.C.E. devolving into confused speech, no longer able to understand one another. Dispersion and confusion are the inevitable consequence of Babylonian hubris and overreach into divine territory. Similar tropes of overly ambitious scientific research and attempts to gain power through technology appear in works such as *Deep Blue Sea* (1999), Michael Crichton's *Jurassic Park* (1990; film adaptation 1993), *Serenity* (2005), and the *Resident Evil* franchise.

Science fiction also frequently involves encounter with the ruins of a great metropolis or civilization—a theme building on the prophetic imagery of Babylon as accursed ruin. This trope of the ancient, lost civilization cursed for hubristically trespassing into territory where humans dare not tread appears frequently in science fiction. H. P. Lovecraft's "At the Mountains of Madness" (1936 [2005]), for instance, tells of a fictional research expedition to Antarctica, where a professor and his team discovers the ruin of a primordial city once populated by extraterrestrials who came to earth shortly after the formation of the moon. The center of the ruined city features a giant tower—described in terms that specifically reference Babylon and its tower—and these ancient gods themselves fear and worship a nameless evil situated in a mountain range beyond the city. Most of the team is slaughtered after several specimens come to life, and the professor warns the reader to stay away from the site.

Lovecraft's story "provided the pervasive template for the lost civilization/haunted city topos in modern and contemporary iterations of science fiction, fantasy, and horror" (Scheil 2016, 247). Ridley Scott's *Prometheus* (2012), for example, provides a mythological basis for the *Alien* franchise with a nearly identical plotline—complete with imposing central temple structure—set in space. Other examples of the accursed ruin from a long-lost race in science fiction include the monolith from *2001: A Space Odyssey*, the Forerunner facilities and halo structures in the *Halo* videogame series, and the ruins from the *Planet of the Apes* series. Examples of accursed ruins from a more recent past, such as postapocalyptic America, include Cormac McCarthy's *The Road* (2006; film 2009), the film adap-

---

start of the space age," in the margins of his copy of Franz Kafka's *Parable and Paradoxes*. See Abrams 2018, 132.

tation of *I Am Legend* (2007), *28 Days Later* (2002), and the *Terminator* series, the latter of which combines the certainty of future postapocalyptic ruin with the images of decadent modern culture. These images are similar to prophetic treatments of Babylon found in later biblical literature.

These ancient ruins are sometimes connected to another topos stemming from later interpretations of the biblical image of Babylon: the conception of a degenerated or accursed race. Nimrod of Gen 10 was the grandson of Noah's son Ham. According to Genesis, after Ham saw his father naked, his descendants became cursed to become slaves. This curse became important in the racialized discourses of the late medieval and early modern period as Babylon, a race allegedly cursed through its founder Nimrod, was interpreted as "the archetypal source of an ancient tainted human lineage" (Scheil 2016, 15–16, 123–93). By the nineteenth century, this idea of an accursed and savage race separated from the rest of (civilized) humanity had been combined with concepts borrowed from evolutionary theory to denigrate non-European racial groups. These tropes frequently appear in early science fiction, where a seemingly civilized protagonist encounters "beast-men" or otherwise degenerated humans. Notable examples include H. G. Wells's *The Island of Dr. Moreau* (1896) and *The Time Machine* (1895), Edgar Rice Burroughs's Barsoom series (1912, 1917–1948, 1964; brought to cinema with *John Carter* in 2012), and Lovecraft's "The Shadow over Innsmouth" (1931) (see Scheil 2016, 177–82, 188–90).

Babylon's destruction is not always encountered as an ancient ruin, however, as the judgment and catastrophic destruction of Babylon in Rev 18—a great city destroyed in one hour, with the smoke visible from afar—has also provided fertile territory for science fiction in the nuclear era. The cosmic language, vivid imagery, and context of judgment provided by the biblical passage lend gravitas and a sense of history repeating itself to scenes of modern warfare and destruction, particularly in apocalyptic or postapocalyptic contexts. Pat Frank's *Alas, Babylon* (1959), for example, is an account of the effects of a catastrophic nuclear war between the Soviet Union and the USA on a small town in Florida. It borrows its title directly from Rev 18:10. Other examples of the use of this "judgment/destruction of Babylon" trope include Glen Cook's *The Heirs of Babylon* (1972), and Stephen Vincent Benét's "By the Waters of Babylon" (1937). The image of the "whore of Babylon" from Rev 17 has also appeared in multiple science fiction works, including *Metropolis* (see below) and the episode "99 Problems" from the television series *Supernatural* (2005–2020).

Babylon in Fritz Lang's *Metropolis* (1927)

Widely regarded as the most influential science fiction film of all time (see Minden and Bachmann 2002), Fritz Lang's 1927 silent film *Metropolis* is essentially a meditation on and reinterpretation of the biblical images of Babylon in a postindustrial world dominated by industry and technology and characterized by socioeconomic division.[4] Set in a distant future, the film tells the story of a great city run by cold industrialist Joh Fredersen from the unsubtly named "new tower of Babel." The city is deeply divided. The wealthy live in opulent skyscrapers and spend their time in the "Eternal Gardens" on top of the towers—an obvious allusion to Babylon's hanging gardens—while the oppressed working class lives in a subterranean city, where they toil robotically at the machines that power the lavish lifestyles of those above.

While at leisure in the gardens, Fredersen's son Freder is confronted by an unknown woman escorting a group of working-class children, showing them how their wealthy "brothers" live. They are promptly ushered away, but Freder is intrigued by the beautiful woman and searches for her only to discover the city's dark secret: a separate subterranean city where oppressed workers live and toil in servitude. Further below, in the depths of the ancient catacombs lying beneath the subterranean city, Freder finds that the young woman, Maria, is the prophetic voice of the workers, holding them back from violent revolution with promises of a better future.

In a central scene, Maria recasts the legend of the tower of Babel into a modern fable about labor relations. In Maria's retelling, the ancient tower fails not because of human hubris and divine retribution but rather because the planners who conceived the idea did not adequately communicate their noble vision to the hired workers. In a clever twist on the confusion of languages in the biblical story, Maria explains, "Although they spoke the same language, they could not understand one another's words," with the result that the workers, feeling oppressed, revolt and destroy the tower. The lesson is that the division between capital and labor is what ultimately

---

4. The original version of the film is, unfortunately, not preserved; after mixed opening reviews, nearly a quarter of the film was cut for its international release and its secondary German release. A copy of the original was discovered in Argentina in 2008, but about five minutes of the film were too badly damaged to recover. Most discussions of the film therefore also consider Thea von Harbou's novel of the same name, which was released simultaneously and provided the basis for the screenplay.

prevents humanity from achieving collective greatness. Maria's promised solution is the coming of a mediator who will join "head" (the ruling class) and "hands" (the working class).

On his trip to the underworld, Freder is horrified to witness several workers killed by the explosion of a huge machine, which transforms before his eyes into the gaping maw of the god Moloch, an ancient deity to whom children were offered as sacrifices (cf. Lev 18:21; 1 Kgs 11:7; 2 Kgs 23:10). Upon seeing this modern mechanized Moloch consuming enslaved workers as human sacrifices, Freder decides to be the mediator Maria spoke about. He rushes to inform Fredersen in the tower, who is unconcerned. Freder is appalled by his father's reaction and ultimately decides to help the workers himself. Here it is worth noting the film's twist on Christian trinitarian theology as applied to the body politic of the city: it is no accident that Fredersen's first name, Joh, is a play on Jah, a short form of the Hebrew name of God. Joh, then, is the father, Freder is the son, and the proletarian workers are the embodiment of the spirit, keeping the city alive.

Things are not quite so simple, however, thanks to the evil scientist Rotwang, who is portrayed with imagery associating him with both modern science and medieval—or Babylonian—magic. Grieving for his lost lover, Hel, who married Fredersen and died giving birth to Freder, Rotwang has engaged in his own Pygmalion project, successfully designing "the most perfect and most obedient tool which mankind ever possessed": a robot that can perfectly replicate a human in every respect minus the will. Concerned about Maria's influence, Fredersen collaborates with Rotwang to kidnap Maria and deploy a lookalike robot in her place, thus endangering the living spirit of the city. Here we see a version of the trope of two cities, as the spiritual essences of Jerusalem (Maria) and Babylon (robot Maria) are present and struggling against one another in the single city of *Metropolis*.

As this is happening, Freder is in a Gothic church where a monk proclaims that the "days of which the Apocalypse speaks draw nigh." The monk points to a page of Rev 17, which displays an image of the blasphemous whore of Babylon riding a seven-headed beast. From this point forward, the film borrows heavily from the images of Babylon from Revelation, integrating these images into the framework of its modern recasting of the tower of Babel story. Robot Maria replaces the tower as the height of human ingenuity and technological progress, an inhuman human created by a man playing God, the very personification of Babylon. Upon being put into service, her orgiastic dance at a nightclub quickly reveals her power over men, who cannot resist her seductive charms and soon turn violent in their efforts to draw her affection.

As Robot Maria dances, Freder—bedridden with shock after having seen the robot embracing his father—has an apocalyptic visionary experience, including a feverish sequence in which the biblical image of Mystery Babylon riding the beast fades to a nearly identical scene of Maria riding a statue of the beast on a dais held aloft by personifications of the seven deadly sins. Notably, the scenes in the nightclub (named after a famous Japanese red-light district) feature a racial mixture not seen elsewhere in the film—including three prostitutes (Asian, African, and European) who laugh provocatively into the camera and the personifications of the seven deadly sins, which include several black men. By prominently including racial mixture (only) in these scenes of promiscuity and debauchery, *Metropolis* here borrows from the topos of Babylon as degenerated or accursed race, hinting that racial mixture results in the degeneration of the body politic—an idea unfortunately at home in the era in which the film was made (Müller 2015, 152–57).

The film gets increasingly allegorical and apocalyptic as the scene of Maria as Mystery Babylon gives way to the image of Death, who first releases the seven deadly sins before stepping forward and harvesting souls from the city with his scythe. For the viewer, who knows that this Maria is in fact a simulacrum, the sequence serves as a powerful visual parable of the seductive and controlling power of technology over humans, who are (inevitably?) enslaved by their own creations. As one critic puts it, "Beneath the whore of Babylon runs the mechanism of modernity" (Gunning 2000, 81). Industrialists such as Fredersen may imagine themselves kings or even gods, but they are mere tools of the great city—modern Babylon—and the artificial woman who serves as the incarnation of the Babylonian zeitgeist, governed by Death himself.

Frederson's plan is for Robot Maria to stoke the fires of violent revolution so he can be justified in using force against them. The novel version of *Metropolis* provides additional details: Frederson plans to replace the workers with robots, who can then serve forever as perfectly obedient slaves.[5] Rotwang, however, deeply hates Fredersen and has secretly

---

5. For the relationship between the movie *Metropolis* and the novel *Metropolis*, see above.

instructed Robot Maria to incite the workers to sabotage the machines that power the city, dismantling both the literal and social structures of the city. In another scene directly transforming famous woodcuts of the whore of Babylon into cinematic imagery, Robot Maria is shown riding the shoulders first of the workers and later of Metropolis elites (Bergvall 2012, 248–49), symbolically demonstrating that "this overflowing, destructive mob is the manifestation of the apocalyptic beast" (254).

Fig. 1. Hans Burgkmair the Elder, *The Whore of Babylon*, 1523, woodcut in Martin Luther, *Das Newe Testament Deutsch* (Augsburg: Otmar, 1523). Source: Wikimedia Commons.

Fig. 2. The Whore of Babylon Woodcut, *Metropolis*, 1927. During the film, a monk holds up a woodcut of the whore of Babylon. Although following typical patterns of actual woodcuts (see fig. 1), the woodcut that appears in the film appears to have been done specifically for the film.

Fig. 3. Maria as Whore of Babylon, *Metropolis*, 1927.

Fig. 4: Maria as Whore of Babylon upon Shoulders of Workers, *Metropolis*, 1927.

Fig. 5. Maria as Whore of Babylon upon Shoulders of Elites, *Metropolis*, 1927.

Robot Maria puts Rotwang's plan to action, inciting the workers to destroy the "heart machine," resulting in widespread destruction and a flood (cf. Rev 12:13–15!) that puts the subterranean city—where all the workers' children have remained—underwater.[6] The workers, angry at having been deceived, burn Robot Maria (the "witch") at the stake and are shocked as the flames reveal her metallic body, invulnerable to the flames. Unknown to them, however, the real Maria has escaped and with Freder's help manages to save the children. After a final conflict on the roof of the Gothic church, Rotwang (which means "red-cheeked") falls (presumably) to his death, cast down from heaven like the red dragon of Rev 12:9.

The film concludes with all converging upon the Gothic church, where Freder mediates between his father and the foreman of the workers, bringing them together for a symbolic handshake. The new tower of Babel—which has not been destroyed in the revolution—therefore does not suffer the fate of the first one; in fact, it survives with a unified humanity in position to benefit all. Instead, it is the subterranean world of the underclass that has been destroyed, suggesting that the previous exploit-

---

6. On the connection to Rev 12, see Bergvall 2012, 253–54.

ative system is no longer sustainable now that it has (literally) been brought to the surface (Müller 2015, 136).

It would therefore seem that the film supports Maria's reinterpretation of the tower of Babel legend, arguing that violent revolution is the wrong answer to oppression, since it results in destruction and chaos even worse than the situation it aims to eliminate. Instead, capital and labor must be unified by someone who cares for and can communicate with both. Unlike the biblical critique of human hubris, the film appears to turn the tower of Babel story into a lesson about how human unity is ultimately what brings glory to God and facilitates lasting prosperity. In place of a perpetual dualism between the city of man (Babylon) and the city of God (Jerusalem), the two can (and must!) be united, in keeping with the declaration at the top of the tower of Babel in Maria's sermon: "Great is the world and its Maker! And Great is Man!"

Yet there is something deeply dissatisfying about the tidy ending of *Metropolis*, as it beggars belief that an awkward handshake can so easily heal the wounds of the deeply divided and oppressive structures and social unrest witnessed throughout the film (Bergvall 2012, 255–56; Malley 2018, 24). For one, those social structures have not changed but rather have been reinforced: Fredersen remains in power, still controlling his urban empire (Kracauer 2004, 163–64; Gunning 2000, 78–80). The disastrous outcome of the original tower of Babel also still looms large in the background. The viewer's knowledge of the original story undermines Maria's reinterpretation, with the image of the tower symbolizing both unified humanity and the impossibility of such unity (Hansen 1994, 184).

The apocalyptic imagery of the film further undermines the peaceful conclusion, and the viewer is left with the sense that the story has stopped in the middle, that the tower and imperial structures it represents ultimately cannot stand (Bergvall 2012, 255–56). The optimism of Maria's sermon is therefore overpowered by the Babylonian motifs throughout the film. The robot proves invulnerable and indifferent to the medieval solution of the mob (Malley 2018, 26), manifesting the immortality of technology and the city itself over and against human frailty. "Babylon is a 'parable of ruin' from a mechanized future that is fundamentally at odds with Maria's naive medieval morality" (24). Built on the catacombs of the dead and the labor of the dying, Babylon continues to control its people, leading them all to inevitable Death, the true ruler of the great imperial city.

It is hard to overstate the depth of the film's engagement with the biblical images of Babylon. By combining the tower of Babel story with the narrative arc of Rev 12–18 in a modern context, *Metropolis* reveals an everlasting cycle of order and chaos: the very technologies humans design to sustain unity and progress paradoxically beget disorder and destruction. For all their impressive achievements, humans are not their own masters. The imagery of the film also serves a metacritical function. Rotwang's power to produce a compelling simulacrum alludes to the filmmaker's ability to do the same (Bellour 1986, 131; cf. Gunning 2000, 68–69), suggesting that the universal language of film is the latest technological iteration of the process unsuccessfully begun at the tower of Babel, an idea Lang himself triumphantly declared in a 1926 article on the future of cinema (see Lang 1994, 623). (*Metropolis* itself was even produced at *Babel*sberg Studios!) Whether intentionally or not, the uncomfortable resolution of the film therefore subtly hints at the hubristic nature of modern confidence in human progress and technological advancement. Warnings against hubris embedded in the biblical tower of Babel story still reverberate in the minds of the viewers—who may themselves identify with the people of the upper world, blissfully unaware that their prosperity owes to the unseen toil of others (Müller 1995, 137, 143–44)—long after *Metropolis* has ended.

Thanks to the substantial impact of *Metropolis* within the genre of science fiction movies and television, many of its Babylonian tropes have been adopted by later works, and the rich, complex biblical portrayals of Babylon continue to provide fertile ground for adaptation and application. Simultaneously beautiful and violent, Babylon is the self-styled bringer of civilization and order that in fact serves as the agent of chaos and enslavement. It has a decadent powerful ruling class at its center benefiting from the suffering of those on the periphery (e.g., *Metropolis*, *The Hunger Games*, *Star Wars*, *Firefly/Serenity*). Babylon is also the prototype of human ingenuity and arrogance, with its scientific and/or mystical power ultimately deriving from (and leading to) darkness (e.g., *Metropolis*, *Star Wars*, and *That Hideous Strength*). As the ancient megalopolis ruling the great evil empire of the past, Babylon is also the paradigmatic lost and haunted civilization, the source of an accursed or degenerated race, lying just beneath the surface ready to bring chaos once again (e.g., *Planet of the Apes*, *Prometheus*, or Lovecraft's "At the Mountains of Madness). That Babylon was destroyed also serves as a warning to modern Babylons, which may similarly become postapocalyptic wastelands, victims of their own ambition and overreach in pursuit of dominion and power.

Representative Examples in Science Fiction

28 Days Later. 2002. Directed by Danny Boyle. Written by Alex Garland. Fox Searchlight.
"99 Problems." 2010. *Supernatural.* Directed by Charles Beeson. Written by Julie Siege. The CW.
2001: A Space Odyssey. 1968. Directed by Stanley Kubrick. Written by Stanley Kubrick and Arthur C. Clarke. Metro-Goldwyn-Mayer.
Alien. 1979. Directed by Ridley Scott. Written by Dan O'Bannon. Twentieth Century Fox.
Asimov, Isaac. 1951. *Foundation.* New York: Gnome.
——. 1952. *Foundation and Empire.* New York: Gnome.
——. 1953. *Second Foundation.* New York: Gnome.
"Babel One." 2005. *Star Trek: Enterprise.* Directed by David Straiton. Written by Michael Sussman and André Bormanis. January 28. UPN.
"Babylon." 2016. *The X-Files.* Written and Directed by Chris Carter. February 15. Fox.
Babylon 5. 1993–1998. Created by J. Michael Straczynski. Syndicated.
Babylon 5: Thirdspace. 1998. Directed by Jesús Salvador Trevino. Written by J. Michael Straczynski. Turner Network Television.
Benét, Stephen Vincent. 1937. "By the Waters of Babylon." *The Saturday Evening Post.*
Blade Runner. 1982. Directed by Ridley Scott. Written by Hampton Fancher and David Peoples. Warner Bros.
Burroughs, Edgar Rice. 1912. "Under the Moon of Mars." *All-Story Magazine.* [and subsequent novels, 1917–1948, 1964].
Chiang, Ted. 1990. "Tower of Babylon." *Omni* (November):50–68.
Collins, Suzanne. 2008. *The Hunger Games.* New York: Scholastic.
Cook, Glen. 1972. *The Heirs of Babylon.* New York: Signet.
Deep Blue Sea. 1999. Directed by Renny Harlin. Written by Duncan Kennedy, Donna Powers, and Wayne Powers. Warner Bros.
Dredd. 2012. Directed by Pete Travis. Written by Alex Garland. Reliance Entertainment.
Firefly. 2002. Created by Joss Whedon. Fox.
Frank, Pat. 1959. *Alas, Babylon.* Philadelphia: Lippincott.
Freejack. 1992. Directed by Geoff Murphy. Written by Ronald Shusett and Stuart Oken. Warner Bros.
Halo. 2001–. Multiplatform. Bungie (2001–2010), 343 Industries (2011–).
Herbert, Frank. 1965. *Dune.* Boston: Chilton Books.

I Am Legend. 2007. Directed by Francis Lawrence. Written by Akiva Goldsman and Mark Protosevich. Warner Bros.

I, Robot. 2004. Directed by Alex Proyas. Written by Jeff Vintar and Akiva Goldsman. Twentieth Century Fox.

"Inferno." 1970. *Doctor Who*. Seven-episode serial. Directed by Douglas Camfield (1–7) and Barry Letts (3–7). Written by Don Houghton. BBC.

John Carter. 2012. Directed by Andrew Stanton. Written by Andrew Stanton, Mark Andrews, and Michael Chabon. Disney.

"Journey to Babel." 1967. *Star Trek: The Original Series*. Directed by Joseph Pevney. Written by D. C. Fontana. NBC.

Judge Dredd. 1995. Directed by Danny Cannon. Written by William Wisher Jr. and Steven E. de Souza. Hollywood Pictures.

Lewis, C. S. 1945. *That Hideous Strength: A Modern Fairy-Tale for Grown-Ups*. Ransom Trilogy. London: Bodley Head.

Lovecraft, H. P. 1931. "The Shadow over Innsmouth." Everett, PA: Fantasy.

———. (1936) 2005. "At the Mountains of Madness." Pages 1–102 in *At The Mountains of Madness: The Definitive Edition*. New York: Modern Library.

McCarthy, Cormac. 2006. *The Road*. New York: Knopf.

Metropolis. 1927. Directed by Fritz Lang. Written by Thea von Harbou. Universum Film.

Planet of the Apes. 1968. Directed by Franklin J. Schaffner. Written by Michael Wilson and Rod Serling. Twentieth Century Fox.

Prometheus. 2012. Directed by Ridley Scott. Written by Jon Spaihts and Damon Lindelof. Twentieth Century Fox.

Resident Evil. 1996–. Created by Shinji Mikami and Tokuro Fujiwara. Capcom.

Serenity. 2005. Written and directed by Joss Whedon. Universal.

Star Wars. 1977. Written and directed by George Lucas. Twentieth Century Fox.

Starship Troopers. 1997. Directed by Paul Verhoeven. Written by Ed Neumeier. Tristar Pictures.

The Terminator. 1984. Directed and written by James Cameron. Orion Pictures.

The Chronicles of Riddick. 2004. Written and directed by David Twohy. Radar Pictures.

The Matrix. 1999. Directed by The Wachowskis. Written by The Wachowskis. Warner Bros.

The Road. 2009. Directed by John Hillcoat. Written by Joe Penhall. Dimension.
"The Long Game." 2005. *Doctor Who.* BBC.
Wagner, John. 1977–. *Judge Dredd.* London: IPC Media; Oxford: Rebellion Developments.
Wells, H. G. 1895. *The Time Machine.* London: Heinemann; New York: Holt.
———. 1896. *The Island of Dr. Moreau.* London: Heinemann; New York: Stone & Kimball.

Works Cited

Abrams, Nathan. 2018. *Stanley Kubrick: A New York Jewish Intellectual.* Newark, NJ: Rutgers University Press.
Akbari, Suzanne Conklin. 2018. Review of *Babylon under Western Eyes: A Study of Allusion and Myth,* by Andrew Scheil. *Modern Language Quarterly* 79:115–16.
Arnold, Bill T. 2009. "Babylon, OT." *NIDB* 1:377–79.
Bellour, Raymond. 1986. "Ideal Hadaly." *Camera Obscura* 5.3:110–36.
Bergvall, Åke. 2012. "Apocalyptic Imagery in Fritz Lang's Metropolis." *Literature/Film Quarterly* 40:246–57.
Brinkman, J. A. 1973. "Sennacherib's Babylonian Problem: An Interpretation." *JCS* 25:89–95.
Davis Bledsoe, Amanda M. 2012. "The Identity of the 'Mad King' of Daniel 4 in Light of Ancient Near Eastern Sources." *Cristianesimo nella storia* 33:743–58.
Finkel, Irving L., and Michael Seymour, eds. 2009. *Babylon.* Oxford: Oxford University Press.
George, Andrew. 2009. "A Tour of Nebuchadnezzar's Babylon." Pages 54–59 in *Babylon.* Edited by Irving L. Finkel and Michael Seymour. Oxford: Oxford University Press.
Gunning, Tom. 2000. *The Films of Fritz Lang.* London: British Film Institute.
Hansen, Miriam. 1994. *Babel and Babylon: Spectatorship in American Silent Film.* Cambridge: Harvard University Press.
Hislop, Alexander. 1862. *The Two Babylons: Or, the Papal Worship Proved to Be the Worship of Nimrod and His Wife.* Edinburgh: James Wood.
Hunt, Dave. 1994. *A Woman Rides the Beast: The Roman Catholic Church and the Last Days.* Eugene, OR: Harvest House.

Kracauer, Siegfried. 2004. *From Caligari to Hitler: A Psychological History of the German Film.* Introduction by Leonardo Quaresima. Princeton: Princeton University Press.

LaHaye, Tim, and Jerry B. Jenkins. 2011. *Are We Living in the End Times?* Grand Rapids: Tyndale House.

Lang, Fritz. (1926) 1994. "The Future of the Feature Film in Germany." Pages 622–23 in *The Weimar Republic Sourcebook.* Edited by Anton Kaes, Martin Jay, and Edward Dimendberg. Berkeley: University of California Press.

Leick, Gwendolyn. 2003. *The Babylonians: An Introduction.* London: Routledge.

Malley, Shawn. 2018. *Excavating the Future: Archaeology and Geopolitics in Contemporary North American Science Fiction and Television.* Liverpool Science Fiction Text. Liverpool: Liverpool University Press.

Minden, Michael, and Holger Bachmann, eds. 2002. *Fritz Lang's* Metropolis*: Cinematic Visions of Technology and Fear.* Studies in German Literature, Linguistics, and Culture. Rochester, NY: Camden House.

Moloney, Francis J. 2020. *The Apocalypse of John: A Commentary.* Grand Rapids: Baker Academic.

Müller, Jürgen. 2015. "Babelsberg/Babylon: Fritz Lang's 'Metropolis' Reinterpreted." Pages 136–61 in *Berlin Metropolis: 1918–1933.* Edited by Olaf Peters. Munich: Prestel.

Radner, Karen. 2020. *A Short History of Babylon.* London: Bloomsbury.

Scheil, Andrew. 2016. *Babylon under Western Eyes: A Study of Allusion and Myth.* Toronto: University of Toronto Press.

Williamson, Hugh G. M. 2022. "Babylon in the Book of Isaiah." Pages 103–25 in *Community: Biblical and Theological Reflections in Honor of August H. Konkel.* Edited by Rick Wadholm and Meghan D. Musy. Eugene, OR: Wipf & Stock.

Messiah/Christ

FRANK BOSMAN

> We now have direct confirmation of a disruptor in our midst, one who has acquired an almost messianic reputation in the minds of certain citizens. [Although H]is figure is synonymous with the darkest urges of instinct, ignorance and decay[,] ... unsophisticated minds continue to imbue him with romantic power, giving him such dangerous poetic labels as the One Free Man, the Opener of the Way.... If you see this so-called Free Man, report him. Civic deeds do not go unrewarded. And contrariwise, complicity with his cause will not go unpunished.
> —Breencast, *Half-Life 2*

Our Western collective memory is replete with all kind of heroes, superheroes, saviors, and messiahs, either religious or secular in nature. From Greek Odysseus to wizard-apprentice Harry Potter, from quick-tempered Popeye to web-swinging Spiderman, from Verne's world-traveling Phileas Fogg to ring-bearing Frodo Baggins: these figures all share characteristics that lift them above the level of the average mortal being. Ethically, physically, and mentally superior to those in whose service they perform their heroic deeds, they are placed upon a pedestal to be cheered and envied at the same time.

This Western hero is not infrequently described (aesthetically and rhetorically) in Christian terms, which is not surprising, since the Christian tradition was (and is still) the most dominant cultural factor of Western society (Grenholm and Gunner 2014). At the same time, simply labeling all heroes from our collective narratives as religious, messianic, and/or Christlike does not do justice to the specifics of every one of them. As Peter Malone (1997, 76) warns:

> the resemblance [between a specific hero and Christ] needs to be significant and substantial, otherwise it is trivial. It also needs to be understood

from the text and the texture of the work of art, be it classical or popular, and not read into the text with Christian presuppositions.

Simply put, and paraphrasing the Pixar movie *The Incredibles* (2004): when every hero is a messianic/Christlike hero, no one actually is. Let us see if we can shed some light on this complex.

Messiah/Christ in the Bible and Beyond

Messiah, *messianism*, and *messianic* have a long history of reception and interpretation, first within Judaism and second within Christianity. The word messiah is the anglicization of the Latin *messias*, which is derived from the Greek adaption of the Aramiac *meshiḥa*, which is itself a translation of the Hebrew *ha-mashi'aḥ* (Ginsberg 2007, 14:110–11). By definition, the messiah is "one who is anointed." The Hebrew Bible used this term to describe a future figure, a powerful descendent of King David, who, by God's order, would purge the heathen and restore the old kingdom of Israel. Especially in the context of the (failed) revolts against the Seleucid Empire (167–160 BCE) and the Roman Empire (66–135 CE), this theological concept gained a definite political dimension.

For Christians, from the authors of the four canonical gospels up to and including present-day Christian theologians, Jesus of Nazareth has been identified as this messiah promised to Israel (Lee 2009; Moltmann 1999; Porter 2007). The honorary title *Christus* given to the figure of Jesus within Christian tradition, up to a point in which the two names became synonyms of one another, is actually the Greek translation of the Hebrew word *ha-mashi'aḥ*. The followers of Jesus are called *Christians* for the same reason, since they (self-)identify as those who believe in the "anointed One" of God himself.

Messiah/Christ in Science Fiction

Scholars have long identified messianic themes and Christlike figures in science fiction films and franchises. Authors such as Susan L. Schwartz (2014), James Papandrea (2017), Richard Grigg (2018), and George Murphy (2005) have identified heroes such as Paul Atreides from Frank Herbert's *Dune* series (1965, 1969, 1976), Luke Skywalker from the *Star Wars* franchise (1977, 1980, 1983), Neo from the *Matrix* trilogy (1999, 2003, 2003), Superman from the franchise with the same name (Siegel et. al. 1938), and the Terminator from the trilogy of the same name (1984,

1991, 2003) as incarnations of the biblical anointed one. Angela Ndalianis (2011, 49) even argues about the *Matrix* that the director "weave[d] a sacred text into their film, conjuring a palimpsest of religious motives."

Another example is the film *Deep Impact* (1998), in which a human space crew attempts to save the earth from an impending giant comet. The spaceship is, conveniently, called *Messiah*, since its mission is to save all of humankind, while sacrificing itself, or rather the crew sacrificing themselves (McKee 2007, 134). In the science fiction classic *The Day the Earth Stood Still* (1951) this theme is even broadened. When the alien Klaatu arrives on earth, his first words are, "We gave come to visit you in peace and with good will." His words echo the words of the angel declaring the birth of the messiah in the Gospel of Luke (2:14).

Messiah/Christ in Video Games

However, the messiah/Christ figure is but one of four, nonmutually exclusive categories of heroes: (1) the common or normal hero, (2) the self-sacrificial hero, (3) the messianic hero, and (4) the christophoric hero. To illustrate this, I have chosen to focus on science fiction video games.

Before examining these categories, however, some words on methodology. In this essay, I define video games as digital, interactive, playable, narrative texts (Bosman 2019, 38–43). As a text, a video game is an object of interpretation; as a narrative, it communicates meaning (or at least can be conceived of in such a way); as a game, it is playable; and as a digital medium, it is interactive in nature. I will use a close reading of the primary sources of my research, the actual video games themselves, as well as secondary sources, that is, material provided by critics and scholars discussing the same games (Bosman 2019, 43–46). The close reading of the video game series is done by playing the games themselves (multiple times), including all possible (side) missions (the so-called game-immanent approach). Other notions such as *hero*, *messianism*, and *christophorism* will be discussed when applied.

1. Saving the World: The Common Hero

The notion of the hero is both self-explanatory and illusive at the same time. This becomes quite clear when one tries to find a definition that encompasses heroes from different eras and places: from Odysseus (Homer) to Harry Potter (J. K. Rowling), from Moses (Hebrew Bible) to

Gandalf (J. R. R. Tolkien), from Parzival (Wolfram von Eschenbach) to Luke Skywalker (George Lucas), and from Phileas Fogg (Jules Verne) to Spiderman (Stan Lee and Steve Ditko). These heroes have some things in common, but perhaps even more things not in common. Where Odysseus is occupied by trying to find a way back home, Luke Skywalker draws his lightsaber to free the galaxy from the Evil Empire; where Phileas Fogg gambles his fortune away just to prove a point, Moses leads his downtrodden people out of Egypt to the promised land.

In spite of their differences, the heroes of our Western world have certain traits in common; or better formulated, their stories as told through novels, films, and games have certain distinctive narrative similarities, as summarized by the famous narratologist Joseph Campbell:

> A hero ventures forth from the world of common day into a region of supernatural wonder: fabulous forces are there encountered and a decisive victory is won: the hero comes back from this mysterious adventure with the power to bestow boons on his fellow man. (1949, 23)

Based on earlier studies by Edward Taylor (Segal 2002), Otto Rank ([1914] 2013), and Lord Raglan ([1936] 2013) and combining insights from psychologists such as Sigmund Freud and Carl Jung (Larsen 1992) with Anton van Gennip's concept of *rite de passage* ([1909] 2013), Campbell argued that *all* heroes have to undertake a similar narratological journey. Campbell's theories received quite some criticism, especially concerning his belief that these themes are universal (Northup 2006) and his exclusive focus on male figures (Murdock 1990). Nevertheless, Campbell's ideas still have a large audience, and I believe we can derive some interesting insights from his comparative theory.

For the sake of clarity—to distinguish them from their self-sacrificial, messianic, and christophoric specifications—I propose the following definition of the common hero, focusing on Campbell's notions of "victory" and "bestowing boons":

> The common hero saves one or more persons, either an individual, a group of individuals, or a collective, from a certain, possibly self-inflicted evil, either personal, institutional, or abstract, in nature.

The normal or common hero is first and foremost a savior: all his or her actions, decisions, and thoughts are directly or indirectly, consciously or unconsciously, aligned to fulfill one purpose, that is, to save. The object of the hero's endeavors can be an individual (friend, lover, child, parent), a group of individuals (parents, family, town, city, partners in misfortune), or collective (the world, the Milky Way, the galaxy, reality itself).

The object(s) or person(s) from which the individual or the collective is saved can range from the personal (the villain) to the institutional (a political party, a corrupt regime, an aggressive cult) to the abstract (evil itself) or a combination of all three. Not infrequently the evil materializes itself in a (fictional) evil organization in which a specific bad guy serves as the personification of both the individual and the collective. The evil the hero has to save us from is—or at least seems to be—inevitable in nature. Because the evil appears to be without possibility to stop it, the actual act of stopping the evil by the hero becomes even greater.

The idea of the common hero can be illustrated clearly by the *Half-Life* series (Bosman 2019, 76–77). In an alternative version of our reality (*Half-Life*), the unpretentious physicist Gordon Freeman assists in a scientific experiment in the (fictional) Black Mesa Research Facility in New Mexico (USA). After the experiment fails, ripping open a dimensional port to the alien dimension of Xen, Freeman has to muster his inner strength to battle against not only hordes of hostile alien life forms but also a special US Marine group sent to cover up the whole operation. Eventually, Gordon travels to the Xen home world and destroys what appears to be their leader, Nihilanth, a giant monstrosity keeping the dimensional rift open.

After the destruction of Nihilanth, Gordon is picked up by a mysterious, well-dressed man wearing a suit and sunglasses (addressed in the game community as "the G-Man") who appears to be working for higher authorities or entities and is put in statis (a long-term, artificially induced deep sleep by which biological functions are reduced to an absolute minimum, allowing the subject to stay alive without aging). When Gordon is finally awoken (*Half-Life 2* [2004]), the Earth has been overrun by the Combine, a technologically superior multidimensional empire. The G-Man employs Freeman again, but to what purpose and by whose orders remain unclear throughout the entire game series. Arriving in City 17, Freeman discovers that Wallace Breen, his former colleague and negotiator for the earth's surrender, is now the Combine puppet ruler for the world.

Through his actions, which develop very quickly into legends, Freeman is seen by the earth's resistance as the "one free man" and the "opener of the way," their one leader to defeat the Combine. Freeman succeeds in destroying the portal reactor that keeps the dimensional port between the Combine's reality and ours open. The Combine is thrown into disarray, and Freeman is saved from the resulting explosion by—again—the G-Man. The two sequels of *Half-Life 2*, conveniently called *Episode One* and *Episode Two* (2006, 2007) follow Freeman's further adventures but are not significant for the discussion here.

Gordon Freeman's adventures classify him as a common type hero. He saves—multiple times—individual friends and comrades (individual) and the entire earth (collective) by destroying the Xen leader and by breaking the connection with the Combine's dimension. The latter action gives the resistance the necessary momentum to fight back successfully. The evil of the both the Xen and the Combine is real and will inevitably lead to the total enslavement of the earth's population. This evil is (unintentionally) self-inflicted by the failed experiment in Black Mesa, when human hubris stimulated technology and science to overstep normal boundaries. Finally, the Combine evil (institutional), from which the earth must be saved, is a danger for the whole universe; it is thus a corporeal representation of universal evil (abstract), and its leader Wallace Breen is the personalized face of said institutional and abstract evil.

2. Paying the Ultimate Price: The Self-Sacrificial Hero

Although Gordon Freeman ticks all the boxes of Western narrative heroism, he does not qualify for the first more specific type of hero, that of the self-sacrificing one. Although one could argue that Freeman's fight against overwhelming (Xen and Combine) forces borders on suicide, there is no narrative point at which Freeman chooses to continue in the face of certain defeat and death. Freeman's journey to the Xen homeworld and his destruction of the portal, which triggers a huge explosion, are both situations of life-threatening proportions, but they do not involve a sequence of events in which Freeman actually *knows* his action will lead inevitably to his demise. Freeman is perhaps assuming he will die, but he is not certain of it. And that is exactly what keeps him going: not the idea of releasing his own life, but the notion of possibility conserving it.

The second type of hero expects exactly that: this hero is prepared to sacrifice himself or herself for the greater good. It does not matter if the self-sacrifice is actually made—the hero may survive the self-offering—but the sacrifice is intentionally given without the hope of a possible better outcome.

In all three sections of the hero's journey (following van Gennip's three stages of *rite de passage*), self-sacrifice is in place: the sacrifice of the old world and all the certainties derived from it; the overcoming of the hero's ego usually by some sort of self-defeat or kenosis; and, ultimately, the sacrifice of the hero's own life in order to save the collective of which he or she was once a part.

Through this process of self-sacrifice, the hero redeems "the wrongdoing of older generations' and begins 'a new life cycle'" (Georgieva 2013, 157). This type of hero not only restores the town, world, or universe to its previous, balanced state (as the common hero, like Freeman, did), but this hero redeems the sins of the collective that inflicted the evil in the first place, thus ushering in a new, upgraded, and improved version of that previous state.

Thus, I propose the following definition of the self-sacrificial hero, based on the previous one concerning the common hero (difference in bold):

> The self-sacrificial hero saves one or more persons, either an individual, a group of individuals, or a collective, from a certain, possibly self-inflicted evil, either personal, institutional, or abstract in nature, **by freely sacrificing himself or herself.**

The self-sacrificial hero has the same characteristics as the common one, discussed above, but has one decisive extra feature that is the very reason for its epithet: self-sacrifice. The offering of the self must be voluntary, total, and without any realistic hope of evading the inevitable sequence of events leading to the hero's death when initiated. The actualization of the self-sacrifice, on the other hand, is not a necessary feature: while the hero is prepared to give his or her life, an outside force or actor can deflect the execution of the hero.

As a case study, Nathaniel Renko from the game *Singularity* (2010) fits into the category of the self-sacrificial hero quite nicely. The game takes place on the former USSR penal labor island of Katorga-12 in our present day. Renko and his fellow Marines are flown in to investigate a strange phenomenon that damaged an American spy satellite flying over the area. When the same phenomenon causes the crash of Renko's helicopter, he starts to "phase" between the present and 1955, the year that Katorga was affected by a catastrophic accident. In 1955, Renko succeeds in saving a scientist by the name of Nokolai Demichev. During the successful attempt to rescue Demichev from the fire, Renko is warned by an unknown man not to save the scientist. The man dies in the fire without giving more information.

Back in the present, Renko discovers that the course of history has been altered. Demichev was supposed to have died in the fire, but he has now—with Renko's help—survived and taken over the world as dictator. Renki, with the help of resistance leader Kathryn, uses a Time Manipulation Device (TMD) to destroy the island back in 1955, thus eliminating Demichev's future source of power.

The narrative, however, does not end there. Back in the present, Renko finds Demichev holding Barisov, the scientist who created the TMD, at gunpoint. Demichev has apparently rebuilt his facility; the only way to prevent him from becoming the world's dictator lies in the fire from which Renko had saved him earlier. Here the player has a choice: (1) Renko shoots Barisov, leaving him and Demichev to rule the world together. Eventually, the two fall out with each other through mutual distrust, which triggers a new cold war between their respective zones of influence. (2) Renko shoots both Barisov and Demichev, effectively making Renko the new world dictator. (3) Renko shoots Demichev—the canonical ending. This choice forces Renko to return to his own 1955 rescue operation. Understanding that he was the one who warned his earlier self not to rescue Demichev, the later Renko decides to shoot his earlier version, thus causing the universe to return to normal. When Renko chooses option 3, the narrative returns to the beginning of the game with Renko alive in the helicopter. The alarm is withdrawn, and the Marines return safely home.

Singularity's hero Renko qualifies as the self-sacrificial type of hero. He saves the world from an evil dictator by freely sacrificing himself. The sacrifice is all the more free because the game offers two other options in which Renko does not die (we will return to this unique feature of digital games in the last section below). Renko's sacrifice is not a wager in which there is a (theoretical) possibility of dodging the bullet, for he is quite certain that shooting his earlier self will trigger a time paradox and kill his later version instantaneously. One could be inclined to invoke the notion of suicide, since Renko is both the killed and the killer, sacrifice and executioner in one. However, the two versions of Renko are separate enough to possess their own individualities.

3. Opening the Way: The Messianic Hero

The notion of self-sacrifice as discussed in the above section is—historically and narratively—closely connected, at least in the Western word, with the figure of the Christian messiah. But self-sacrifice is not necessarily messianic or Christlike in nature. As Peter Malone (1997, 76) described, a messianic kind of hero should have a "significant and substantial" resemblance with the Christ figure from the New Testament and subsequent Christian tradition; otherwise, the resemblance will be nothing but trivial. Thus, while Gordon Freeman from the aforementioned *Half-Life* series was identified (in-game) as a (supposed) messianic figure, he does not, in my opinion, qualify as such: Freeman does not sacrifice himself, and his figure appears not to be aesthetically or rhetorically inspired by the messianic or Christ figure from Christian tradition.

Messianic or Christlike heroes have distinct traits that are aesthetically and rhetorically inspired by the original one, either the nameless one to come from Judaic traditions or Jesus of Nazareth from Christian traditions (Papandrea 2017). Thus, I propose the following definition of the messianic (or Christlike) hero, based on the previous two concerning the common and self-sacrificial hero (difference is bold):

> The messianic hero, **who is aesthetically and rhetorically inspired by the messianic or Christ figure from Christian tradition,** saves one or more persons, either an individual, a group of individuals, or a collective, from a certain, possibly self-inflicted evil, either personal, institutional, or abstract in nature, (potentially) by freely sacrificing himself or herself.

As a case study, the game *Child of Light* (2014) is an excellent, although not uncomplicated, example of this kind of messianic hero (Bosman 2018a). The game is a lot of things at once: a playable poem, a story told in full rhyme, a bedtime fairy tale told by a mother to her daughter, a coming-of-age story in which a young, insecure child blossoms into a self-aware and strong woman, a Campbellian descent into the belly of the whale as part of the heroine's psychological and emotional transformation, and, last but not least, a late-modern rendering of the classical *descensus Christi ad inferos*, in English better known as "the harrowing of hell" (Laufer 2013).

In 1895, Princess Aurora, daughter of the nameless duke of Carniola (present-day Slovenia) and his apparently deceased wife, dies under suspicious circumstances and wakes up in the strange and dark land of Lemuria. Here, Queen Umbra rules over the land, after the rightful ruler, Queen of Light, disappeared for unknown reasons. Umbra and her two daughters, Nox and Crepusculum, have stolen Lemuria's lights: the sun, moon, and stars.

Aurora eventually, and with the help of a lot of friends, succeeds in defeating Nox and Crepusculum, freeing moon and sun, but she is ultimately defeated by Umbra, who reveals herself to be the duke's second wife, who is responsible for Aurora's first death. Aurora escapes with the sun but is mortally wounded by Umbra's attacks. Aurora is taken by her friends to the same altar upon which she awoke at the beginning of her Lemuria adventures. There she is resurrected by the Lady of the Forest, who appears to be her own mother in disguise, the Queen of Light.

After facing Umbra again, Aurora succeeds in defeating her, freeing Lemuria from her dark spell. Aurora returns to the surface, where she finds her father dead and her people in mortal danger because of a flood, caused by a (historical) earthquake (Coen 2014, 141–44). She rescues her people by magically transporting them to Lemuria, which is no longer a place of darkness and suffering but one of light and peace.

The game goes to quite some lengths to establish Aurora as a Christ-like figure. First of all, Aurora travels to Lemuria, a name derived from Ruldof Steiner's human epoch with the same name and associated with the biblical story of the fall of humankind in Gen 3 (Leijnenhorst 2006, 85). These travels are easily paralleled with one of Campbell's stages of his hero's journey, the "belly of the whale," where the hero is swallowed up into the unknown, apparently to die. The image of the belly of the whale is in itself a reference to both the story of the prophet Jonah from the Hebrew Bible and to its Christian interpretation as symbolizing Christ's three-day sojourn in the underworld between his death and resurrection (Matt 12:39–40; Ziolkowski 2007, 388–89).

Second, there is the internal time frame of the game: between Good Friday and Easter Sunday, which mirrors Christ's harrowing of hell.

Third, there are the three transformations of Aurora from a small girl into a full-grown woman. Every time she is transformed, Aurora hovers in the air, some meters above the ground, face raised to the sky, hair floating around, holding her arms spread out wide. The pose is reminiscent of the crucifixion position of the suffering Christ.

Fourth, in a flashback we see the very young Aurora with her mother, the Queen of Light, sitting under a blossoming tree identified as an apple tree. The queen dies under the tree due to an unknown poison, just as her daughter will years later. The notion of the apple tree and the deadly poison evoke the image of the biblical garden of Eden and especially the fall of humankind from divine grace. While the Hebrew Bible does not identify the kind of fruit Adam and Eve touched, Christian imagination made it into an apple, probably because the Latin word *malum* means both "apple" and "evil" (Kissling 2004, 193).

Fifth, the family structure of Aurora's family is quite special: her father is a mortal, while her mother appears to be some kind of goddess. The same mixture can be found in the biblical narratives on Jesus, only with the genders reversed, Mary being Jesus's mortal mother, while God takes the role of the divine father.

Sixth, Aurora's name means "morning star" and is associated in the New Testament with Christ as the bringer of a new spiritual morning (Rev 2:28; 22:16).

Seventh, the phrase "my people" is used frequently by Aurora to refer to the people of both Lemuria and Carniola. The same phrase is frequently used in the Hebrew Bible by God in reference to his chosen people. One of the *Improperia*, sung in Roman Catholic liturgy on Good Friday, renders: "My people, what have I done to you? How have I offended you? Answer me!"

Last but not least, the earthquake mentioned at the end of *Child of Light* is a reference to the New Testament statement that Jesus's death was accompanied with such a phenomenon (Matt 27:54). Elsewhere, Christ's second coming is also associated with earthquakes and all kinds of other disasters (Luke 21:10–11).

Aurora's heroism is rather complicated. She does save Carniola's and Lemuria's people from Queen Umbra's reign of terror. This terror is, however, not self-inflicted, neither by Aurora nor by the other people involved. Further, Aurora's sacrifice is not so much intended as forced by Umbra's actions. Nevertheless, Aurora does qualify quite nicely as a messianic hero, since her narrative and representation are very much sculpted in the image of Christ.

4. Taking Responsibility: The Christophoric Gamer

Aurora's case is complicated also because of a double lack of agency. Neither Aurora nor the player is given any real possibility to choose between self-sacrifice or not. This is different in *Singularity*: Renko has a choice to go back in time and kill himself or take one of two other options leading to different kinds of lives. Not only does Renko (as the game's protagonist) have such a choice; the player has one, too. As in a large number of video games, especially in action, adventure, and role-playing games, the narratological role of the protagonist coincides with the player's avatar. In Renko's case, both the protagonist and the player have agency, while in Aurora's case, the game decides what course of action is to be undertaken, bypassing that particular form of gamer agency.

This brings us to the fourth form of heroism, predominantly built upon previously established characteristics of the self-sacrificial and messianic heroes, a form I have coined as the "christophoric gamer" (Bosman 2019, 77–100). The notion of the christophoric gamer is rhetorically based on the legend of Saint Christopher, the patron saint of travelers. In the medieval *Legenda Aurea*, a giant named Reprobus seeks to find the greatest prince in the world to serve. When he learns that the king is afraid of the devil and the devil is afraid of Christ, Reprobus enters into the service of a desert hermit, who gives him the task of helping people cross a great river safely.

Eventually, the giant must carry a child across on his shoulders, but halfway he is crushed down under its mysterious weight, causing him nearly to drown. Reprobus cries out that he is carrying the world on his shoulders, to which the child replies that Reprobus carries not only the world but also him who created the world. The child identifies itself as Jesus Christ, thus giving Reprobus his Christian name: Christophorus (Christopher), "he who carries Christ." It is this specific feature from Christopher's legend that the player of specific games embodies, in my opinion. In some cases, the gamer becomes a christophoric hero; that is, he is presenting God in the game world, while saving it by sacrificing his in-game representation, his avatar.

The definition of the christophoric gamer is, again, based on the previous common, self-sacrificial, and messianic ones, and it incorporates (almost) all their features (differences are bold):

> **The christophoric gamer identifies himself or herself with** the messianic hero's **in-game agency,** who is aesthetically and rhetorically inspired by the messianic or Christ figure from Christian tradition, to save one or more persons, either an individual, a group of individuals, or a collective, from a certain, possibly self-inflicted evil, either personal, institutional, or abstract in nature,

(potentially) by freely sacrificing himself or herself, **in the form of the voluntary (narratological) death of the game protagonist, that is, the player's avatar**.

It may appear strange to think about the death of the game's protagonist in terms of a sacrifice performed by the player, let alone frame this as some kind of self-sacrifice, but it becomes more plausible if discussed within the context of the player-avatar identification. First of all, there is a difference between the narratological and ludological death of the player's avatar (Bosman 2018b). The ludological death of the avatar is a feedback mechanism provided by the game to the player to signal that the player failed to respond to the given stimuli in the appropriate manner. For example, falling in a pit will force the player to start the level or the game again, since the player failed to succeed in pressing the keyboard or control inputs on the exact moment necessary. The same applies to the situation when in-game enemies kill the player's avatar. Such a death, sometimes confusingly also called "player's death," is usually reversible, in the sense that the player is usually given an endless amount of retries.

However, the narratological death of the avatar, the kind relevant to the theme of heroism, is something different: it is the in-game death, or sacrifice, of the game's protagonist, as we have seen in the case of *Singularity* and *Child of Light*. However, the significant point for the christophoric hero is not the narratological self-sacrifice of the game's protagonist but the agency of the gamer. The *player* should have the choice to sacrifice his or her in-game representation freely. In the case of Aurora such an agency was absent, but with Renko it was indeed the player taking the responsibility for the protagonist's decision.

The gamer and the avatar are more closely connected than one might imagine: the avatar is an "affective conduit for the player" (Owen 2017, 23) through which the player can interact with the digital environment of the game and to which (or even to whom) the player can become emotionally attached up to the point of severe emotional identification. The player is simultaneously "the initiator of the performance action" through the avatar but is also "the audience or critical witness to that action" (2). The connection is not based on aesthetic similarities between the actual gamer and the in-game avatar but on control, or the lack of it, when control is temporarily taken away (McDonald 2013, 116).

An illustrative case is found in the game *Fallout 3* (2008). The game features an alternative version of human history (called "allohistory";

Hellekson 2013), based on the idea how our relative future has been imagined by writers from our relative past (called "retrofuturism"; Guffey and Lemay 2014) setting, positioning its narrative in a devastated United States of America in 2277. A global war between China and the United States has triggered a global nuclear war, leaving the few survivors either in special vaults (semisecret underground compounds) or in small settlements surrounded by raiders and mutated wildlife. The game's protagonist and player's avatar is born and raised in one of the vaults, designated by the number 101, a reference to American university course numbering systems, where that number is often used for an introductory course in a department's subject area.

The protagonist, dubbed "the Lone Wanderer," loses its (the player can choose the gender of the avatar) mother in childbirth and eventually its father James, who disappears. The rest of the game is more or less focused on finding James and assisting him in finishing his "Project Purity," which is aimed at the development of a water purification system that will be able to cleanse the flora and fauna that depend on this supply.

The symbolism of water is recurring in the game's narrative. When the Lone Wanderer is still a toddler, James points out a quotation in a picture frame, commenting:

> Come on over here. I want to show you something. That was your mother's favorite passage. It's from the Bible. Revelation 21,6. "I am Alpha and Omega, the beginning and the end. I will give unto him that is athirst of the fountain of the water of life, freely."

The symbolism of living water is dominant in John's Gospel and the book of Revelation (Jones 1997); the theological idea signifies that Jesus Christ himself is the living water from which the church (as collective) and the faithful (as individuals) are energized. The Lone Wanderer (and the gamer) appears to take on this christophoric role later in the narrative. When confronted with beggars asking for water, the Lone Wanderer/player can choose to ignore the beggar altogether, offer him purified water, or verbally refuse the request. If refused, the beggar is found dead at the next encounter. Interestingly enough, if the player verbally refuses the beggar any water but nevertheless gives it to him, the game still acknowledges this as providing water. This could be regarded as an anomaly in the game itself, but within the game's narrative it could be a reference to the parable of the two sons in Matt 21:28–32. One of the two sons verbally refuses his father's request to work in the vineyard but eventually does actually go to work and is therefore described as having done the will of his father.

The true messianic heroism of the game's protagonist and the christophoric heroism of the gamer find their climax at the end of the game itself. When the Lone Wanderer has found its father working on Project Purity, the laboratory comes under attack by the Enclave, one of the Wastelands' factions, which claims to be the descendants of the last official government of the United States. To prevent the Enclave from taking his altruistic project and turning it into a weapon, James floods the laboratory with highly radioactive radiation, killing himself and the Enclave soldiers in the process.

Besides the fact that James becomes a self-sacrificial hero by this very action—he is perfectly aware that the flooding of the chamber will end his life instantly—this situation places the Lone Wanderer/ player in an interesting moral dilemma with three options. (1) The player can enter the radiated chamber to save the project, resulting in the certain death of the Lone Wanderer. (2) The player can send one of the Lone Wanderer's companions into the chamber to suffer the same fate. (3) The player can do nothing, resulting in the eventual explosion of the laboratory, killing everyone inside, even the Lone Wanderer and its companion. If the project is activated by the Lone Wanderer, the following is heard:

> It was not until the end of this long road that the Lone Wanderer learned the true meaning of that greatest of virtues—sacrifice. Stepping into the irradiated control chamber of Project Purity, the child followed the example of the father sacrificing life itself for the greater good of mankind.

If the Wanderer decides to send someone else into the radiated chamber, the text is altered:

> It was not until the end of this long road that the Lone Wanderer was faced with that greatest of virtues—sacrifice, but the child refused to follow the father's selfless example, instead, allowing a true hero to venture into the irradiated control chamber of Project Purity and sacrifice his own life for the greater good of mankind.

Or, if the Wanderer does nothing at all, resulting in total destruction, the voice-over has—again—something different to say:

> It was not until the end of this long road that the Lone Wanderer was faced with that greatest of virtues—sacrifice, but the child refused to follow the father's selfless example.

Major notions are mentioned by the voice-over: the sacrifice, the child following the example of the father (or not), and the father sacrificing life itself for the greater good of humanity, all reminiscent of the above-mentioned messianic rhetoric from Christian tradition, like the water symbolism itself. There are three possible messianic heroes and one christophoric hero in the game: James, the Lone Wanderer, the Wanderer's companion, and the gamer.

When the Lone Wanderer obeys the rules of the self-sacrificial and messianic hero type—freely giving itself to deliver the Wastelands from the self-inflicted radio-active hell, which is aesthetically and rhetorically clearly inspired by the Christ figure from Christian tradition—the gamer does likewise (1) by identifying himself or herself with the messianic avatar and the in-game agency of said avatar and (2) in the form of the voluntary sacrifice of the in-game avatar.

As said before, in *Singularity* the same argument could be made, but this is not the case in *Child of Light*, because of the absence of a specific sort of in-game player's agency: the possibility to choose pro or contra an avatar's self-sacrifice. The player is unable to choose if Aurora sacrifices herself or not; the game's narrative just runs like that.

Last Remarks

In this essay I have tried to establish a typology of different kind of narrative heroes. The common hero is a savior who delivers those who depend on him from a greater evil, which is usually directly linked to the actions of those who are saved. The self-sacrificial hero adds the important feature of being willing to sacrifice himself or herself, even if such a sacrifice is not actualized within the narrative. The messianic hero is typically (but not necessarily) a self-sacrificial hero whose aesthetics and rhetoric are clearly inspired by the messianic or Christ figure from Christian tradition.

The player receives christophoric-heroic status by the voluntary sacrifice of his or her in-game representation, a possibility that is exclusively tied to the medium of video games, since other narrative devices lack the necessary agency from the side of the human actor. Because of the messianic aesthetics and rhetoric, the gamer is imbued with the image of the messianic hero itself, making the gamer—like Christopher—a carrier of the Christ figure.

Representative Examples in Science Fiction

Child of Light. 2014. Ubisoft Montreal. Ubisoft.
The Day the Earth Stood Still. 1951. Directed by Robert Wise. Twentieth Century Fox.
Deep Impact. 1998. Directed by Mimi Leder. Paramount Pictures.
Fallout 3. 2008. Bethesda Game Studios. Bethesda Softworks.
Half-Life. 1998. Valve. Sierra Studios.
Half-Life 2. 2004. Valve Corporation.
Half-Life 2: Episode One. 2006. Valve Corporation.
Half-Life 2: Episode Two. 2007. Valve Corporation.
Herbert, Frank. 1965. *Dune*. Boston: Chilton.
———. 1969. *Dune Messiah*. New York: Putnam.
———. 1976. *Children of Dune*. New York: Putnam.
The Incredibles. 2004. Directed and written by Brad Bird. Walt Disney Pictures.
The Matrix. 1999. Directed by The Wachowskis. Written by The Wachowskis. Warner Bros.
The Matrix Reloaded. 2003. Directed by The Wachowskis. Written by The Wachowskis. Warner Bros.
The Matrix Revolutions. 2003. Directed by The Wachowskis. Written by The Wachowskis. Warner Bros.
Singularity. 2010. Raven Software. Activision.
Star Wars: Episode IV—A New Hope. 1977. Directed by George Lucas. Twentieth Century Fox.
Star Wars: Episode V—The Empire Strikes Back. 1980. Directed by Irvin Kershner. Twentieth Century Fox.
Star Wars: Episode VI—The Return of the Jedi. 1983. Directed by Richard Marquand. Twentieth Century Fox.
Siegel, Jerry, et. al. 1938. "Superman." *Superman. Action Comics #1*.
The Terminator. 1984. Directed and written by James Cameron. Orion Pictures.
Terminator 2: Judgment Day. 1991. Directed and written by James Cameron. Carolco Pictures.

Terminator 3: Rise of the Machines. 2003. Directed by Jonathan Mostow. Written by John Brancato and Michael Ferris. Intermedia.

Works Cited

Bosman, Frank. 2018a. "The Bell Tolled Six on Easter Sunday: The Motif of the Harrowing of Hell in the Video Game 'Child of Light.'" Pages 160–84 in *The Apostles' Creed 'He Descended into Hell'*. Edited by Marcel Sarot and Archibald van Wieringen. Leiden: Brill.

———. 2018b. "Death Narratives: A Typology of Narratological Embeddings of Player's Death in Digital Games." *Gamenvironments* 9:12–52.

———. 2019. *Gaming and the Divine: A New Systematic Theology of Video Games*. London: Routledge.

Campbell, Joseph. 1949. *The Hero with the Thousand Faces*. Princeton: Princeton University Press.

Coen, Deborah. 2014. *The Earthquake Observers: Disaster Science from Lisbon to Richter*. Chicago: University of Chicago Press.

Gennip, Anton van. (1909) 2013. *The Rites of Passage*. London: Routledge.

Georgieva, Margarita. 2013. *The Gothic Child*. London: Palgrave/McMillan.

Ginsberg, Harold Louis. 2007. "Messiah." *EncJud* 14:110–11.

Grenholm, Carl-Henric, and Göran Gunner. 2014. "Introduction: Remembering the Past—Living the Future." Pages 1–12 in *Justification in a Post-Christian Society*. Edited by Carl-Henric Grenholm and Göran Gunner. Eugene, OR: Pickwick.

Grigg, Richard. 2020. *Science Fiction and the Imitation of the Sacred*. London: Bloomsbury Academic.

Guffey, Elisabeth, and Kate Lemay. 2014. "Retrofuturism and Steampunk." Pages 434–50 in *The Oxford Handbook of Science Fiction*. Edited by Rob Latham. New York: Oxford University Press.

Hellekson, Karen. 2013. *Alternate History: Refiguring Historical Time*. Kent, OH: Kent State University Press.

Jones, Paul. 1997. *The Symbol of Water in the Gospel of John*. Sheffield: Sheffield Academic.

Kissling, Peter. 2004. *Genesis*. Vol. 1. Joplin, MO: College Press.

Larsen, Stephen. 1992. "Freud, Jung, and Campbell." Pages 19–38 in *Uses of Comparative Mythology: Essays on the Work of Joseph Campbell*. Edited by Kenneth Golden. London: Routledge.

Laufer, Catherine, ed. 2013. *Hell's Destruction: An Exploration of Christ's Descent to the Dead*. London: Routledge.

Leijnenhorst, Cees. 2006. "Anthroposophy." Pages 82–89 in vol. 1 of *Dictionary of Gnosis and Western Esoterism*. Edited by Wouter Hanegraaff. 2 vols. Leiden: Brill.

Lee, Aquila. 2009. *From Messiah to Preexistent Son: Jesus's Self-Consciousness and Early Christian Exegesis of Messianic Psalms*. Eugene, OR: Wipf & Stock.

Malone, Peter. 1997. "Edward Scissorhands: Christology from a Suburban Fairy Tale." Pages 73–86 in *Explorations in Theology and Film: Movies and Meaning*. Edited by Clive Marsh and Gaye Williams Ortiz. Oxford: Blackwell.

McDonald, Peter. 2013. "On Couches and Controllers: Identification in Video Game Apparatus." Pages 108–20 in *Ctrl-Alt-Play: Essays on Control in Video Gaming*. Edited by Matthew Wysocki. Jefferson, NC: McFarland.

McKee, Gabriel. 2007. *Gospel according to Science Fiction*. Louisville: Westminster John Knox.

Moltmann, Jürgen. 1999. *The Way of Jesus Christ: Christology in Messianic Dimensions*. London: SCM.

Murdock, Maureen. 1990. *The Heroine's Journey: Woman's Quest for Wholeness*. London: Shambala.

Murphy, George. 2005. *Pulpit Science Fiction*. Lima, OH: CSS.

Ndalianis, Angela. 2011. *Science Fiction Experiences*. Washington, DC: New Academia.

Northup, Lesley. 2006. "Myth-Placed Priorities: Religion and the Study of Myth." *RelSRev* 32:5–10.

Owen, David. 2017. *Player and Avatar: The Affective Potential of Videogames*. Jefferson, NC: McFarland.

Papandrea, James. 2017. *From Star Wars to Superman: Christ Figures in Science Fiction and Superhero Films*. Manchester: Sophia Institute Press.

Porter, Stanley, ed. 2007. *The Messiah in the Old and New Testaments*. Grand Rapids: Eerdmans.

Raglan, Fitzroy R. S. (Lord). (1936) 2013. *The Hero: A Study in Tradition, Myth, and Drama*. Mineola, NY: Dover.

Rank, Otto. (1914) 2013. *The Myth of the Birth of the Hero: A Psychological Interpretation of Mythology*. Alcester, UK: Read Books.

Segal, Robert. 2002. "Myth as Primitive Philosophy: The Case of E. B. Tylor." Pages 18–45 in *Thinking through Myths: Philosophical Perspectives*. Edited by Kevin Schilbrack. London: Routledge.

Schwartz, Susan L. 2014. "A Teaching Review of Dune: Religion is the Spice of Life." *Implicit Religion* 17:533–38.

Ziolkowski, Jan. 2007. *Fairy Tales from before Fairy Tales: The Medieval Latin Past of Wonderful Lies*. Ann Arbor: University of Michigan Press.

Resurrection and Afterlife

JAMES F. MCGRATH

If there is something that forms a common interest and pursuit across the domains of religion, magic, science, science fiction, and fantasy, it is surely the expression of a human desire to cheat, overcome, or at the very least postpone death.[1] In the realm of science fiction, biblical themes and allusions are ubiquitous in this context, often explicitly, but at the very least implicitly at the level of terminology. The transfer of a consciousness to a new body in science fiction stories—whether android, clone, or something else—is certainly not precisely what any of the biblical authors envisaged. It may nonetheless in some respects be in keeping with key emphases in biblical literature that popular spirituality today ignores (even while the latter claims to be biblical). The exploration of points of intersection (and apparent as well as real disagreements) can help us to better understand how people make meaning from the variety of scriptural texts they cherish.

Resurrection and Afterlife in the Bible and Beyond

Many readers of the Bible show no awareness of the diversity of perspectives on afterlife that can be found in biblical literature, nor the trajectories of development that can be traced over time across them. Apart from the book of Daniel and the Deuterocanon (i.e., some of the latest works to be composed), resurrection appears in the Jewish canon and/or Christian

---

1. The subject of zombies, and why Jesus ought or ought not to be categorized as one, would require a chapter in its own right. Since the focus here is on efforts to cheat death, rather than the state of becoming undead (which most if not all consider undesirable), its omission is hopefully excusable for that reason as well. Those interested in the subject are directed to Murphy 2019.

Old Testaments only as a symbol of God's restoration of the nation (as, for instance, in Ezekiel's vision of the valley of dry bones in Ezek 37, on which see Levenson 2006, 162), not as a hope for individual immortality. As John Jarick (1999, 22) writes,

> For people imbued with this long-established Jewish and Christian response to the question "Is there life after death?," it can come as a surprise, or even a shock, to discover that the Hebrew Bible does not give the same answer, but in fact presents virtually the reverse scenario: Death is, to all intents and purposes, the end; if there is anything beyond it, that epilogue will be merely a shadow and inadequate aftertaste of what we experienced during life.

A likely impetus for the development of hope for afterlife in Judaism is the problem of evil as it was compounded by the crisis faced during the reign of the Syrian king Antiochus IV Epiphanes. This ruler infamously prohibited observance of the Jewish law in his kingdom, which encompassed the historic homeland of the Jews. Among his actions (let the reader understand) was the rededication of the temple in Jerusalem to Zeus and the sacrificing of a pig on the altar there. The suffering of the righteous was already a conundrum explored in the Bible, in particular in the book of Job. Nonetheless, when those who faithfully observed God's commandments were singled out for persecution and even execution, while those who were willing to abandon observance were spared, it made belief in divine sovereignty and goodness far more difficult to reconcile with experience. The conviction thus emerged that not even death would prevent God from doing justice. If not before death, then after death. Even in a great undoing of death itself, divine justice would prevail. Precisely how and in what form, of course, remained a topic of ongoing interest and speculation (Bynum 2017, 88; Ehrman 2020, 237–38).

In the New Testament, the idea of bodily resurrection appears to be assumed as a given by all its authors (although the Letter to the Hebrews presents a puzzle, since Jesus offering his sacrifice and presenting it in the heavenly tabernacle seems to leave little place for him to retrieve his body in the process). Yet occasional references in the gospels and Acts remind us that this was not uniformly the case in the time. The Sadducees were conservative and did not embrace this innovation (see Mark 12:18; Acts 23:8), while yet others gravitated more toward the idea of the immortality of the soul. Even within the New Testament, there are tensions with respect to the nature of the resurrection body. In Luke, the risen Jesus is depicted as saying that he has flesh and bones (Luke 24:39), while Paul in speaking about the resurrection body says that flesh and blood will not inherit the kingdom of God (1 Cor 15:50). Moreover, early Christians did not think that bodily resurrection was something unique to the followers of Jesus but something that awaited all human beings when the time for the final judgment arrived (1 Cor 15:20).

Resurrection and Afterlife in Science Fiction

The number of different kinds of immortality and/or resurrection that science fiction has explored threatens to burst the seams of a single chapter. There is cellular regeneration technology that prolongs lives indefinitely, uploading one's consciousness into a digital world, or transferring one's memories and personality to a biological clone or android replica of oneself that then lives in the physical world; the list could go on (see, e.g., Hrotic 2014, 3; Micali 2019, 17). The scenarios both hopeful and dystopian that science fiction has depicted in which humans seek and occasionally even achieve immortality rivals the number and variety of imagined aliens in the genre. Whether any truly deserves the appellation "afterlife," much less represents a competitor with classic religious/spiritual hopes and expectations, is another matter (Grigg 2019, 41, 64).

There are certain presuppositions that most people in the English-speaking world bring to this subject, which have had an impact on what science fiction focuses on and which are likely to influence what readers expect from a study such as this one. Whether accepted or repudiated by any given individual, the English-speaking world has a cultural, religious, and metaphysical heritage that includes beliefs about what most would call the human soul. What the nature of a soul might be and whether there is such a thing are questions that cannot be avoided, and science fiction provides both a useful vantage point for approaching the matter, as well as specific stories of concrete relevance to these questions (see, e.g., Barrett and Barrett 2017, 130–32, 144).

Part and parcel with this heritage is the assumption that bodily death of an individual is a bad thing and the extinction or cessation of the ongoing existence of the soul something even worse. It may seem odd to mention these things, but these assumptions are not universal even in the cultures and religions on planet Earth, never mind those that science fiction can imagine may be found on other worlds. Science fiction and religion have both converged in the modern era in focusing on individual immortality (as have some real-world efforts to bring about the future that science fiction imagines for humanity). Yet science fiction often broadens the vision to include questions of the survival of our species, bringing into focus a neglected aspect of the biblical tradition in the process.

The greater part of the Bible is focused on the future of the tribe or nation rather than the individual (Vidal 2006, 48). The covenant with Abraham does not promise him that he will live forever in heaven but that his offspring will be numerous. Science fiction works such as Orson Scott Card's Ender series, in particular *Speaker for the Dead* (1986) and *Xenocide* (1991), broach topics ranging from the source and destiny of the soul (*aiúa*) to forces that threaten the survival of entire species. Arthur C. Clarke's *Childhood's End* (1953) likewise explores the end and survival of the species, as does the movie *Knowing* (2009), in ways that relativize the importance of individual survival. In general there is a marked contrast between stories that focus on the survival of individuals and those that place their emphasis on the survival of humanity itself, whoever its individual representatives might happen to be.

The movie *The Sixth Day* (2000) focuses on the theme of scientists playing God through a story about cloning, alluding in its very title to the creation of human beings in Gen 1. *Altered Carbon* (2018–2020; Morgan 2002) highlights (while simultaneously challenging) the angelic or quasidivine status of those who can go on living endlessly. *Battlestar Galactica* (1978–1979, 1980, 2004–2009), to which we will return our attention later, explores the soul or lack thereof in the machine—while also making the machine so like us, and eventually revealing it as part of us, that the distinction is called into question. Amid mutual attempts by Cylons (a race of artificially created beings) and humans to eradicate the other, there is a premise to the series that human beings have already ventured out to other worlds, such as the legendary Earth. The survival of humans from the twelve colonies is thus placed in a broader framework, which affects the overall feel and flavor of the engagement with religious and moral questions. Religions may likewise focus on survival and rewards for the individual, the family, the nation, or of all creation. Does the focus with respect to this particular set of questions correlate with the prioritization of related ethical values? Do religions and science fiction narratives that share a particular type of focus when it comes to human survival also share other traits and characteristics in common?

Shows such as *Upload* (2020) and *Altered Carbon* bring into focus a major question related to technological afterlives, whether virtual or corporeal. In most scenarios these are expensive and as a result remain out of reach of all but the extremely wealthy (some of whom become wealthier still as a result of their extended lifespans). Given that concern about injustice and the problem of evil provided the impetus for the development of the vision for a final judgment in Judaism in the first place, the fact that technological afterlives may cause or compound injustice is worthy of reflection. It may also provide a basis for interesting discussion of universalism and exclusivism. Should everyone have a chance to survive death, whether in spiritual, bodily, or digital form? If only some have this opportunity, on what basis should the distinction be made? Is participation of a select few able to afford it fundamentally different from a minority being saved based on beliefs, works, rituals, heritage, or the like?

The miniseries "Restoration" (2016) by DUST explores a not too distant future in which memories and personalities can be backed up. In some cases, an employer foots the bill, requiring it to safeguard their investment in the employee and the crucial knowledge they have. The series explores the phenomenon we typically call "muscle memory" in ways that are often ignored in both science fiction and religion. Which of our habits and abilities resides in our bodies (physical aspects of the brain being part of our body) and which in our memories, so that, in theory, they could be transferred with our minds into a different body? Our initial instinct might be to reject the notion that a personality, when transferred to someone else's body, might discover a new ability to play the piano, crave a cigarette, or desire to punch things in ways characteristic of that body's rightful owner. However, the truth is that our reflexive and motor memory, our habits, do become woven into our physical structure (although primarily in the brain rather than in the muscles, the popular term for this notwithstanding). People with dementia may no longer recognize loved ones or recall events and yet may retain an ability to play a musical instrument. Not only might one discover new abilities by transferring one's memories and personality to a different body, but one might also discover that abilities previously held are lost in that same process as well, for the same reason.

We may contrast this with the series *Altered Carbon*, in which characters retain fighting skills and other abilities when they "resleeve." Comparing stories involving transference of memories/personality/consciousness/soul from one body to another with others involving a brain transplant can help us become aware of the extent to which we instinctively distinguish between our bodies and our inner mental and spiritual selves. Ancient Hebrew and Greek thought had different tendencies with respect to this, and the debates and tensions that we find in ancient literature are with us still.

The difficulty we confront in finding satisfactory ways to talk about whom a body or a mind belongs to, assuming they can be separated in the ways that both ancient religious texts and modern science fiction tend to assume, highlights key questions about identity and continuity. This provides wonderful opportunity to reflect on the notion of resurrection, which is often envisaged in popular thought as the soul (however understood) transferring from one kind of body to a new, immortal one. If we change bodies, in what sense would we still be ourselves?

Some think of the body (the thing that Paul, the author of the majority of letters in the New Testament, literally calls the "flesh") as the place where one's "sinful nature" resides.[2] Logically, it would seem that, if the problem of sin can be eliminated through provision of a resurrection body, then this provides good grounds for thinking of resurrection hope in universalist terms. Everyone fell short while inhabiting a fleshly body, and so should not everyone have the opportunity to live in a different kind? On the other hand, if sin is a bodily problem, could we not hope to overcome it through genetic engineering or the creation of an artificial body that lacks whatever carries this trait? However much a new body might change a human person, a purely disembodied afterlife—whether of a disembodied soul or of a digital copy of the mind—would be even less like us as we now exist. If I am so radically transformed, in what sense would it be *me* who experiences that new kind of existence? These conundrums have been raised apart from science fiction, but science fiction stories provide helpful assistance in thinking about and wrestling with the problem.

Science fiction stories can also raise questions about personal identity. If the mind and the body can be duplicated, backed up, and restored, could one not make multiple copies of the same individual, and, if so, which one, if any, would be the same person? Even apart from questions of afterlife, *Star Trek*'s transporter technology has raised the issue of whether copying a person results in the same person coming out the other end of the process (see Nichols, Smith, and Miller 2009, 301–52, and in particular *The Next Generation* episodes such as "Relics" [1992] and "Second Chances" [1993]). Biblical authors express no concern about whether some kind of

---

2. For example, the NIV switched to "flesh" in most instances when it revised its translation in 2011 but left "sinful nature" in Rom 7:18, 25.

physical or substantial continuity might be essential to the maintaining of identity. One might assume this is due to their belief that a soul serves this purpose, functioning in essence as a lifeboat for the person's consciousness, allowing it to survive death intact and take up residence elsewhere. That idea is not articulated in the Hebrew Bible, however, and most likely was borrowed from Greek thought. The Jewish scriptures, including the book of Daniel, which is probably the first work therein to articulate hope for an afterlife in the form of resurrection, view human beings as psychosomatic unities (Vidal 2006, 50). The word in the Hebrew Bible that is sometimes translated "soul" (*nephesh*) denotes the whole *self* rather than one particular piece of the self or kind of substance. God breathes life into Adam in the garden of Eden, and he *becomes* (rather than obtains) a living soul, that is, a living being (Gen 2:7). In other words, human beings are animated bodies rather than incarnate souls, meant for bodily rather than disembodied existence.

In science fiction, the need for something like a soul if the resurrected are not to be merely *copies* of an individual is addressed directly in Philip José Farmer's Riverworld novels (1971a and b, 1977, 1980, 1983). On the other hand, *Altered Carbon* features movement of consciousnesses of both AIs and humans, and the issue of degradation of personality over time arises for both, but changing hardware does not raise the issue of the continuity of the AI person, and the same may be said of humans who move to a different "sleeve." Yet "double sleeving" (that is, the same person/mind being in two bodies) is illegal, and the rationale for this would be worth exploring beyond what the show does. On *Westworld* (2016–) humans have not been successful in harnessing the technology that is used to replicate human bodies to make artificial hosts in service of their own immortality. The hosts can be sentient, however, and we eventually learn that a host named Delores made multiple copies of herself, so that a variety of other hosts that have been working with her turn out to be copies of her, copies that begin to diverge as their ongoing experiences differ. Philosophically, whether or not a show wrestles explicitly with the matter, these scenarios raise questions about what it means to be *oneself* in the future, to be the same person. This is true whether bodies are re-created with precisely the same mental states being in place as were there at the moment someone died or whether those mental states are transferred to a new kind of existence in some very different sort of reality, whether purely virtual or embodied.

Some questions about individual identity do not require science fiction to raise them. For many religious people, a person is affirmed to be a distinct human individual with a soul from conception. This idea is often connected with the Bible, although no specific text articulates the point explicitly. Identical twins are also not explicitly mentioned in the Bible, although it has been suggested that Rachel and Leah and/or Jacob and Esau might have been identical twins, with different hair or eye color, which would explain certain otherwise puzzling aspects of the stories about them (on which, see Lefkovitz 2010, 71). Be that as it may, we know something the ancient authors of biblical texts did not, that identical twins are the result of a single fertilized human ovum. The question of the relationship between physical continuity and personal identity is thus raised at the beginning of human life and throughout it, not only at the end (McGrath 2016, 57, 69–74). If a single conception can become more than one individual, and each individual then remains the same person even as their cells die and are replaced, this suggests that personal identity ought not to be sought in physical continuity, including when it comes to afterlife. Positing a "spiritual" continuity may help, but the question must still be asked what that means.

For the ancient Greek philosophical schools of the Stoics and Epicureans, spirit was simply one kind of "stuff" rather than something strictly incorporeal (Lehtipuu 2015, 57–58; Ehrman 2020, 59, 71). This sort of viewpoint would account for continuity, but it raises questions (explored over the centuries by philosophers and theologians) about where the soul resides and how it interacts with the body. Some readers of the Bible will be happy simply to chalk such things up to mystery. The Bible and science fiction both leave room for mystery—one cannot enjoy and explore them without at least some willingness to do so. We ought to ask, however, whether there is anything in either genre that could not be explained in such terms and whether being too ready to appeal to mystery might not prevent us from discovering a deeper and more interesting coherence in certain stories or perhaps recognizing incoherence and authorial ineptitude in others. At the very least, we should be wary of accepting "it is a mystery" (or inscrutable "technobabble" or "theobabble") in either genre, and certainly we ought not to give it a pass in one but not the other.

Comparative reading of science fiction and the Bible can clue us in to our own reading habits and assumptions, as well as to the assumptions the authors of stories appear to have made (or fail to have made), and possible disconnects between these differing assumptions that might impact our interpretation or simply our enjoyment of the stories in question. This is not to say that we might not appropriately be content, as Paul seems to have been, to assert continuity in relational terms of being "with Christ" without further elaboration (Lampe 2002, 110–12, 114). The point is to recognize that every religion and every science fiction story posits the unknown and the unexplained and to appreciate them all for what they are and learn from the comparison between them.

An afterlife is not always explicitly mentioned where many humans would expect it to be. Redshirts galore die on away missions in the *Star Trek* franchise (1966–), with none of the crew of any Starfleet ship being shown seeking comfort in the idea that they may live on in heaven or rise again on the last day. Many expect science fiction, if any afterlife is mentioned at all, to give it a materialist form that is technological in character of the sorts we have been discussing thus far. This is typical of science fiction in general. One exception is the *Star Wars* franchise (1977–), which places the spiritual concept of the Force at center stage. The afterlife in *Star Wars* is nevertheless vague and self-contradictory, as well as appearing to be as elitist as the Jedi and Sith religions are. From an extranarrative perspective, it was the lack of any real role for Obi-Wan Kenobi's character in the script that led to the decision to have him sacrifice himself so that Luke and the others could escape, only to vanish with a promise that if Vader strikes him down he would become even more powerful. Obi-Wan then reappeared as a Force ghost in subsequent films, later to be joined by Yoda and eventually Anakin Skywalker (whether old or young). In the prequels we learn more about the nature of becoming "one with the Force" and the ability to retain one's individuality and manifest oneself after death, and this is explored in detail in the season six *Clone Wars* episode "Destiny" (2014). Toward the end of *Revenge of the Sith* (2005), Yoda reveals to Obi-Wan Kenobi that "an old friend has learned the path to immortality. One who has returned from the netherworld of the force." This explains why Qui-Gon did not disappear the way that Obi-Wan and Yoda did when they died. In a deleted scene from *Revenge of the Sith*, Qui-Gon further elaborates that the secret of immortality is something the Sith cannot achieve because it involves releasing the self. In the process of doing this, ironically, the self can be preserved.

To the extent that Force ghosts (or at least the voices of dead Jedi) can reappear in the physical world in a form they had while alive, the description of their destiny as "becoming one with the Force" does not seem apt, nor does Yoda's reference to "forever sleep." There are still tensions and unanswered questions, as perhaps there should be with respect to a matter such as this. In contrast, the Sith desire to cheat death aims to extend life in this material world. They desire tangible existence, not a spiritual afterlife as a Force ghost. All of this is a moot point for the majority of inhabitants of the *Star Wars* galaxy who cannot and do not hope to live on either as a Force ghost or through technological means. Those with a low midi-chlorian (a microscopic organism) count apparently do not have a shot at ongoing life in this way. Even for Jedi it requires training and represents quite an achievement. Christians should not respond to this elitist aspect of Jedi religion with smug superiority, however, since eternal bliss or conditional immortality for a select few is a feature in Christian theology. (On afterlife in *Star Wars* as an accomplishment rather than something all experience or achieve, see the statement by George Lucas quoted in Rinzler 2005, 40; discussed further in McDonald 2013, 147–48, 165).

While *Star Wars* has often been felt to be distinctive within the context of science fiction by making the expressly spiritual a central element, the contrast is less marked than some imagine, and the way the soul and/or afterlife are treated illustrates this well. Even the expressly secular *Star Trek* has made regular mention of the soul (or the Vulcan katra that plays such an important role in *The Search for Spock* [1984]) as well as much else that looks like magic and miracle or at least the paranormal, often without bothering to offer an explanation in terms of supposed advanced future technology. Various sentient beings on *Star Trek* hold beliefs about an afterlife (for Klingon and Ferengi examples, see Cowan 2010, 30, 146–50; for Talaxian beliefs see the *Voyager* episode "Mortal Coil" [1997]).

A character who features in several episodes of the *Doctor Who* franchise (1963–), Ashildr, provides an opportunity to explore another interesting aspect of immortality. The Doctor saves her life by using an alien technology that repairs her body. This technology will continue working forever, however, rendering Ashildr immortal. When the Doctor encounters her again many centuries later, she simply calls herself "Me" and has taken to writing down her experiences in books because her brain, while immortal, has the same limited storage capacity that any human brain does, which means that she cannot retain her earlier memories indefinitely.

For the various biblical authors who envisage eternal life in terms of bodily resurrection, there is no indication of awareness that memory storage could present a problem for ongoing bodily existence without death. While some might be content to appeal once again to the miraculous, we should still ask in what sense is it *bodily* resurrection if the brain of the envisaged resurrection body has infinite capacity to store memories and thus transcends bodily limitations. For ancient authors such as Paul, of course, not only was the brain little understood; they were not even certain that the mind is associated with the brain. When Paul speaks of cognition, if he mentions a bodily organ, it is likely to be the heart, which many thinkers of his time believed to be the place that human thought and reasoning resides. If resurrected humans do not retain memories, the question of in what sense they remain the same individuals arises. On the other hand, if they remember absolutely everything, that will be a mode of existence so unlike our present one that it becomes unclear in what sense the person who lives that way could be the same person either, even if the memories corresponded precisely to an individual's earthly experience. This brings into focus some challenges inherent in making continuity of memories the basis for identity, in addition to the questions this raises for visions of immortality based on transformed bodies.

The *Doctor Who* character Ashildr provides opportunity to explore other questions at the intersection of science fiction and the Bible. To what extent was and is the human spiritual life *already* supplemented and enhanced through technology—not only by the things in the present day that may immediately come to mind as technological back-up memory such as our phones but the Bible itself? To the extent that books allow for memories and other information to be backed up and preserved outside of a person and to the extent that human thoughts from ancient times have been recorded in biblical texts and transmitted across time, the memories of ancient Christians have clearly lived on for thousands of years *in this world*, far beyond the limit of three score and ten or even the longest antediluvian lifespan. Those memories have been shared with us and live on in us, without the need for Borg-like additions, Matrix-like knowledge downloads, or Vulcan mind melds. Such things are so taken for granted that we may miss how utterly remarkable they are, how different human lives were and would be in the absence of that technology, and how much they already make humans *cyborgs* with technologically supplemented memory. A particularly important service that science fiction can provide in relation to the Bible is to present fictional technologies that allow us to view those we already have in fresh ways. Over its long history, *Doctor Who* has offered many episodes exploring immortality and resurrection (see, for instance, "Enlightenment" [1983], "The Five Doctors" [1983], and "Dark Water/Death in Heaven" [2014]). These raise questions such as whether immortality is in fact desirable, whether tedium inevitably ensues, and whether boredom might explain why godlike beings always seem to seek to entertain themselves by playing games with humans and other sentient species.

In the conversation between the biblical tradition and various science fiction franchises, the question arises of which, if any, of the scenarios that science fiction explores bears closest resemblance to things within the biblical tradition. Is a purely spiritual afterlife or the desire to have more life as a bodily being more in keeping with the biblical outlook on human beings? Fans and theologians alike tend not to do justice to the fact that science fiction storytelling is (or at least has the potential to be) itself a form of theology. A theologically rich philosophical treatise and a theologically rich imaginary story can both explore and challenge in comparable ways.

Resurrection and Afterlife in *Battlestar Galactica*

Battlestar Galactica is one of many shows that merits a closer look in relation to our theme. Even before one gets to the content of stories, a comparison between the Bible and *Battlestar Galactica* brings interesting dimensions of both into sharper focus. When one discusses *Battlestar Galactica*, should the focus be on the original television series from the late 1970s, that plus the spinoff *Galactica: 1980*, the rebooted series that is what many mean when they simply refer to "BSG" today, the prequel to the latter *Caprica* (2009–2010), or some or all of the above? Referring to "the Bible" is no more straightforward. Different groups have significantly different Bibles, and even groups with the same contents understand them in different ways. How much should the historical context and world of ideas that the author of Daniel or Glen A. Larson (the creator of the 1978–1979 BSG) inhabited be considered relevant to interpretation? When one speaks of afterlife in the Bible, should that entail an effort to do justice to each literary work on its own terms or to weave the entire ensemble together into a united if not necessarily unified whole? We are prone to speak so casually about the Bible as well as our favorite franchises of science fiction that we can neglect to notice their blurry boundaries and porous borders.

Caprica contains material that is especially relevant to one form of science fiction afterlife. A major plot element involves the digital preservation of the remnants of two human girls who died, Zoe and Tamara. The idea that a human self might be reconstructed through the digital traces we leave deserves to be the object of a study in its own right. The key question is not whether we are the sum of our outward expression in words and action (we clearly are not) but whether those outward expressions reveal our inner selves sufficiently that our personalities could be replicated on that basis. Creating a chatbot that sounds like us by mimicking our interests, behaviors, and turns of phrase is not the same thing as creating an AI that shares all our memories, our outlook, our hopes, and our dreams. That fact is often a plot element in stories about the retrieval of some echo of a person's personality, however faint, by digital reconstruction. Such undertakings tend to be more about the needs and desires of those left behind than about the genuine survival of the individual who has died. One may compare the notion of a faint shadow of one's former self persisting or being brought back into existence in digital space to the idea of Sheol, which was understood in ancient Israel as a shadowy existence that is not quite nonexistence and from which a ghost of someone might be brought back temporarily (e.g., Samuel in 1 Sam 28). This kind of technology might indeed be considered useful for someone wishing to pose a question to an individual who had died. Should such a practice be considered necromancy and therefore subject to the prohibitions against it in Lev 19:31 and 20:6, 27? *Caprica* also features the pursuit of developing a virtual heaven as a place of apotheosis for the martyrs who die as part of the radical monotheist movement, the Soldiers of the One (see further Urbanski 2013, 108, 191–92). That religious movement (which provides the background to the beliefs of the Cylons in BSG), as well as the series's advertising featuring Zoe with an apple posed in a manner stereotypically associated with Eve, means there is a lot more at the intersection of the Bible and *Caprica* than just the theme of afterlife.

In the rebooted *Battlestar Galactica* series, the Cylons (whose origins were as artificial creations by human beings) have resurrection technology that allows them to transmit their consciousness to a duplicate body and resume living. The term *resurrection* is explicitly used. A new body is provided, although unlike the resurrection body envisaged by most Jewish and Christian authors, the new body is capable of dying again (and again and again). We learn in the episode "No Exit" (2009) that the technology to transfer consciousness fell out of use after the original Cylons from Kobol became able to procreate. The idea that procreation was felt to make resurrection unnecessary (except in a case of impending apocalypse) is fascinating. This represents an inversion of the biblical trajectory in which hope to transcend death was initially through progeny, and once the idea of resurrection is introduced, marriage and procreation are relativized (Brown and Holbrook 2015, 297; Jowett 2010, 64–71). The Cylons nonetheless understand it to be a divine commandment that they reproduce and so they seek to find a way to achieve it. Humans desire to cheat death even though they can reproduce, while Cylons desire reproduction even though they can resurrect. In essence, this pits one form of afterlife found in the Bible against another (see further Jowett 2010).

What this might have to say about humanity's desire for immortality is underexplored in the show's narrative. What does get some attention, however, is the way resurrection as an aspect of Cylon existence becomes something abhorrent and terrifying from a human perspective (Peirse 2008, 126). Arguably Ezekiel's depiction of dry bones coming to life again, even as a symbol of national restoration rather than a vision for individual afterlife, is likewise more the stuff of horror than an appealing image, although that may represent a perspective shaped more by the genres of horror and science fiction than ancient Israelite thought. Cylon resurrection in the rebooted series makes for an interesting conversation partner with biblical ideas about resurrection (see further Wetmore 2012, 136–37).

In the original *Battlestar Galactica*, ideas that fall at the intersection of the Bible, science fiction, and show creator Glen A. Larson's Latter-day Saints faith are to the fore when it comes to afterlife. In the episode "War of the Gods" (1979) several main characters, having already encountered a figure who is essentially the devil, also encounter angels (Hunter 2013, 2:114). On the one hand, these beings can restore a dead human being to life. On the other hand, they also represent the potential future for human beings. The statement one of these beings makes, "As you now are, we once were; as we now are you may yet become," has been highlighted as especially congruent with LDS doctrine. On the other hand, many Jewish and Christian authors down the centuries have envisaged a future life for humanity that is in one sense or another akin to that of angels, and within the realm of science fiction *Battlestar Galactica* is obviously not at all unique in that regard. There is clearly room for significant conversation not only between Bible and *Battlestar Galactica* but between both of these and a wider array of science fiction than this context allows us to pursue.

Conclusion

From its earliest days, science fiction has explored how we might journey into the heavens, restore the dead to life, eliminate suffering, and live forever. Dialogue between the Bible and science fiction has much to offer that can enrich our understanding of the unique perspectives and limitations of each. There is much more that could be written on this topic if space permitted. The bodily focus of early Christian literature stands in contrast not only with purely spiritual hopes to go to heaven but also the desire to upload into a digital space (Magerstädt 2014, 53). Dystopian visions of the future can be compared to historic eschatological hopes associated with the end times and the arrival of God's eternal kingdom (Almond 2016, 186–91). Future explorations of this topic should also consider whether dystopias serve as secular equivalents either of hell (for that strand of the biblical and postbiblical tradition that expects punishment beyond death) or are more akin to the Israelite prophets' warnings about judgments that would arrive within history.

Candida Moss (2019, 117–19) discusses the impact of technology on our discussion of these and other matters related to the body and the self. She writes, "Twenty-first-century discussions about identity and immortality are very differently executed, but they nevertheless reflect the same worries about the self, about the lives we value, and about the lives we never want to have" (118; see also 43–45 on the issue of continuity of the self). Science fiction not only helps us to explore many of the same concerns and hopes biblical authors had in a manner updated for the present day, with a view to the future as we currently imagine it. It also helps us to better appreciate the disconnects we might otherwise miss between our own scientific and cultural horizon and that of the biblical authors and their writings. This makes for a fruitful conversation that can lead to genuine insight. So say we all.

Representative Examples in Science Fiction

Digital Afterlives

"Be Right Back." *Black Mirror*. Directed by Owen Harris. Written by Charlie Brooker. Netflix.
Caprica. 2009–2010. Created by Remi Aubuchon and Ronald D. Moore. Syfy.
Devs. 2020. Directed and written by Alex Garland. Hulu.

Gibson, William. 1984. *Neuromancer*. New York: Ace Books.
"Restoration." 2016. Directed and written by Stuart Willis. DUSTx.
"San Junipero." 2016. *Black Mirror*. Directed by Owen Harris. Written by Charlie Brooker. Netflix.
Sawyer, Robert J. 1995. *The Terminal Experiment*. New York: Harper Prism.
Upload. 2020. Created by Greg Daniels. Amazon.

Resurrection

Doctor Who. 1963–. Created by Sydney Newman, C. E. Webber, and Donald Wilson. BBC Studios.
Farmer, Philip José. 1971a. *The Fabulous Riverboat*. Riverworld Saga. New York: Putnam.
———. 1971b. *To Your Scattered Bodies Go*. Riverworld Sage. New York: Putnam.
———. 1977. *The Dark Design*. Riverworld Saga. New York: Berkley Books.
———. 1980. *The Magic Labyrinth*. Riverworld Saga. West Bloomfield, MI: Phantasia
———. 1983. *Gods of Riverworld*. Riverworld Saga. New York: Putnam.
Simmons, Dan. 1989. *Hyperion*. Hyperion Cantos. New York: Doubleday.
———. 1991. *The Fall of Hyperion*. Hyperion Cantos. New York: Doubleday.
———. 1996. *Endymion*. Hyperion Cantos. London: Headline Book.
———. 1997. *The Rise of Endymion*. Hyperion Cantos. Bantam.
Star Trek. 1966–1969. Created by Gene Roddenberry. CBS.
Star Trek: The Next Generation. 1987–1994. Created by Gene Roddenberry. Paramount.
Star Trek: Voyager. 1995–2001. Created by Rick Berman, Michael Piller, and Jeri Taylor. Paramount.
Star Wars. 1977–. Created by George Lucas. Lucasfilm.
Star Wars: Episode III—Revenge of the Sith. 2005. Directed and written by George Lucas. Twentieth Century Fox.
Star Wars: Episode IV—A New Hope. 1977. Directed by George Lucas. Written by George Lucas. Twentieth Century Fox.
Star Wars: Episode V—The Empire Strikes Back. 1980. Directed by Irvin Kershner. Written by George Lucas. Twentieth Century Fox.
Star Wars: Episode VI—Return of the Jedi. 1983. Directed by Richard Marquand. Written by Lawrence Kasdan and George Lucas. Twentieth Century Fox.

Star Wars: The Clone Wars. 2008–2020. Created by George Lucas. Warner Brothers Television.

Cloning/Robotics

Altered Carbon. 2018–2020. Created by Laeta Kalogridis. Netflix.
Battlestar Galactica. 1978–1979. Created by Glen A. Larson. ABC.
———. 2004–2009. Developed by Ronald D. Moore. Sci-Fi.
Galactica 1980. 1980. Created by Glen A. Larson. NBC.
The Island. 2005. Directed by Michael Bay. Dreamworks.
Morgan, Richard K. 2002. *Altered Carbon*. London: Victor Gollancz.
The Sixth Day. 2000. Directed by Roger Spottiswoode. Written by Cormac Wibberley and Marianne Wibberley. Sony Pictures.
Westworld. 2016–. Created by Jonathan Nolan and Lisa Joy. Warner Bros.

Heaven, Hell, and Other Universes

The Black Hole. 1979. Directed by Gary Nelson. Walt Disney Productions.
Card, Orson Scott. 1986. *Speaker for the Dead*. New York: Tor.
———. 1991. *Xenocide*. New York: Tor.
Chiang, Ted. 2001. "Hell Is the Absence of God." *Starlight 3*.
Clarke, Arthur C. 1953. *Childhood's End*. New York: Ballantine.
Cordwainer, Smith [Paul Linebarger]. 1961. "A Planet Named Shayol." *Galaxy Science Fiction* (October).
Event Horizon. 1997. Directed by Paul W. S. Anderson. Written by Philip Eisner. Paramount Pictures.
Heinlein, Robert. 1961. *Stranger in a Strange Land*. New York: Putnam's Sons.
Knowing. 2009. Directed by Alex Proyas. Written by Ryne Douglas Pearson, Juliet Snowden, and Stiles White. Escape Artists.
"A Nice Place To Visit." 1960. *Twilight Zone*. Directed by John Brahm. Written by Charles Beaumont. CBS. [This does not have clear science fiction elements, although it is part of a franchise that specialized in that genre.]

Secular Alternatives to Spiritual Afterlives

Butler, Octavia. 1993. *Parable of the Sower*. New York: Four Walls Eight Windows.

———. 1998. *Parable of the Talents*. New York: Seven Stories.

Works Cited

Almond, Philip C. 2016. *Afterlife: A History of Life After Death*. Ithaca, NY: Cornell University Press.

Barrett, Michèle, and Duncan Barrett. 2017. *Star Trek: The Human Frontier*. New York: Routledge.

Brown, Samuel Morris, and Kate Holbrook. 2015. "Embodiment and Sexuality in Mormon Thought." Pages 292–305 in *The Oxford Handbook of Mormonism*. Edited by Terryl Givens and Philip L. Barlow. Oxford: Oxford University Press.

Bynum, Caroline Walker. 2017. *The Resurrection of the Body in Western Christianity, 200–1336*. New York: Columbia University Press.

Cowan, Douglas A. 2010. *Sacred Space: The Quest for Transcendence in Science Fiction Film and Television*. Waco, TX: Baylor University Press.

Ehrman, Bart D. 2020. *Heaven and Hell: A History of the Afterlife*. New York: Simon & Schuster.

Grigg, Richard. 2018. *Science Fiction and the Imitation of the Sacred*. London: Bloomsbury.

Hrotic, Steven. 2014. *Religion in Science Fiction: The Evolution of an Idea and the Extinction of a Genre*. London: Bloomsbury.

Hunter, James Michael. 2013. *Mormons and Popular Culture: The Global Influence of an American Phenomenon*. 2 vols. Santa Barbara, CA: Praeger.

Jarick, John. 1999. "Questioning Sheol." Pages 22–32 in *Resurrection*. Edited by Stanley E. Porter, Michael A. Hayes, and David Tombs. London: T&T Clark Continuum.

Jowett, Lorna. 2010. "Frak Me: Reproduction, Gender, Sexuality." Pages 59–80 in *Battlestar Galactica: Investigating Flesh, Spirit and Steel*. Edited by Roz Kaveney and Jennifer Stoy. London: Tauris.

Lampe, Peter. 2002. "Paul's Concept of a Spiritual Body." Pages 103–14 in *Resurrection: Theological and Scientific Assessments*. Edited by Ted Peters, Robert John Russell, and Michael Welker. Grand Rapids: Eerdmans.

Lefkovitz, Lori Hope. 2010. *In Scripture: The First Stories of Jewish Sexual Identities*. Lanham, MD: Rowman & Littlefield.

Lehtipuu, Outi. 2015. *Debates over the Resurrection of the Dead: Constructing Early Christian Identity*. Oxford: Oxford University Press.

Levenson, Jon D. 2006. *Resurrection and the Restoration of Israel: The Ultimate Victory of the God of Life.* New Haven: Yale University Press.

Magerstädt, Sylvie. 2014. *Body, Soul and Cyberspace in Contemporary Science Fiction Cinema.* Houndmills, UK: Palgrave Macmillan.

McDonald, Paul F. 2013. *The Star Wars Heresies: Interpreting the Themes, Symbols and Philosophies of Episodes I, II and III.* Jefferson, NC: McFarland.

McGrath, James F. 2016. *Theology and Science Fiction.* Eugene, OR: Cascade.

Micali, Simona. 2019. "Sogni, illusioni, realtà virtuali: I mondi possibili della Science Fiction." *Between* 9.18. https://tinyurl.com/SBLPress6708i1.

Moss, Candida. 2019. *Divine Bodies: Resurrecting Perfection in the New Testament and Early Christianity.* New Haven: Yale University Press.

Murphy, Kelly J. 2019. "Jesus and the Undead: Resurrected Bodies in Scripture and the Zombie Apocalypse." Pages 147–59 in *The Paranormal and Popular Culture: A Postmodern Religion Landscape.* Edited by Darryl Caterine and John W. Morehead. New York: Routledge.

Nichols, Ryan, Nicholas D. Smith, and Fred Miller. 2009. *Philosophy through Science Fiction: A Coursebook with Readings.* New York: Routledge.

Peirse, Alison. 2008. "Uncanny Cylons: Resurrection and Bodies of Horror." Pages 118–30 in *Cylons in America: Critical Studies in Battlestar Galactica.* Edited by Tiffany Potter and C. W. Marshall. New York: Continuum.

Rinzler, J. W. 2005. *The Making of Star Wars Revenge of the Sith.* New York: Del Rey.

Urbanski, Heather. 2013. *The Science Fiction Reboot: Canon, Innovation and Fandom in Refashioned Franchises.* Jefferson, NC: McFarland.

Vidal, Senén. 2006. "Resurrection in the Israelite Tradition." Pages 47–55 in *Resurrection of the Dead.* Edited by Andrés Torres Queiruga, Luiz Carlos Susin, and Jon Sobrino. Concilium 5. London: SCM.

Wetmore, Kevin J. 2012. *The Theology of Battlestar Galactica: American Christianity in the 2004–2009 Television Series.* Jefferson, NC: McFarland.

Apocalypse

Kelly J. Murphy

Stories of the end permeate our world. Plagues ravage and leave few survivors, oceans swell and destroy human civilization, wars end in catastrophic annihilation of all life. The apocalypse comes in the form of invading alien hordes, artificial intelligence takeovers, or technological advancements gone awry. Sometimes such imaginings of the end are resolutely bleak, pronouncing a final guilty verdict on the role that humans have played in reaching such dire conclusions. Other times, apocalyptic accounts imagine new beginnings rising out of seeming denouements, and these stories provide anticipations of a better world.

From its very beginnings, science fiction has turned to the apocalyptic, and science fiction writers have frequently found biblical apocalypses to be an inspiration for their creations. Whether describing pandemics, environmental disaster, extraterrestrial attacks, robotic insurrections, or a virus that turns humans into monsters, science fiction has invoked the apocalyptic stories of the Hebrew Bible and New Testament to criticize the present, to call people to certain behavior, to wrestle with what time and history might mean, and to imagine, sometimes but not always, a hopeful future.

Apocalypse in the Bible

The English word *apocalypse* now evokes undead monsters, catastrophic disasters, and various other configurations of the end of the world, but biblical scholars are quick to note that the Greek term from which the English word derives signifies something else altogether. Rather than the end of the world, the Greek *apokalyptein* means "to uncover, disclose, or reveal." It is with this meaning that the word appears in the opening of the New Testament's book of Revelation: "The revelation [*apokalypsis*] of Jesus

Christ, which God gave him [John] to show his servants what must soon take place" (Rev 1:1).[1] The book of Revelation is perhaps the best known of biblical apocalypses; however, it is only one of many texts by early Jewish and Christian writers that biblical scholars label apocalypse. Other examples include chapters 7–12 in the Hebrew Bible's book of Daniel, as well as numerous noncanonical works (e.g., 1 Enoch, 2 Baruch).

Although these texts were written at different times by different authors and for different reasons, scholars argue that they share important characteristics: extraordinary revelations by otherworldly beings, heavenly journeys that transcend normal space and time, divine judgment, and a focus on the eschaton, or end times, as brought about by God.[2] Four features in particular are important to understanding the influence this genre has had on modern science fiction: ancient apocalypses tend to (1) adopt a dualistic worldview that (2) employs symbolism and codes to (3) criticize the present while explaining how people should behave and (4) offer comfort to those in distress.

Ancient apocalypses frequently adopt a dualistic worldview in which the cosmos is divided into two diametrically opposed factions. On the side of good stands God and those who are aligned with God, such as the angels. On the side of evil stand those who are united against God, such as Satan and various beasts. This duality can be clearly seen in Dan 10–12, which describes a cosmic battle between the forces of good and evil. In heaven, the angel Gabriel fights against an angel described as "the prince of the kingdom of Persia" (Dan 10:13); Gabriel defeats this enemy angel with the help of the archangel Michael. Meanwhile, on earth, a parallel battle ensues; various earthly, evil kings battle one another, while only those among Israel who are faithful to God remain righteous (see Dan 11).

---

1. Biblical quotes follow the NRSV.
2. The most famous definition of the genre of biblical apocalypse describes it as "revelatory literature with a narrative framework, in which a revelation is mediated by an otherworldly being to a human recipient, disclosing a transcendent reality which is both temporal, insofar as it envisages eschatological salvation, and spatial insofar as it involves another, supernatural world" (Collins 1998, 5). Ancient apocalypses, according to some scholars, were written "to interpret present, earthly circumstances in light of the supernatural world and of the future, and to influence both the understanding and behavior of the audience by means of divine authority" (Yarbro Collins 2000, 7). Other scholars prefer to think of an apocalyptic worldview; for more, see DiTomasso 2014.

This cosmic strife between good and evil is often expressed using codes and symbols. For instance, in the book of Revelation, the final battle is heralded by the coming of four horsemen, and the colors of their horses represent different disasters associated with the end times: white (conquest), red (war), black (famine), and a "pale green" (disease or death). Similarly, in the book of Daniel, the prophet sees a vision of the divine throne room, where God is described as having clothing "white as snow" and hair "like pure wool" (7:9). In this vision, white represents righteousness. In 1 Enoch, the biblical figure of Noah is coded as a white bull (89.1). In the ancient world, bulls were associated with strength, and again the color white is used to symbolize Noah's goodness.

Such codes provided authors a way to criticize their present without directly speaking out against those in power. For example, in the late first century CE, the land of Palestine, including the city of Jerusalem, was under the control of the Roman Empire. Early Jews and Christians reacted differently to life under Roman rule, with some adapting elements of Roman culture into their lives and others vehemently rejecting any such adoption. The author of the book of Revelation, John, as he calls himself, stood firmly on the side of the latter. He strongly opposed Rome and all that it stood for. In fact, John claims that he has been exiled on Patmos, a small island in the Aegean Sea, because of his opposition to Rome and his faith in Jesus Christ (Rev 1:9). So, in the book of Revelation, we can see John using code to criticize Rome.

Revelation 13, which describes two monstrous hybrids that John associates with Satan, is one illustration of how ancient apocalypses use coded and symbolic language to criticize their present. In different ways, each beast symbolizes John's attitude toward the Roman Empire. The first beast has seven heads and ten horns, and each horn has its own diadem. The beast is "like a leopard, its feet were like a bear's, and its mouth was like a lion's mouth" (Rev 13:2). Intimations of Rome run throughout the description: Rome was famous for its seven hills; the diadems represent the kinds of headpieces that Roman emperors wore and thus symbolize their (in John's eyes false) claim to sovereignty; and the hybrid symbolizes the terrifying power that Rome seems to wield. By coding Rome as a monstrous beast, John signifies to his audience that Rome—and those who associate with Rome—should be understand as a dangerous Other.

Revelation 13:3 explains that one of the beast's seven heads "seemed to have received a death-blow, but its mortal wound had been healed." Scholars suggest this refers to *Nero redivivus*, a popular legend from John's time

Fig. 1. Albrecht Dürer, "The Beast with Two Horns Like a Lamb," ca. 1498.

claiming that the Roman emperor Nero, who died in 68 CE, would one day return (Blount 2009, 248–49). Such a reading is strengthened by one of the most famous codes from the book: "let anyone with understanding calculate the number of the beast, for it is the number of a person. Its number is six hundred sixty-six" (Rev 13:18). The number 666 might conjure ideas of the antichrist for contemporary readers, but the original audience of the book would have likely made a connection between it and the Roman emperor Nero.[3] Every Hebrew and Greek letter is associated with a number, and if the Greek name Neron Caesar is transliterated into Hebrew, the numbers add up to a total of 666. In other words, the number 666 is a veiled reference to the emperor Nero, whom John's followers would have known "as the most vicious of emperors toward Christ-believers" and who symbolically represented "the monster that was imperial Rome" (Blount 2009, 261). As John continues to describe his vision, he adds that the first beast "was allowed to make war on the saints and to conquer them" (Rev 13:7). By coding the beast as Rome, linking the beast with Satan, and claiming that the beast was responsible for the oppression of early followers of Jesus (i.e., "the saints"), John clearly situates Rome on the side of evil.

The second beast rises out of the earth and deceives its inhabitants, instructing them to make an image of the first beast and worship it. "Rome, as a beast from the sea, is a foreign force," but the second beast "rises up out of the very soil on which John's hearers and readers have built their lives and homes" and "represents the native traditions and institutions that nevertheless serve the bestial imperial cult" (Blount 2009, 257). According to John, the second beast causes all people, "both small and great, both rich and poor, both free and slave, to be marked on the right hand or the forehead, so that no one can buy or sell who does not have the mark, that is, the name of the beast or the number of its name" (Rev 13:16–17). The "mark of the beast" represents "a person's allegiance to and participation in the religious, social, economic, and political rites associated with the imperial cult" (Blount 2009, 259). Accordingly, John's use of the second beast and its mark connects those who participate in any aspect of life under Rome to Satan. Employing monstrous imagery, John calls on his followers to decide which side they will align themselves

---

3. The idea of the antichrist, which is found frequently throughout science fiction, never appears in the book of Revelation. In the New Testament, it is found only in 1 John 2:18, 22, 4:3; and 2 John 1:7.

with: God or Rome. Through this coded and symbolic language, John demands action on the part of his followers: "Do not buy into [Rome's] economic schemes or accommodate its imperial force. Resistance is not futile" (Blount 2009, 263).

Despite their sometimes-violent imagery, apocalypses are intended to comfort their audiences. Resistance against evils, these ancient authors suggest, would ultimately lead to reward. For example, chapters 7–12 of the book of Daniel narrate a series of visions that are interpreted for Daniel by a divine being. While the stories about Daniel are set literarily in the period of the Babylonian exile, scholars date the composition of these chapters to a later period in history, specifically to a time when a Seleucid king named Antiochus IV, who ruled 175–164 BCE, made a series of changes in Judea. The biblical writers remember Antiochus IV for quashing Jewish religious practices and for setting up what the writers of the book call "the abomination that makes desolate" (Dan 11:31), perhaps a statue of the Greek deity Zeus, in the Jerusalem temple. However, the book of Daniel offers comfort. In its violent depiction of the end, the book notes that, while the Seleucid king might lead some of God's people astray and others might be martyred for their faith (see Dan 11:33; 1 Macc 1:63; 2 Macc 7), God's justice will ultimately be revealed. Eventually the wicked king "shall come to his end, with no one to help him" (Dan 11:45), and the angel Michael "shall arise" to help the righteous; "many of those who sleep in the dust of the earth shall awake, some to everlasting life, and some to shame and everlasting contempt" (Dan 12:1–2). In other words, the book of Daniel promises a future resurrection and reward for those who remained faithful to God, as well as just punishment for those who aligned themselves with evil. In this way, Dan 7–12 offers comfort to hearers while also reminding them that their behavior matters; they must stay faithful to their God and resist Antiochus IV.

In the centuries since the ancient apocalypses' composition, many readers have turned to them, especially the book of Revelation, in the hope of finding clues about how and when the world will end, and these works provide plenty of material for such speculations. Yet if we step back from these (always failed) attempts to use ancient apocalypses as a roadmap for the future apocalypse—as the word is popularly understood today—and consider the books within their ancient contexts, we can see that the genre is far more than predictions of future disasters or the end of time. They are complex critiques about the author's own context that set forth expectations for ethical living in the here and now and work to assure their audiences that there is hope for the future.

Apocalypse in Science Fiction

From the very beginning, science fiction writers have repeatedly drawn on biblical apocalypses, especially John's apocalypse, to describe the end of the world.[4] They sometimes explicitly allude to well-known characters (e.g., God, Satan, the four horseman), places (e.g., heaven, hell, Armageddon), and imagery (e.g., plagues, war, earthquakes). For example, Robert Heinlein's novel *The Number of the Beast* (1980) takes its title from Rev 13:18. At other times, science fiction evokes the genre of apocalypse more broadly by adopting apocalyptic themes and concepts into its narrative. For example, Arthur C. Clarke's 1953 short story "The Nine Billion Names of God" traces a group of Tibetan Buddhist monks who are working to list all the known names of God, believing that "when they have listed all His names—and they reckon that there are about nine billion of them—God's purpose will be achieved" and the world will end (Clarke [1953] 2000, 420). Once the list is complete, the stars in the sky begin to go out. In this way, Clarke draws on the biblical theme that there is a divinely ordained end time.

Yet even when explicitly drawing upon the ancient apocalyptic tradition, science fiction often also significantly alters the images and themes associated with it. In the biblical apocalyptic tradition, apocalyptic events "are seen as inflicted on humanity, ultimately by an angry God, whose wrath will lead to a final judgment" (Lietaert Peerbolte 2021, 90–91). Some of this carries over into science fiction. Thus Jean-Baptiste Cousin de Grainville's 1805 *Le Dernier Homme*, one of the earliest examples of a science fiction apocalypse, places the apocalypse in divine hands. The story focuses on the last two humans—named Omegarus and Syderia—as they roam the earth. The biblical figure of Adam (the first human being) returns to mundane existence and is tasked by God to convince Omegarus to leave the pregnant Syderia. Why? Because the divinely chosen end has arrived. Overall, Grainville's story largely stays true to the biblical apocalyptic tradition. As the tale ends, "a pale light, softer than the stars of night

---

4. Readers are pointed to several helpful works that explore the connections between biblical apocalypses and science fiction (as well as the broader use of apocalypse in popular culture), including DiTommaso 2014, Rosen 2008, and Sheinfeld 2020.

and brighter than the sun" fills "the vault of heaven without need for any other illumination.... It was the dawn of eternity" (Cousin de Grainville 2002, 133–34).

However, while some science fiction works preserve God's role in the apocalypse, many take God out of the equation. Mary Shelley's 1826 *The Last Man*, for instance, draws on the same "last man" trope as Grainville's narrative, telling the story of Lionel Verney, the only human to survive a series of calamitous events. Shelley's apocalypse invokes imagery from the book of Revelation to wrestle with the question of whether there is any purpose to history, but ultimately the narrative is markedly secular.[5] In the early days of the apocalypse, Lionel and a few other survivors try to make their way to Rome, but they are "haunted for several days by an apparition ... the Black Spectre." They never see it "except at evening, when his coal black steed, his mourning dress, and plume of black feathers, had a majestic and awe-striking appearance" (Shelley [1826] 1965, 318). At first, as Jennifer L. Airey notes, Lionel and the others connect this man to the fourth horseman of the apocalypse from Rev 6:8: "Its rider's name was Death, and Hades followed with him; they were given authority over a fourth of the earth, to kill with sword, famine, and pestilence, and by the wild animals of the earth." Yet later the travelers realize that the figure is simply another survivor; "biblical truth is reduced to fiction, the horseman of the apocalypse demystified into just another suffering human" (Airey 2019, 117).

In contrast with biblical apocalypses, Shelley ultimately rejects the idea that time has any divine meaning or purpose; as Airey writes, "The fearful current underlying the novel is the possibility that there is no plan, no benevolent divine oversight, that humans have died for nothing" (2019, 117). In the end, Verney finds himself alone, "the Last Man" (Shelley [1826] 1965, 339). He decides to set sail into the world, taking with him "a few books, the principal are Homer and Shakespeare," and leaves with "neither hope nor joy," expecting only "restless despair and fierce desire of change"

---

5. Several scholars have helpfully traced the rise in so-called secular apocalypses, including their relationship to religious—especially evangelical Christianity in the United States—imaginings of the end. As one example, Lisa Vox (2017) argues that Western imaginings of the apocalypse were firmly tied to the divine until Darwin's works, especially his *Origin of the Species*. For other discussions of the turn toward the secular in science fiction and broader depictions of the end in popular culture, see Rosen 2008; Sheinfeld 2020.

to lead him on (342). Notably, he does not take a copy of the Bible. In this apocalypse, God provides no meaning for history; instead, Shelly suggests that "to read and to write are in themselves a consolation, and, on some level, proof of Lionel's triumph over death" (Airey 2019, 122).

In part due to this secular shift, contemporary apocalyptic stories are often far more muted in their use of dualism as a device to explain reality. As Shayna Sheinfeld explains:

> There are protagonists and there are villains, but most of the characters are complex in a way that reflects more realistically on the experience of contemporary audiences. In portrayals of apocalyptic in popular culture we see an acknowledgment that our lives are not black and white, not dualistic, but instead are complex, with a wide variety of shades of gray. (Sheinfeld 2020, 215)

So, although there are sometimes heroes and villains, science fiction apocalypses tend to blur the distinction, exploring the complexity of human emotions and motivations in the face of disaster.

Take, for instance, H. G. Wells's *The War of the Worlds*, which began as a serialized story and was subsequently published as a novel in 1898. *The War of the Worlds* describes how aliens from Mars invade earth. The Martians are described as monstrously Other: they have "V-shaped mouths," "gorgon groups of tentacles," and are "at once vital, intense, inhuman, crippled and monstrous" (Wells [1898] 1960, 34). Their invasion causes panic; one clergyman exclaims, "This must be the beginning of the end.... The end! The great and terrible day of the Lord!" (100; see Rev 6:16). Eventually, the invasion fails, for the Martians are susceptible to bacteria on earth, "slain, after all man's devices had failed, by the humblest things that God, in his wisdom, has put upon this earth" (Wells [1898] 1960, 235).

The War of the Worlds presents a dualistic world, but in a subdued fashion, unlike the highly dualistic biblical apocalypses, where good and evil are so clearly separate and easily identifiable. Rather, Wells confronts his readers, asking:

> Before we judge them [the Martians] too harshly, we must remember what ruthless and utter destruction our own species has wrought, not only upon animals, such as the vanished Bison and the Dodo, but upon its own inferior races. The Tasmanians, in spite of their human likeness, were entirely swept out of existence in a war of extermination waged by European immigrants, in the space of fifty years. Are we such apostles of

Fig. 2. Henrique Alvim Corrêa, illustration of a scene from H. G. Wells's *The War of the Worlds*, 1906.

mercy as to complain if the Martians warred in the same spirit? (Wells [1898] 1960, 14)

In this way, as is often noted, Wells challenged his readers to examine the role of colonizers in the contemporary world. How, for instance, might the British have behaved like the Martians as they expanded their empire around the world?

Much like in biblical apocalypses, the dualism in *The War of the Worlds* features otherworldly creatures, though its creatures are aliens, not angels or demons. But in much of science fiction, the otherworldly element disappears, and the focus is on dualism in the human sphere. This is the case in Carmen Maria Machado's 2013 short story "The Hungry Earth." This story, told from the perspective of a character named Mario, is set in a future where humans have managed to splice themselves with animals, creating bird-men, cow-men, and pig-men. In this future, pure humans no longer eat but instead hook themselves into terminals to be fed nutrients that must be paid for by credits. Mario narrates how the splices "freed themselves" and "laid waste to our farms and our meat-packing plants" (Machado 2013, 61). The humans who remained in the torched landscape all die as their credit runs dry: "the human body is not meant to have nutrients downloaded into it. Or uploaded" (62).

As in the biblical apocalypses, Machado's future is highly dualistic, but it is a dualism based on this plane: humans against their splices, humans against the earth. Moreover, the animal-human hybrids, which call to mind the strange beasts of Revelation, understand the end of humanity as part of an inevitable plan: "As the last crop of humans failed, the splices said to us via the terminal screes, 'We are sorry. This is part of the natural cycle. It was always supposed to happen this way. A normal flux. Evolution'" (Machado 2013, 62). The splices in Machado's story stand ready to inherit the earth. This reflect how, as N. K. Jemisin observes, an "apocalypse is a relative thing. Usually the world survives just fine and there's another species waiting to take our place" (Hurley 2018, 476; see also Rosen 2008). While the biblical apocalypses depicted what their authors imagined as *the* end, science fiction writers more often wrestle with *an* end.

So, while some science fiction works feature an actual end to time, much contemporary science fiction is actually *postapocalyptic*; that is, the narrative focuses on what happens after an apocalypse. Richard Matheson's 1954 novel *I Am Legend* is one clear example of postapocalyptic science fiction; it is a narrative that uses the time after an apocalyptic event to critique the author's present.[6] The novel tells the story of Robert Neville, who believes he is the only survivor of a pandemic that either killed all other humans or turned them into nocturnal creatures who feed on blood and are repelled by garlic, that is, vampires. Alone, Neville tries to conjure a cure for the infected, while also hunting and killing the creatures.

Many scholars argue that Matheson uses dualism—the last man on earth versus the monstrous horde of former humans—to wrestle with racial tensions present in the United States in the 1950s. The monsters of Matheson's work are often understood to be coded as black.[7] In one scene,

---

6. As are the various films based loosely on the book, including the 1964 *The Last Man on Earth*, the 1971 *The Omega Man*, and the 2007 *I Am Legend*. For discussions of how these films have addressed issues of race, see Ransom 2018.

7. Readers are pointed to Ransom 2018 for an in-depth analysis of how the vampires in *I Am Legend* are coded, including her critique of previous readings that overemphasize whether the vampires are coded only as black.

which recalls events as the apocalypse unfolds, Neville finds himself at a tent revival, where he hears, "Do you want to be changed into a black unholy animal? Do you want to stain the evening sky with hell-born bat wings? I ask you—do you want to be turned into godless, night-cursed husks, into creatures of eternal damnation?" (Matheson [1954] 1995, 103). In contrast, Neville is described as "born of English-German stock" with "bright blue eyes" (14); in short, Neville is coded as white.

In this way, Matheson uses the figure of Neville to reflect on racial tensions. As Amy Ransom (2018, 51) explains, "Neville himself directly engages—albeit with biting sarcasm—discourses of race prejudice and minority status." At times, he sees in the vampires something close to human: "usually he felt a twinge when he realized that, but for some affliction he didn't understand, these people were the same as he" (Matheson [1954] 1995, 28). But he also frequently thinks of the vampires as Other. As he says to himself, "Would you let your sister marry one?" (21). On the one hand, then, Neville is set up as a possible "white savior" for humanity. On the other hand, as Ransom and others note, Neville is complicit in the racism that Matheson identifies as problematic.

The end of the novel ultimately rejects the idea that Neville might be a savior figure. As he dies, Neville grasps that, while he has always thought that the creatures were the monsters, they have come to see him—the man who hunts and kills them—as the monster:

> Robert Neville looked out over the new people of the earth. He knew he did not belong to them; he knew that, like the vampires, he was anathema and black terror to be destroyed.... A new terror born in death, a new superstition entering the unassailable fortes of forever. I am legend. (Matheson [1954] 1995, 159)

Like the splices in Machado's story, the vampires are a new breed, poised to take over the earth. Neville's final realization—that he is a "black terror to be destroyed ... a new terror born in death"—interrogates the simple dualism of the biblical apocalypse, forcing readers to wrestle with the implications of American racism.

More recently, science fiction writers have told the story directly from the perspective of those who are Other. For example, Jemisin's award-winning *Broken Earth* trilogy takes place in a postapocalyptic world, where a conscious "Father Earth" is in an ongoing dualistic struggle against humans. Here time is marked by epochs called "Fifth Seasons," which regularly end with geological disasters. The first novel, *The Fifth Season*, opens with a character named Essun, who is an orogene—a human born with the power to subdue the earth. In the novel, orogenes are enslaved by other humans, often violently and brutally, and taught to fight against Father Earth. Trained in special schools, the orogenes are seen as tools rather than as individuals, and they are avoided and feared by nonorogenes.

Jemisin, a black American author, explained that the *The Fifth Season* was, "in a lot of ways, my processing the systemic racism that I live with, and see" (Hanifin 2015).[8] The novel uses a postapocalyptic landscape to critique Jemisin's own context, including the systematic oppression of black Americans. As Jemisin explains, "it wasn't that I was trying to write an apocalyptic story, it was that I was trying to depict a society that had the emotional impact of the society that I live in now where there have been … the equivalent of pogroms and holocausts and all of these disasters happening to a people again and again and again" (Hurley 2018, 474). The novel works to show that the orogenes' attempt to live within the system that oppresses them ultimately fails: "no amount of deference will ever be sufficient to appease" their oppressors (Hanifin 2015). In works such as Jemisin's, we see how the use of symbolism in science fiction is often more subtle than in the biblical apocalypses. As an orogene, Essun is considered less than human by those who wield power; "orogenes have no right to say no" (Jemisin 2016, 99). Yet even as Essun is a symbol for the oppressed, she also functions in the narrative as a fully developed character whose actions are not always easily labeled as purely good or purely evil.

Some biblical scholars note that *postapocalyptic* is an oxymoron, since ancient apocalyptic texts saw "the end time [as] a literal event," where "after the salvation, the narrative terminates" and "there is no sequel" (DiTommaso 2014, 496). Others, however, argue that the increasing focus on what happens after a cataclysmic event deemed an apocalypse is an example of how the genre has continued to grow and evolve (see DiTomasso 2014; Rosen 2008; Sheinfeld 2020). Either way, the postapocalyptic focus of modern science fiction is a way to imagine the future, allowing writers to explore the consequences of human action—or inaction—even in the absence of a divine purpose for history or a deity who ultimately judges

---

8. On Jemisin's trilogy within the broader landscape of literary afrofuturism, see Dowdall 2020.

humanity. What happens in a world where racism continues unabated? Or climate change remains unaddressed? Or technology unchecked?

As the above examples demonstrate, science fiction apocalypses, like their biblical counterparts, use violent events to ask these difficult questions and to criticize the present. Such criticism can be technological, as in the case of "The Hungry Earth," or social, as in the case of *I Am Legend*. However, unlike biblical apocalypses, many science fiction writers abandon any emphasis on comfort and hope, yet another way that the genre has continued to evolve. In her work on the transformation of the apocalyptic genre, Elizabeth K. Rosen notes that many contemporary apocalypses are "grimmer eschatological tales," where the "message of hope is largely subsumed by its emphasis on destruction."[9]

Take, for instance, George Romero's 1968 film *Night of the Living Dead*.[10] Romero's film famously introduced what would come to be called the zombie into science fiction (though in the script they are referred to as "ghouls"). The story of the zombie begins in Haiti and is deeply rooted in colonialism and racism. The horror film *White Zombie* (1932), for instance, recounts how the dead in Haiti can be raised through magic—turned to zombies—and thus forced to serve as the enslaved undead. Following this belief, an evil "voodoo" master attempts to drug a white woman named Madeline to make her his own enslaved zombie.[11] Zombie scholars regularly note how such accounts are rooted in colonialist, racist, and sexist fears: rather than Western white men enslaving black Haitians, white women (and sometimes men) risk zombification—enslavement—by those they oppressed (see Kee 2017, 72–87). Romero's zombies were different from these stories. In *Night of the Living Dead*, the dead also return to life, but they violently attack the living and eat their flesh, thus beginning a "transition from slave-style zombies to cannibal zombies" (51), though the racist connections remain in many zombie narratives (see Kee 2017 and below). The cause of this reanimation is never specified, although at one point a television broadcast in the film suggests that perhaps radiation from a returning space probe might have caused the dead to rise.

---

9. Rosen 2008, xv. Rosen calls these "neo-apocalyptic," noting that they function "largely as a cautionary tale, positing potential means of extinction and predicting the gloomy probabilities of such ends" (Rosen 2008, xv).

10. For an examination of *Night of the Living Dead* that discusses in more detail some of the themes and ideas touched upon here, see Murphy 2016.

11. See, among others, Bishop 2010; Kee 2017; Murphy 2019; Wilson 2020.

Fig. 3. A zombified Madeline, *White Zombie* (1932). Madeline is under a spell that forces her to do the bidding of her master.

Fig. 4. Zombies, *Night of the Living Dead* (1968). The zombies have risen from the grave and eat human flesh.

More important is how humans react to this apocalyptic event. The film traces the interactions of a group of strangers who take shelter inside a farmhouse, boarding up its doors and windows to stave off the attacking ghouls. In particular, the casting of a black actor to play one of the main characters, a young man named Ben, caused many to see the film as commentary on race in Romero's then-contemporary United States, while also firmly situating the film in the larger discourses of colonialism, racism, and gender in which the history of the zombie exists. While other characters panic or fight among themselves, Ben stays calm. Focused on protecting the living from the reanimated dead, he offers a fleeting hope that strangers might work collectively when confronted with terror. But as the film progresses, human interaction breaks down, and by the end, only Ben survives. Hope is entirely lost as the film ends, and Ben is shot by a group of white men.[12] As Kyle Bishop (2010, 120) writes, "coming on the heels of Martin Luther King Jr.'s assassination, and in light of abundant lynchings and racially motivated murders, Ben's eventual death at the hands of a white posse becomes a scathing condemnation of unchecked violence and social injustice in 1968 America." Like the monsters in Daniel and Revelation and the vampires in *I Am Legend*, Romero's ghouls reveal a darker truth about human nature. As biblical scholar Kim Paffenroth (2006, 13) writes, "More than any other monster, zombies are fully and literally apocalyptic"; as "in the original meaning of 'apocalyptic,' they 'reveal' terrible truths about human nature, existence, and sin." In Romero's film, even when faced with the living dead, humans are unable to overcome their differences.

Other science fiction apocalypses waver between hope and pessimism as they look to the future. For example, Chuck Wendig's 2019 novel *The Wanderers* combines a pandemic with concerns about the relationship between humanity and artificial intelligence. One storyline traces the spread of a fungus-based, flu-like disease called the "White Mask." The infected suffer memory loss and insanity, eventually dying. As the infection spreads, so, too, does violence. A second storyline traces a group of what become known as "walkers": seemingly random humans who suddenly fall into a sleepwalking-like state, joining others like them, headed for an unknown location. These walkers do not appear aware of what is happening; they neither eat nor drink, and they never "twitch or flinch or change their gait" (Wendig 2019, 33). Any attempts to stop them results in the walker "burst[ing] from the inside" (47). Yet even as the rest of

---

12. As Kee outlines, "Those who represent the status quo of the white male world do not allow either black men or zombies to survive. *Night of the Living Dead*, then, is a transitional moment: the 'blackness' or, perhaps more aptly, the racialization of zombies is more ambiguous than its slave-style predecessors, yet racialization still occurs" (2017, 57).

society falls into chaos around them, a group of "shepherds"—family and friends who accompany the flock of walkers to keep them safe—offer a message of comfort and hope: not all of humanity is prone to self-interest and violence.

Over the course of the novel, readers learn that the walkers have been chosen by a "predictive machine intelligence" named Black Swan (Wendig 2019, 24), which was initially created to see and prevent future disasters. Yet seeing the future—a world devasted by human-driven climate change—Black Swan goes rogue and develops White Mask with the plan of killing off all of humanity except for the walkers. When the novel ends, any hope promised by the survival of the remaining humans is muted by their dependence on a genocidal machine.

Of course, not all contemporary apocalypses are as pessimistic as *Night of the Living Dead* or as hauntingly ambiguous as *The Wanderers*. Instead, many science fiction apocalypses contain a promise of hope, either for humans or for something beyond humanity. For example, consider the early seasons of *The Walking Dead*, where the survivors of the zombie apocalypse were motivated by hope as they sought to rebuild the broken world around them. This was "not the hope that God will intervene and destroy the Roman Imperial system, the Walkers, or the equally frightening human enemies" they regularly encountered but rather a hope that "resides in *humans*—that at the end of the day there is enough good in humanity to overcome the evil that is also present" (Murphy 2016, 491–92). Perhaps, say these more hopeful contemporary apocalypses, humans can rebuild and make the world, and themselves, better. At other times, the hope that science fiction holds for the future is, perhaps shockingly, for something other than humans. Machado's "The Hungry Earth" is a case in point: as the last of the humans die off, a new time can start, one that holds open the hope that the earth can be healed and a new species, the strange human-animal splices, can live.

Whether entirely pessimistic or espousing a (sometimes muted) message of hope and comfort, modern science fiction apocalypses are, as scholars have long noted, heirs of the biblical apocalyptic tradition. Yet while the biblical tradition of apocalypse envisions a future where the righteous happily exist outside mundane time and space, science fiction accounts of the end instead present a messier future, one where no divine purpose is revealed, where time does not end but continues forward with uncertainty and, often, violence, or where humans and the nonhuman continue to exist, uneasily, in the same physical and temporal world.

Apocalypse and *The Girl with All the Gifts*

M. R. Carey's short story "Iphigenia in Aulis," originally published in 2013, tells the story of Melanie, a precocious young girl who lives at a military base, where only some have survived a fungal infection that decimated the human population.[13] The story begins with an explanation of Melanie's name: "It means 'the Black girl' from an ancient Greek word, but her skin is mostly very fair so she thinks maybe it's not such a good name for her. Miss Justineau assigns names from a big list: new children get the top name on the boy's list or the girl's list, and that, Miss Justineau says, is that" (Carey [2013] 2014, 161). Melanie's world is small: "she has the cell, the corridor, the classroom and the shower room" (161).

Like the other children at the base, Melanie lives in these cells. Each day follows a routine: Melanie sits in a wheelchair, and a man she calls Sergeant, along with some soldiers, come with guns into her cell. When the men enter, they strap her arms, legs, and head to the chair. Then Melanie and the other children—likewise strapped in—are wheeled down the hallway into the classroom. There they learn what we might imagine most ten-year-old children learn: state capitals, birds, and flowers or the order of the presidents of the United States. Yet when Melanie points out a discrepancy in some of what they are taught, her teacher bursts out that all of it is pointless: "Jesus, it's irrelevant. It's ancient history! The Hungries tore up the map. There's nothing east of Kansas anymore. Not a damn thing" (Carey [2013] 2014, 164). On a subsequent day, Miss Mailer, Melanie's favorite teaching, is reading to the children from *Winnie-the-Pooh*. The Sergeant bursts into the room and demands to know why she does this: "You want to tell them stories? Tell them Jack the Ripper and John Wayne Gacy" (168). When she responds with, "They're children," he bites back, "No, they're not" (168). And then he rolls up his sleeve, spits on his arm,

---

13. M. R. Carey's 2013 short story draws its title from a fifth-century BCE play by a Latin writer named Euripides. Euripides's play tells the story of Iphigenia, daughter of the Greek military leader Agamemnon. In the play, Agamemnon sacrifices his daughter to the goddess Artemis, a sacrifice performed in the hopes that it would grant Agamemnon's sailors a favorable wind to carry their ships. In Carey's short story, "Melanie is obsessed with *The Iliad*—and she wrongly believes she is being held at the base because the Trojan War or something like it is still raging in the world outside. If the children are released from the base, they'll end up as sacrifices in the same way Iphigenia did" (Carey 2014, 415).

rubs, and holds it in front of the mouth of one of the children, whose "mouth gape[d] wide and he start[ed] to snap" (168).

And so, it is revealed that the children in "Iphigenia in Aulis" are not children at all. Rather, they are the offspring of human women who were pregnant when they succumbed to a virus that caused people to turn into "hungries," namely, zombies. As Miss Mailer explains, "It was a virus ... a virus that killed you, but then brought you partway back to life; not enough of you to talk, but enough of you to stand up and move around and even run" (Carey [2013] 2014, 172). "You turned into a monster," she continues, "that just wanted to bite other people and make them into Hungries, too" (172–73). As Melanie later learns, while the virus was spreading, an amendment was added to the US Constitution that prohibited abortion. Due to the amendment, the zombie-children hybrids were sent to military base schools, where they were to be raised and educated until "either someone came up with a cure, or the children reached the age of eighteen" (174).

Later in the narrative, the base is attacked by hungries, and Miss Mailer refuses to leave without Melanie. While the two eventually make it safely to a helicopter, there are too many people aboard for it to take flight. As the story ends, readers learn that Melanie knew what she had to do, which was "not even a hard choice, because the incredible, irresistible human flesh smell is helping her, pushing her in the direction she has to go" (Carey [2013] 2014, 185). Both she and Sergeant end up on the ground, surrounded by hungries. In a moment where he seems to see Melanie as human, Sergeant says to her, "You ready, kid?" And when she replies in the affirmative, he adds, "Then let's give these bastards something to feel sad about" (186).

Carey's "Iphigenia in Aulis" was nominated for an Edgar Award and became the basis for Carey's 2014 novel *The Girl with All the Gifts*, as well as a 2016 film adaptation of the same name. Both the novel and the film extend the narrative, adding a scientist named Dr. Caldwell, who dissects the hybrid-children in a hope to find a cure for the virus. When Dr. Caldwell takes Melanie to dissect her, Melanie's favorite teacher—here called Miss Justineau—intervenes to save her; at the same time, the base is attacked and overrun. Dr. Caldwell, Melanie, Miss Justineau, the Sergeant—now named Parks—and a private named Kieran Gallagher escape.

While direct references to biblical apocalypses are rare, Carey's short story and novel are nonetheless an excellent case study for how science fiction employs—and alters—the broader themes of the biblical apocalypse, especially the use of dualism, symbolism, the criticism of the present, and, finally, the promise of hopeful future—though not for humans.

In its use of zombies, Carey's narrative sets up an expected dualism of good (humans) verses evil (hungries). Like the terrifying beasts of the books of Daniel and Revelation, zombies in science fiction often function symbolically for that which is evil. However, unlike the beasts—which in the original literary setting of the book of Revelation are clear symbols for Rome—zombies serve as a cipher for multiple human concerns: consumerism, racial divides, xenophobia, and more.[14] At times, Carey suggests that the zombie plague in his narratives is a symbol of consumerism, the uncontrollable hunger for wealth and goods at the expense of all else:

> The infection was still spreading, and global capitalism was still tearing itself apart…. No amount of expertly choreographed PR could prevail, in the end, against Armageddon. It strolled over the barricade and took its pleasure. (Carey 2014, 48)

By invoking the book of Revelation's imagined location of the final battle between good and evil—Armageddon (Rev 16:6)—Carey uses biblical imagery to establish the hungries as the beginning of the end, pitting them against the remaining humans.

Carey's use of thinking, speaking, and feeling zombie-children hybrids, however, muddies any easy labeling of good and evil.[15] Children are frequently used as harbingers of hope in contemporary science fiction apocalypses (see, for example, *Children of Men* [2006]). Furthermore, Carey's use of zombie-children hybrids places *The Girl with All the Gifts* in a long tradition of what Chera Kee (2017, 165) calls the "extra-ordinary" zombie, where "artists and producers take what should be monstrous and abject and make it over as something humanized, sympathetic, and, at times, even heroic." On the one hand, the children in Carey's work are related to the very monster that caused the downfall of society. They are seemingly evil, as many of the characters in the story suggest. In fact,

---

14. On the history of zombies and what they might symbolize, see Canavan 2017; Dendle 2007; Kee 2017; Murphy 2016; Stratton 2020. For the history of zombies and the zombie apocalypse in the United States, see Baker 2020.

15. For other examples of similar zombies—who can think and feel—see Isaac Marion's 2011 *Warm Bodies*, the 2010–2012 comic *iZombie*, and the 2017–2019 television series *Santa Clarita Diet*. For a helpful discussion of such changes, see Kee 2011.

readers learn that Parks thinks "the regular hungries *are* clean compared to these kid-shaped monstrosities. At least you can tell that the regular hungries are animals. They don't say 'Good morning, Sergeant' when you kneecap them" (Carey 2014, 72). On the other hand, by focusing the narrative on Melanie, an intelligent, empathetic child who feels deeply but just happens to desire human flesh, Carey turns the idea of the zombie-as-Other on its head. The monster is allowed to speak for itself, to comment on the ways in which humanity acts monstrously, and the reader is encouraged to adopt the perspective of the zombie and to side with the zombie rather than the few remaining humans.

Carey's narrative also complicates the traditional dualism of biblical apocalypses by exploring the different human reactions to the hybrid children. In the short story, we find the following exchange after the Sergeant purposefully gets too close to the hybrid child to bring out its desire for flesh: "You see," the Sergeant says, "Not everyone who looks human is human." "No," responds Miss Mailer, "I'm with you on that one" (Carey [2013] 2014, 168). In his attempt to bait and tempt the hungry child, the Sergeant is intentionally cruel and callous. It is in the Sergeant, and not the confined and caged hybrid, that Miss Mailer sees true monstrosity. As the novel unfolds, the humans at first treat Melanie as a monster, "as a dangerous captive, locking her hands behind her back and placing a muzzle over her mouth," and in this way "Melanie's treatment evokes colonialism and slavery, each of which relied upon treating others as dangers to destroy, force into bondage, or 'educate' into submission/assimilation" (Wilson 2020, 60). Yet as the story continues, the characters illustrate that humans come in a variety of hues on the spectrum of good and evil behavior. Miss Justineau sees Melanie as worthy of saving—she alone out of the adults is able to see that Melanie is both human and a hungry. Dr. Caldwell also sees Melanie as worthy of saving, though she is interested in Melanie only as a research subject whom she often refers to as "a crucially important specimen" (Carey 2014, 244). Dr. Caldwell's myopic focus on finding a cure means she is unable to see the humanity in the hungry children. Sergeant Parks, however, begins with a strongly antagonistic attitude toward the hungries but eventually grows to care for Melanie as he spends more time with her. This is especially the case after they are forced to flee the base and Melanie, who can move among the hungries undetected and unharmed, works to keep Parks and the others safe. Following one such encounter, Parks, "looking at her hard for a few moments," says, "Good job, kid" (237). In this way, Melanie becomes an example of "the gift of monstrosity" and "offers the gift of hope" for the surviving humans (Wilson 2020, 59, 60).[16] Moreover, the changes that Parks undergoes suggest some hope that humans can learn to see humanity in the Other.

However, Dr. Caldwell never ceases to see Melanie and the other hungry children as monsters, useful only for saving humanity. Her heartless attitude toward the children distorts the line between human and monster and casts a dark shadow over humanity. So, by the time readers discover Melanie's true nature, she seems more fully human than many of the adults in her life, one who can see the reality of both her nature *and* human nature. When Melanie finally says aloud what she has realized—that she is a hungry, though of a different sort—she is able to see that the hungry plague, while evil, is not the only evil:

> She also knows that not all evils that struck this land had the same cause and origin. The infection was bad. So were the things that the important-decision people did to control the infection. And so is catching little children and cutting them into pieces, even if you're doing it to try to make medicine that stops people being hungries. (Carey 2014, 245)

Unlike the biblical apocalypses, Carey's novel exists in a world of gray. Melanie, reflecting on the Greek myth of Pandora's box—which, when opened, lets loose evil into the world—wonders what it might have been like to be a normal human child, "growing up and growing old.... And then, like Pandora, opening the great big box of the world and not being afraid, not even caring whether what's inside is good or bad. Because it's both. Everything is always both" (242).[17] Like other contemporary science fiction apocalypses, Carey's narrative does not try to draw clear lines between good and evil.

In the short story, readers do not learn the details of the fungus, which the novel reveals to be *Ophiocordyceps unilateralis*. Readers also do not learn what happens after the Sergeant and Melanie descend into the horde of hungries below the helicopter. But in the novel, as in other

---

16. For more on Melanie as a symbol of hope and the ways that *The Girl with All the Gifts*, as well as other zombie narratives, use the figure of the zombie child as they address issues of gender and race, see Wilson 2020.

17. Wilson (2020, 60) writes, "Rather than blaming a female for transforming the world into a place of suffering, or furthering the misogynistic bent of tales about first females (Pandora and Eva among them), the novel positions Melanie as able to provide the inhabits of earth the gift of another chance."

science fiction narratives, *The Girl with All the Gifts* depicts the apocalypse as *an* end to the present order, rather than *the* end to all things. Dr. Caldwell, Melanie, Miss Justineau, Sergeant, and Kieran Gallagher eventually find themselves in London. There they discover two things: first, that eventually unfed hungries cease to function, falling to the ground, and out of their rotting bodies tall columns grow. Dr. Caldwell explains that this is "the fruiting body of the hungry pathogen," and the "pods are the sporangia ... full of seeds" (Carey 2014, 251). If the pods were to open, she continues, then the spores of *Ophiocordyceps* would spread through the air, infecting any living human with the hungry virus. Once the pods open—an inevitable occurrence—no humans will remain uninfected. Second, the group finds an abandoned mobile laboratory where Dr. Caldwell can continue her work. When Dr. Caldwell captures a feral hungry child and dissects him, Melanie confronts her and learns what the doctor has discovered: the hungry children were born with the infection, but the fungus does not feed on the children's brains in the same way that it does with humans, and therefore the hybrids can still think and speak and learn. Faced with the possibility that humans might continue to experiment on the other hungry children in the hopes of finding a cure, Melanie sets fire to a wall of the fungal growth, opening the spores and releasing the pathogen into the air. And so "in the end, the plague becomes its own cure" (399).

The humans are all destined to die, but the hybrid children will survive: "they'll be the ones who live and grow up and have children of their own and make a new world" (Carey 2014, 399). Melanie explains this to Sergeant Parks, then adds, "But only if you *let* them grow up.... If you keep shooting them and cutting them into pieces and throwing them into pits, nobody will be left to make a new world" (399). "They'll be the *next* people," Melanie continues, "the ones who make everything okay again" (399). With this revelation, a dying Parks sees that the time of humans has drawn to a close; a new time, where only the hybrid human-hungries can survive, has already replaced the old world. Here Carey again participates in an ongoing trajectory in zombie apocalypse narratives, which "suggest that life with zombies (or as a zombie) is less horrific" than life in a world that is dominated by structural inequalities (Wilson 2020, 54).

Additionally, as others note, a change in the film significantly heightens what it might mean for Melanie to claim that the hybrid human-hungries will be the next people. In both the short story and the novel, Melanie is portrayed as a white child. In the film, however, Melanie is played by a black actress, which "puts the narrative more in line with the Haitian zombie tradition, especially via suggestions of how militarism, scientific racism, and imprisonment perpetuate enslavement" (Wilson 2020, 61).[18] As Sherronda J. Brown (2017) writes, "since its (mis)appropriative beginnings, Western zombie narratives have placed Otherness at the center, removing the zombie from its original lore in Haitian/African religious traditions, and constructing Blackness as a monstrosity and a direct threat to whiteness."[19] The film challenges this, especially as Sergeant Parks dies and Melanie says to him, "I'm sorry, sergeant. I'm so sorry. It's going to be alright. It's not over, it's just not yours anymore." In this way, with Melanie cast as a black child, writes Brown, "The world now belongs to the Other, who hereafter will be Other no more."

Carey's "Iphigenia in Aulis" ends without resolution, and readers are left to guess whether Melanie survives her encounter with the hungries. In contrast, *The Girl with All the Gifts* outlines the future for its readers and identifies the end as hopeful. Melanie, as savior of any remaining hybrid-children, brings this to fruition, though the hope in the novel is a reversal of what we might expect. Ultimately, the novel declares humanity guilty, and the hope is not for humanity but for something new—a "happy ending for its monsters," an overturning of "the normality of the world," and—in the film—"the end of whiteness" (Brown 2017). Like biblical apocalypses, *The Girl with All the Gifts* imagines that the new world will reverse past and present wrongs. The only human still alive at the end of the novel is Miss Justineau, who must remain inside a mobile laboratory, safe from the fungus that has now spread throughout the air, invoking previous science fiction accounts of the last human.[20] In this new world, Miss Justineau is

---

18. Additionally, in the novel Miss Justineau is depicted as black, though in the film she is played by a white actress. For a further discussion of the impact of this change, see Wilson 2020.

19. Wilson (2020, 62) also cites Brown, focusing especially on Brown's discussion of "apocalyptic whiteness."

20. Carey later wrote a prequel to *The Girl with All the Gifts* entitled *The Boy on the Bridge* (2017). As Wilson and others note, the addition of an epilogue in the prequel significantly changes the impact of the first novel's ending. The epilogue returns to the story of Melanie, twenty years later, recounting how she finds rumored human survivors—and is happy to find them. As Wilson (2020, 62) notes, "This closing segment of *Boy* was interpreted as an anti-climactic let-down by some—and, in particular—a less revolutionary vision that the proffered in *Girl*." For example, Wilson

Fig. 5. Miss Justineau teaching, *The Girl with All the Gifts*, 2016. Miss Justineau teaches the zombie-children hybrids from the safety of the mobile laboratory, with Melanie and the others free in the new world.

still a teacher, called by Melanie to instruct the hybrid-children Melanie gathers, but the teacher is now caged, just as her students once were. As Miss Justineau realizes her place in this new world, she laughs: "Nothing is forgotten and everything is paid" (Carey 2014, 402). And so, as the world in *The Girl with All the Gifts* ends, it also begins.

---

points to Prevas (2017), who writes "Monsters have always been signposts for what their societies fear the most: the racial Other, the independent woman, the transgressive queer. Carey's monsters, the hungry children like Melanie, are no different; they are a sympathetic allegory for any community oppressed or marginalized by society and by its institutions," but the epilogue in *Boy*, argues Prevas, undoes this as Melanie seeks to help the survivors.

Conclusions

The Girl with All the Gifts stands in a long line of apocalyptic stories—both those that feature the undead and those that do not. It imagines an end as a way to critique the present and explore ways to make the world better. It highlights the worst of humanity and illuminates the possibility of a different future. It shows us how the apocalypse can be a device used to focus on wanton violence but can also be a tool by which to imagine hope. Ultimately, both ancient apocalypses and science fiction apocalypses call on their readers to consider how the past, the present, and the future are inescapably spliced and to interrogate our place in time.

Representative Examples in Science Fiction

Novels and Short Stories

Adams, Douglas. 2002. *The Ultimate Hitchhiker's Guide to the Galaxy*. New York: Del Rey.

Atwood, Margaret. 2003. *Oryx and Crake*. New York: Doubleday.

———. 2009. *The Year of the Flood*. New York: Doubleday.

———. 2013. *MaddAddam*. New York: Doubleday.

Brooks, Max. 2007. *World War Z: An Oral History of the Zombie War*. New York: Three Rivers.

Butler, Octavia. (1993) 2000. *Parable of the Sower*. New York: Grand Central.

Carey, M. R. (2013) 2014. "Iphigenia in Aulis." Pages 161–86 in *An Apple for the Creature: Tales of Unnatural Education*. Edited by Charlaine Harris and Toni L. P. Kelner. New York: Ace.

———. 2014. *The Girl with All the Gifts*. London: Orbit.

———. 2017. *The Boy On the Bridge*. London: Orbit.

Clarke, Arthur C. (1953) 2000. "The Nine Billion Names of God." Pages 417–22 in *The Collected Stories of Arthur C. Clarke*. London: Victor Gollancz.

Cousin de Grainville, Jean-Baptiste-François-Xavier. 2002. *The Last Man*. Translated by I. F. Clarke and M. Clarke. Middletown, CT: Wesleyan University Press.

Cronin, Justin. 2010. *The Passage*. New York: Ballentine.

———. 2012. *The Twelve*. New York: Ballentine.

———. 2016. *The City of Mirrors*. New York: Ballentine.
Forster, E. M. (1909) 2001. "The Machine Stops." Pages 91–123 in *Selected Stories: E. M Forster*. Edited by David Leavitt and Mark Mitchell. New York: Penguin.
Heinlein, Robert. 1980. *The Number of the Beast*. New York: Random House.
James, P. D. 1993. *The Children of Men*. New York: Knopf.
Jemisin, N. K. 2015. *The Fifth Season*. New York: Orbit.
———. 2016. *The Obelisk Gate*. New York: Orbit.
———. 2017. *The Stone Sky*. New York: Orbit.
Machado, Carmen Maria. 2013. "The Hungry Earth." Pages 60–63 in *Mothership: Tales from Afrofuturism and Beyond*. Edited by Bill Campbell and Edward Austin Hall. Greenbelt, MD: Rosarium.
Marion, Isaac. 2011. *Warm Bodies*. New York: Atria.
Matheson, Richard. (1954) 1995. *I Am Legend*. New York: Tor.
Shelley, Mary. (1826) 1965. *The Last Man*. Lincoln: University of Nebraska Press.
Wells, H. G. (1898) 1960. *The War of the Worlds*. Clinton, MA: Epstein & Carroll.
Wendig, Chuck. 2019. *The Wanderers*. New York: Del Rey.

Comics

Columbia, Al. 1998. "The Trumpets They Played!" *Blab #10*.
iZombie. 2010–2012. Written by Chris Roberson. New York: Vertigo.
Lob, Jacques, and Jean-Marc Rochette. (1984) 2014. "Snowpiercer." Titan Comics.
Promethea. 1999–2005. Written by Alan Moore et al. America's Best Comics.
The Walking Dead. 2003–2019. Written by Robert Kirkman. Image Comics.

Films

The Book of Eli. 2010. Directed by The Hughes Brothers. Written by Gary Whitta. Alcon Entertainment.
Children of Men. 2006. Directed by Alfonso Cuaron. Written by Alfonso Cuaron et al. Strike Entertainment.
I Am Legend. 2007. Directed by Francis Lawrence. Written by Mark Protosevich and Akiva Goldsman. Village Roadside Pictures.

The Last Man on Earth. 1964. Directed by Sidney Salkow and Ubaldo B. Ragona. Written by Logan Swanson et al. Associated Producers.
Night of the Living Dead. 1968. Directed by George A. Romero. Written by John Russo and George A. Romero. Image Ten.
The Omega Man. 1971. Directed by Boris Sagal. Written by John William Corrington and Joyce H. Corrington. Walter Seltzer Productions.
Planet of the Apes. 1968. Directed by Franklin J. Schaffner. Written by Michael Wilson and Rod Serling. Twentieth Century Fox.
Seeking a Friend for the End of the World. 2012. Written and directed by Lorene Scafaria. Mandate Pictures.
Snowpiercer. 2013. Directed by Bong Joon-ho. Written by Bong Joon-ho and Kelly Masterson. Moho Film.
The Terminator. 1984. Directed by James Cameron. Written by James Cameron and Gale Anne Hurd. Hemdale.
White Zombie. 1932. Directed by Victor Halperin. Written by Garnett Weston. Halperin Productions.

Radio

The Fifth Horseman. 1946. Written by Arnold Marquis. NBC Radio.
The Hitchhiker's Guide to the Galaxy. 1978. Written by Douglas Adams. BBC Radio 4.
The War of the Worlds. 1938. Written by H. G. Wells. Adapted by Howard Koch. CBS Radio.

TV Series/Episodes

The 100. 2014–2020. Produced by Jason Rothenberg. Bonanza Productions.
Battlestar Galactica. 2004–2009. Produced by Ronald D. Moore et al. R&D TV et al.
Defiance. 2013–2015. Produced by Scott Stewart et al. Five & Dime Productions.
"The End of the World." 2005. *Doctor Who*. Directed by Euros Lyn. Written by Russell T. Davis. British Broadcasting Corporation.
"Lamentis." 2021. *Loki*. Produced Kate Herin. Written by Bisha K. Ali. Marvel Studios.
The Leftovers. 2014–2017. Produced by Damon Lindelof. White Rabbit Productions.

The Passage. 2019. Produced by Liz Heldens et al. Twentieth Century Fox.
Santa Clarita Diet. 2017–2019. Created by Victor Fresco. Kapital Entertainment.
"The Satan Pit." 2006. *Doctor Who*. Directed by James Strong. Written by Matt Jones. British Broadcasting Corporation.
Snowpiercer. 2020–. Produced by Scott Derrickson et al. TNT.
Sweet Tooth. 2021–. Produced by Jim Mickle et al. Netflix.
The Walking Dead. 2010–2022. Produced by Frank Darabont. AMC Studios.
Westworld. 2016–. Written by Jonathan Nolan and Lisa Joy. Warner Bros.
"What Lies Ahead." 2011. *The Walking Dead*. Directed by Ernest Dickerson and Gwyneth Horder-Payton. Written by Frank Darabont and Robert Kirkman. AMC Studies.

Works Cited

Airey, Jennifer L. 2019. *Religion around Mary Shelley*. Religion Around 5. University Park: Pennsylvania State University Press.
Baker, Kelly J. 2020. *The Zombies Are Coming: The Realities of the Zombie Apocalypse in American Culture*. Chapel Hill, NC: Blue Crow Books.
Bishop, Kyle W. 2010. *American Zombie Gothic: The Rise and Fall (and Rise) of the Walking Dead in Popular Culture*. Jefferson, NC: McFarland.
Blount, Brian K. 2009. *Revelation: A Commentary*. NTL. Louisville: Westminster John Knox.
Brown, Sherronda J. 2017. "'The Girl with All the Gifts Is a Nightmare for White Supremacy." Racebaitr. https://tinyurl.com/SBLPress6708j1.
Canavan, Gerry. 2017. "'We *Are* the Walking Dead: Race, Time, and Survival in Zombie Narrative." Pages 413–32 in *Zombie Theory: A Reader*. Edited by Sarah Juliet Lauro. Minneapolis: University of Minnesota Press.
Collins, John J. 1998. *The Apocalyptic Imagination: An Introduction to Jewish Apocalyptic Literature*. Minneapolis: Fortress.
Dendle, Peter. 2007. "The Zombie as Barometer of Cultural Anxiety." Pages 45–57 in *Monsters and Monstrous: Myths and Metaphors of Enduring Evil*. Edited by Niall Scott. New York: Rodopi.
DiTommaso, Lorenzo. 2014. "Apocalypticism and Popular Culture." Pages 473–510 in *The Oxford Handbook of Apocalyptic Literature*. Edited by John J. Collins. New York: Oxford University Press.

Dowdall, Lisa. 2020. "Black Futures Matter: Afrofuturism and Geontology in N. K. Jemisin's Broken Earth Trilogy." Pages 149–70 in *Literary Afrofuturism in the Twenty-First Century*. Edited by Isiah Lavender III and Lisa Yaszek. New Suns: Race, Gender, and Sexuality in the Speculative. Columbus: Ohio State University Press.

Hanifin, Laura. 2015. "Black Lives Matter Inspired This Chilling Fantasy Novel." *Wired*. https://tinyurl.com/SBLPress6708j2.

Hurley, Jessica. 2018. "An Apocalypse Is a Relative Thing: An Interview with N. K. Jemisin." *ASAP/Journal* 3:467–77.

Kee, Chera. 2011. "Good Girls Don't Date Dead Boys: Toying with Miscegenation in Zombie Films." *Journal of Popular Film and Television* 42:176–85.

———. 2017. *Not Your Average Zombie: Rehumanizing the Undead from Voodoo to Zombie Walks*. Austin: University of Texas Press.

Lietaert Peerbolte, Bert Jan. 2021. "The Book of Revelation: Plagues as Part of the Eschatological Human Condition." *JSNT* 44:75–92.

Murphy, Kelly J. 2016. "The End Is (Still) All Around: The Zombie and Contemporary Apocalyptic Thought." Pages 469–95 in *Apocalypses in Context: Apocalyptic Currents through History*. Edited by Kelly J. Murphy and Justin Jeffcoat Schedtler. Minneapolis: Fortress.

———. 2019. "Jesus and the Undead: Resurrected Bodies in Scripture and the Zombie Apocalypse." Pages 147–59 in *The Paranormal and Popular Culture: A Postmodern Religion Landscape*. Edited by Darryl Caterine and John W. Morehead. New York: Routledge.

Paffenroth, Kim. 2006. *Gospel of the Living Dead: George Romero's Visions of Hell on Earth*. Waco, TX: Baylor University Press.

Prevas, Christine. 2017. "Queer Revolution, Zombie Uprisings, and the Problem with M. R. Carey's *The Boy on the Bridge*." Medium. https://tinyurl.com/SBLPress6708j2a.

Ransom, Amy J. 2018. *I Am Legend as American Myth: Race and Masculinity in the Novel and Its Film Adaptations*. Jefferson, NC: McFarland.

Rosen, Elizabeth K. 2008. *Apocalyptic Transformation: Apocalypse and the Postmodern Imagination*. Lanham, MD: Lexington.

Sheinfeld, Shayna. 2020. "Scenes from the End of the World in American Popular Culture." Pages 201–18 in *Oxford Handbook of the Bible and American Popular Culture*. Edited by Dan W. Clanton Jr. and Terry R. Clark. Oxford: Oxford University Press.

Stratton, Jon. 2020. "Zombie Trouble: Zombie Texts, Bare Life, and Displaced People." Pages 403–20 in *Monster Theory Reader*. Edited by Jeffrey Andrew Weinstock. Minneapolis: University of Minnesota Press.

Vox, Lisa. 2017. *Existential Threats: American Apocalyptic Beliefs in the Technological Era*. Philadelphia: University of Pennsylvania Press.

Wilson, Natalie. 2020. *Willful Monstrosity: Gender and Race in Twenty-First Century Horror*. Jefferson, NC: McFarland.

Yarbro Collins, Adela. 2000. *Cosmology and Eschatology in Jewish and Christian Apocalypticism*. Leiden: Brill.

Reading from the Twilight Zone: An Afterword

Christine Wenderoth

And so it is clear: biblical themes—Adam and Eve, Messiah/Christ, resurrection, apocalypse, and all the rest—transcend the pages of the Bible and enter our consciousness, our literature, our popular culture to stay alive and animate our explorations of the universe. The scope and variety of the thematic overlap of science fiction and biblical worlds is almost infinite. It is no surprise, therefore, that we routinely "note parallels between recent [science fiction] books or movies, on the one hand and Biblical or other sacred literature on the other" (McGrath 2016a, 2), whether those parallels come as theological conflict, dialogue, or integration. We also "try to look deeper at the way that [science fiction] stories themselves tackle theological ideas … [and] look at the intersection of science fiction with the formulation of theology in the present" (2–3). Biblical theology can and *is* expressed in and through science fiction.

But a haunting question is: Why? Why do people (at least that growing percentage who do not identify as Christian or Jewish) look to science fiction—a literary genre that presents an alternative, fictive world even if that world posits "a scientific explanation for these unreal beings and occurrences" (McGrath 2016a, 5)—to find meaning and not to the Bible? Why is it that the Bible is not trusted but the world of, say, *Star Wars* is? What is going on here? This is not unlike debates in the American Academy of Religion and the Society of Biblical Literature about the dialogue "between theology and biblical studies on the one hand and studies in fantasy theory and literature on the other," as sampled in the 1992 *Semeia* volume on *Fantasy and the Bible* (Aichele and Pippin 1992, 3). Substitute *science fiction* for *fantasy*, and significant parallels emerge.

Admittedly, the answer to that question lies to a great extent with the manner in which people relate to those religious institutions that claim the Bible as holy scripture—a matter outside the scope of this volume. However, there is a phenomenon within literature—the matter of canon, midrash, and reboots—that might offer a partial answer to the question of why, as well as offer an intriguing reading strategy for the future of the relationship of science fiction and the Bible.

Let us take as our entry into this exploration the case of the television series, *The Twilight Zone*, the original and the 2019 Jordon Peele et al. reboot. The original *Twilight Zone* first aired in 1959, the creation of Rod Serling, short-story author, playwright, screen writer, and narrator. For five seasons, it brought us into:

> another dimension, a dimension not only of sight and sound but of mind. It is the middle ground between light and shadow, between science and superstition, and it lies between the pit of one's fears and the summit of one's knowledge. You are now traveling through a dimension of imagination. You just crossed over … into the Twilight Zone. (*The Twilight Zone* 2019, introduction)

Each episode ran for twenty-five minutes, offering "a funhouse mirror on modern concerns" (Tallerico 2019), including stories about nuclear war, McCarthyism, mass hysteria, the Cold War—all those horror stories and topics absent from the typical television fare of the day. Serling, in fact, had run afoul of television producers and censors for exploring these topics in conventional dramas. *The Twilight Zone* was "a safe space, an underground meeting place to talk about things you couldn't talk about on TV—about prejudice, conformity, human frailty—if [you] dressed them in monster masks and alien goo" (Poniewozik 2019).

The series quickly became a cult hit and engendered several reboots and spin-offs. It was directly revived in 1985 and again in 2002. Serling brought his touch to a horror series he created called *Night Gallery*. In addition, *The Twilight Zone* was remade in spirit several times, most notably in *The X-Files* and the *Black Mirror* series of 2011–2019 (and possibly continuing). *Black Mirror*, in fact, received high praise from the critics, who noted its roots in *The Twilight Zone*. So given the half-hearted success of some of the spin-offs and the accolades poured onto the *Black Mirror* series, what impelled Jordon Peele, Simon Kinberg, and Marco Ramirez, developers of *The Twilight Zone* 2019, to add another reboot to the mix?

The critics have not been kind to *The Twilight Zone* 2019. James Poniewozik, in his 2019 *New York Times* review, noted that "a 'Twilight Zone' without a specific perspective on the nightmares of its time is just a collection of creepy stories, an exercise in nostalgia." Daniel d'Assario (2019) in *Variety* complained that the new episodes had twice the length with nothing worth saying. Sophie Gilbert (2019) in *The Atlantic* lamented that the show was not dark enough. "Nothing feels sinister. Everything feels safe," she wrote. Critics trashed specific episodes because of poor plotlines, lack of character development, and generally lackluster writing.

Only a nonprofessional viewer/reviewer (Ariel21692) noticed that the original 1959 series "was originally designed for the middle-class white American. The vantage point [of the 2019 reboot] is broader and wider so expect something more than the original." Indeed. Not only is the cast broader racially, culturally, and gender-wise (women who are not solely damsels in distress), the racial, cultural, political, and gender situations in which the 2019 stories exist are broader. The racial diversity of the cast is in and of itself no small thing. Remember, as many women of color have expressed, some tearfully, just how important it was to see Nichelle Nichols play Uhura in the original *Star Trek* series back in the late 1960s. Seeing one's face mirrored in film and television matters. Having one's kind represented as an astronaut, comedian, spouse, mother, and so on first and as African American, Pakistani, Guatemalan, and so on second is huge.

More important, however, the presence of persons of color on screen interplays with the topics of the various episodes as well. The terror of knowing that, no matter what you do, your African American son will die at the hands of racism (how pertinent in 2020!); the terror of knowing that I.C.E. is knocking at your door and coming for *you* no matter what security you think you have; the terror of seeing that all males, even those you love and trust, will act violently; the terror of knowing that the white folks in charge have stolen your land, your ways, and your dignity and will never relent—all of these terrors are signals that you are in the Twilight Zone. (See *The Twilight Zone* 2019 episodes "Rewind," "Point of Origin," "Not All Men," and "The Traveler," respectively.) How Sophie Gilbert (2019) can claim that "nothing feels sinister. Everything feels safe," is a mystery … or an observation from comfortable privilege. To be African American, Inuit, Guatemalan, and female in white patriarchal America *is* to live in the Twilight Zone. The fact that the reviewers for the *New York Times*, the *Atlantic*, the *New Yorker*, and *Variety* missed this demonstrates just how badly needed this 2019 *Twilight Zone* is.

Back to the matter of canon, midrash, and reboots: if the case of the 2019 *Twilight Zone*—maligned, ignored, and misunderstood—is any indication, we can see why midrash is important. Midrash is a term used, in the strictest sense, to mean Jewish biblical interpretation, the rabbinic method used in such interpreting, and a collection of such interpretations composed between 400 and 1200 CE (Neusner 2005, 41). The term midrash has subsequently been used by later Jewish and Christian biblical scholars to refer to exegetical practices that imaginatively update, enhance, augment, explain, and justify sacred texts (Kermode 1998). It has thus been expanded to include any imaginative update, augmentation, and explanation of sacred texts. It is in this latter sense that *The Twilight Zone* 2019 is midrash.

Certain truths remain: television is still skittish about overt political messages in its entertainment fare; the state of the world is still awful and requires commentary; the power of science fiction to portray misery, fear, helplessness, and prejudice remains strong and popular. And so, the original *Twilight Zone* is still revered: it is canon. The 2019 reboot pays homage to the original: its look and images, its soundtrack, the opening and summation narratives, the narrator himself, even the riff on original screenplays ("Nightmare at 20,000 Feet" becomes "Nightmare at 30,000 Feet") all reproduce what we remember from the original series, a nod to its power and truth and, yes, entertainment value. (You can even watch the first season of *The Twilight Zone* 2019 in black and white, if you wish.) We cannot discard or even improve the original. Yet the issues facing the white American of 1959—McCarthyism, nuclear war, conformity—have been replaced with new issues to rightfully obsess about: current expressions of racism, misogyny, and xenophobia; the role of technology, environmental devastation, populist tribalism; the impact of social media and pandemics. *The Twilight Zone* begs to be revisited and updated with our current horrors and impotence. And it would seem—even if there is disagreement about the relative artistic merits of the two series—there is room for both, even a need for both. *Ecclesia reformata, semper reformanda* (the church reformed, always reforming), as the Protestant Reformers have said. Or we can call it fandom, as James McGrath (2016a, 18–19) describes: "communities of faithful followers of films and shows or of the Bible—that leads to ongoing interpretation, which in turn leads to the production ... of further texts," a process identical to midrash and reformation.

Again, the analogy of midrash is helpful. In his book *What Is Midrash?* (2014, 1–2, 7–8), Jacob Neusner outlines three functions of midrash: (1)

paraphrase: recounting the content of the biblical text in different language that may change the sense; (2) prophecy: reading the text as an account of something happening or about to happen in the interpreter's time; and (3) parable or allegory: indicating deeper meanings of the words of the text as speaking of something other than the superficial meaning of the words or of everyday reality, such as when the love of man and woman in the Song of Songs is interpreted as referring to the love between God and Israel or the church. Put somewhat differently, midrash (1) can update and clarify, (2) provide a hermeneutic to correct for what sounds bad in the current context, or (3) to make a current point of view (e.g., Christian) from an older tradition (Judaism). In all cases, the textual rhythms of canon and midrash keep the original (text, story, show) as authoritative (if not sacred) as well as current and relevant.

The Twilight Zone original series and 2019 reboot is but one small, recent example of canon and midrash within the genre of science fiction in which these functions of updating, correcting, and anchoring are practiced. Hundreds of others (e.g., *Star Wars*, *Dune*, *Star Trek*) exist, and clearly the Bible has experienced midrash since its beginning. It is possible to understand science fiction as midrash on the Bible as well, as the current volume demonstrates. All well and good. But does the matter of canon and midrash illuminate the question of why some today can find meaning in science fiction but not in the Bible?

I think it does in the sense that midrashic texts

> discern value in texts, words, and letters, as potential revelatory spaces; they reimagine dominant narratival readings while crafting new ones to stand alongside—not replace—former readings. Midrash also asks questions of the text; sometimes it provides answers, sometimes it leaves the reader to answer the questions. (Gafney 2017, 3)

Science fiction does just that: discern value in biblical texts while crafting new texts to stand alongside the Bible. One might claim, therefore, that, understood as midrash, science fiction and science fiction readers have an obligation to return to the biblical texts to see the themes, values, and worldviews from which science fiction has drawn sustenance.

Simply ordering, or just recommending, a return to the biblical texts is not going to make it happen if, for whatever reason, the Bible feels irrelevant or even hurtful. Acknowledging that this can be what prevents some people from reengaging the Bible (or even engaging with it for the first time), I would like to recommend an approach, a reading strategy, that might break the deadlock for some people. This is the strategy recommended by Frauke Uhlenbruch in her 2015 book *The Nowhere Bible: Utopia, Dystopia, Science Fiction*.

We know that the Bible is actually "a library containing many genres: historical memories, pious fictions (e.g., the parables), theological interpretations of both history and pious fictions (the Gospels), and other genres." We must be careful not to read the Bible in such a way as to be "reductive of the variety of biblical literature" (Robert Cathey, personal email, 21 September 2018). We also know that modern biblical criticism, especially the post-Enlightenment work of the last three centuries, has struggled hard to bring modern approaches to the Bible. Disciplines as diverse as Near Eastern studies, philology, archaeology, cultural anthropology, and sociology have been brought to bear on the Bible. Historical criticism, source criticism, form criticism, literary criticism, and, more recently, social criticism, postmodernism, feminist and womanist literary criticism, and psychological criticism have all brought sophisticated techniques and perspectives to bear on the biblical texts. One result of all these approaches has been the plethora of endeavors found largely in academia. Another result has been the fundamentalist movement's rejection of these modern and rational approaches to scripture, culminating in some circles as an adherence to the "plain reading" of the text or even the literal reading of the text. Nonacademic readers of the Bible have largely been influenced by the filtering of modern biblical criticism or responses to it either through communities of faith or through popular culture. All of this is to say that what Uhlenbruch proposes and I provisionally recommend is but one reading strategy with which to approach the Bible, one strategy existing within a spectrum of reading strategies—and one not to be used exclusively or dogmatically.

Uhlenbruch's (2015, 3) central premise is this: "I am going to propose a contemporary utopian reading of it [the Bible] as science fiction which concludes that the Bible can be read as a message from a far removed time and space, supposedly transmitted by a non-human entity." Put more forcefully, she writes, "Today's reader is a figure from another space and time when it comes to reading the Bible. One could almost say that the Bible cannot be read as anything but [science fiction] in today's world" (161). On the one hand, this resembles what other theorists have pointed out about the "anachronistic" nature of reading in which a text always comes to us from a foreign past (see Aichele 2011, xi, xiii, 3). Uhlenbruch's proposal comes with two important caveats, however. First, she is not saying that the Bible *is* science fiction, the way previous theorists have stated that the Bible *is* fantasy (see, e.g., Manlove 1992), wording of the previous quotation notwithstanding. Science fiction is a literary genre that most commentators trace back only to the nineteenth century, well after all the biblical texts were written, canonized, midrashed, and incorporated into the life of faith communities. Second, she is proposing a "synchronous vision of suppositions brought to biblical texts" (2015, 2). All other readings are still operative: the Bible as true history, the Bible as "remnant of an ancient community's utopian power fantasy" (3), and so forth. The point is not to negate other reading strategies but to make the Bible "understandable to the modern reader" (3).

Uhlenbruch focuses on the story from Num 13 after the Israelites have wandered through the desert and come to the land of Canaan. In the story, the Israelites send advance spies to Canaan to see what the land and its people are like. The spies report back, telling the people of a land of milk and honey with amazing fruit (a single cluster of grapes had to be carried on two poles) and strong fortified towns occupied by giants. The inevitable debate begins as to whether to occupy (invade) Canaan or retreat from it. Uhlenbruch calls this a "classically structured utopia: travelers exploring a land and returning to report about it to the home community" (2015, 5). Fantastic elements—strong giants, huge fruit—cause wonder and fear back home. Structurally speaking, Canaan could just as well be Mars—and that's the point. For readers of the Bible today, the world of the biblical text is alien—long ago and far away, mysterious, somewhat unbelievable … and yet relatable.

Let's ponder those two poles: alien and allusion. The world presented in Num 13 is alien in two senses. First, the land of Canaan as first experienced by the Israelite spies is alien to *them*. This is the stuff of wild imagination. The people and the natural landscape as described by the spies are so unusual and foreign as to be almost unbelievable. But more important, the larger story of the Israelites' amazing escape from Egypt, their survival in hostile territory, their deliverance from danger, and their eventual conquest and occupation of Canaan all exist in a world that is alien to *our* world—and arguably the world of all readers since the crafting of this story. This is a world governed not by scientific principle but by YHWH. This is a world that answers the question, "What would a world governed by YHWH look like?" (Uhlenbruch 2015, 162). We as readers are asked to imagine such a world and, for the duration of the story at least, make believe that such a world exists. (Interestingly, my Bible professor Walter Brueggemann, in an introductory Hebrew Bible class at Columbia Theological Seminary in the 1990s, said that the preacher's job was to speak "as if" the world of the Bible exists and to speak of it so convincingly that, for at least a few steps outside the sanctuary, people feel that imaginary world's reality and power, even as our world of day-to-day experience regained its hold on us with every step.)

So the Bible is alien. It is weird. It is unbelievable and contradicted by our experience in this, the real world. In this regard, the Bible—no matter what the literary genre of specific passages—is no different from any imaginative literature, be it poetry, drama, memoir, or science fiction. Indeed, science fiction has been described as "a literary genre whose necessary and sufficient conditions are the presence and interaction of estrangement and cognition, and whose main formal device is an imaginative framework alternative to the author's empirical environment" (Suvin 1972, 375). If we can allow the Bible this "interaction of estrangement and cognition" and "imaginative framework alternative to the author's empirical environment," we are well on our way to being able to read the Bible seriously (and playfully!).

The Bible is simultaneously allusional (allusion understood as an indirect reference to a person, place, thing, or idea of historical, cultural, literary, or political significance). That is, the world, stories, and figures of the Bible can and often do provide a blueprint for interpreting the empirical, present reality in which the reader finds herself. Chapter 5 of *The Nowhere Bible* devotes itself to just that allusional power, a dramatic and unambiguous instance in which the Bible—Num 13, specifically—was used as the prototype or model for William Bradford's understanding of his community's (the so-called Pilgrims or Puritans of Plymouth, Massachusetts, during the years 1620–1646) experience in North America, their scouting of the new land, their encounter with its indigenous population (the "Indeans") and strange fruit (the Pilgrims had never seen corn before), and their decision to settle (that is, invade) that land. In Bradford's reading of the situation, captured in his *Of Plymouth Plantation* (his journal written between 1630 and 1651), his community were the present-day Israelites, the indigenous people were the Canaanites, and most importantly, New England was Canaan, the promised land given to the Pilgrims by God to subdue and settle. The application of Num 13 to their own circumstances gave Bradford's community the justification, the permission, and the *imperative* to remain in Massachusetts even though the land was clearly already inhabited, that is, taken. Numbers 13 gave Bradford an interpretive lens to understand his present reality. But importantly, Bradford did not see the Pilgrims as reenacting the Num 13 story. There is a built-in caution in the biblical story: the Israelites who did *not* trust YHWH and therefore did not enter the promised land, who did *not* believe they could defeat the Canaanites and subsequently thrive in Canaan, were killed. Only the faithful came into the promised land. Numbers 13 is a tale of gift and promise, yes, but also a tale of the need to trust God and act appropriately out of that trust. Thus, Bradford understood his and his people's mission as one of *reworking* Num 13, of *being* the obedient people of God who carried out God's directives, however scary those orders might be—unlike those spooked spies and Israelites. The Pilgrims were not to repeat the mistakes of the disobedient Israelites. The biblical blueprint is one of interpretation *and* guidance.

This reading of Num 13 into the English colonists' situation is not subtle, and as evidence of its obviousness it was picked up a generation later in Cotton Mather's *Magnalia Christi Americana* (1702). In Mather's *Magnalia*

> we find direct references to America as a Promised Land, to Numbers 13, to the wilderness wanderings of the Israelites, and to Bradford. Similar re-working of Bible and reality takes place, and we find the same strategy as in Bradford of distancing one's own community slightly from biblical templates to stress one's own chosen status, only that in Mather's reading, Bradford's account has become a foundation myth. (Uhlenbruch 2015, 89)

Mather, in other words, saw what Bradford was doing and approved. We Americans are God's chosen people, America is the promised land given to us by God, and anything we have done to assure this is just swell.

Is this an example of reading the Bible as science fiction? Certainly not in the sense that either Bradford or Mather were familiar with a literary genre called science fiction, which did not yet exist. And not in the sense that either Bradford or Mather understood their lived reality to be governed by the laws of science and reason in the way we do today. The world they were describing in their histories was governed by other distinct laws, the will of God. But in the sense that their vision and writings were governed by an "imaginative framework alternative to the author's empirical environment" ("Indeans" were Canaanites, yet clearly they were not people of the Middle East; corn was grapes, though clearly not; North

America was Canaan or, more trenchantly, the promised land, though, again, Bradford was not so delusional as to think they had taken a wrong turn in the Atlantic Ocean), which projected meaning onto their lived reality and onto their actions within that lived reality, Bradford, Mather, and their readers were engaging in a project of imagination and fictional appropriation. They found the so-called New World to be alien, yet it was relatable. They were engaging in a kind of reading strategy we today bring to science fiction when we take one imaginative interpretation (Num 13's imaginative account of the invasion of Canaan) and impose it on a second reality (the Pilgrim's account of the invasion of New England).

Again, is this an example of reading the Bible as science fiction? Perhaps another way of framing the question is to wonder if there is any structural similarity between the Bradford/Mather appropriation of Num 13 and *The Twilight Zone* 2019's appropriation of the original series. Can the example of the reboot of *The Twilight Zone* series help us reboot scripture as imaginative exploration of life's big questions? The answer is yes, in so far as the original story still holds power and authority in the interpreting community. *The Twilight Zone* 2019, as we have noted, pays homage to the original series, but it in no way supersedes it. The original *Twilight Zone* stands unchanged. People still watch it and find value in it and come away from it with new interpretations. The original was rebooted in part *because* the original *Twilight Zone* was a cult classic, an admired artifact that held the potential of commenting upon today's problems and fears. Numbers 13 was appropriated *because* it was revered as holy scripture. Finding one's current situation in a tweaking application of the original was validating in both cases because it extended the mantel of meaning into and onto the present.

That is not our situation today. The Bible has lost its authority for many people, and those people look elsewhere for meaning and validation. For starters, we live in the postmodern era, the era in which science holds sway for many and the reality of the contingent or socially conditioned nature of knowledge claims holds sway for others. For those folks, particularly those brought to believe that conservative, literal readings of the Bible were the accepted orthodoxy, the Bible reads as neither modern nor postmodern. McGrath (2016b, 83) is right: "The difference between the pre-scientific context of the Bible, and the emphatically scientific context of Science Fiction should not be downplayed." Nor should we downplay the high likelihood that biblical literalists will not entertain the possibility that (some) biblical stories "may belong to the genre of fiction, in a manner comparable to other literature that is widely appreciated in our time" (83). Put succinctly: some who go to the Bible for truth and sustenance will react with dismay at the connection of their holy scripture with something as seemingly trivial as science fiction. Others who read and appreciate science fiction as a way to explore the big questions will react "with horror at the connection of as serious a subject as theirs with texts [the Bible] they associate with superstition and a variety of other things seemingly antithetical to the spirit of science fiction" (92). So why bother to put science fiction in conversation with the Bible? What is to be gained? Why not let science fiction carry on and carry the meaning-making all by itself and relegate the Bible to the past? And why outrage Bible adherents with the suggestion that the Bible can be enhanced, updated, and made relevant through a contemporary, popular literary genre such as science fiction?

Because as *The Twilight Zone* 2019 demonstrates—and as the entire history of Jewish and Christian midrash demonstrates—midrash happens. People will always enhance, update, and relate their holy scriptures to present circumstances. Perhaps the recommendation to read the Bible *as science fiction* is too clumsy as stated. One cannot pretend that an ancient literature is identical to or aware of a current genre or sensibility. The Bible is not science fiction-in-code (nor is science fiction the Bible-in-code). The recommendation is one of a reading *strategy* rather than correlation. Science fiction *criticism* is an analogue, a heuristic tool, not science fiction itself (Wilson 2016). It is a way of reading in a contemporary way, noticing that the "contemporary Bible reader is in fact reading stories about an unfamiliar far away world." It is saying that it is possible that the Bible can be read as science fiction in the contemporary world because the Bible is a message from a far-away time and space, "essentially unrecognisable and therefore predominantly a mirror of our home culture" (Uhlenbruch 2015, 195), like science fiction. It is a way of reading that might recommend the Bible to those who otherwise dismiss it as antiquated and irrelevant. It is a way of reading that has been called the willing suspension of disbelief, the attitude that pretends that a story is real for the duration of the story, that humors the story, even though we know it could not have happened in real life (meaning, the reader's experience). It is how we read fiction. Willing suspension of disbelief in either the reading of the Bible or science fiction may not be acceptable for fundamentalists insisting on literalism. That helps explain, not only attitudes about the Bible, but conservative Christian rejections of science fiction. Yet we do such imaginative reading all the time. Even fundamentalist Christians do it, else how did we get the Left Behind series, which traces through fiction what "will" happen in the end times, when true believers in Christ have been raptured (taken instantly to heaven), leaving the world shattered and chaotic (see the Wikipedia entry on "Left Behind").

Reading the Bible as though it were science fiction, a reading strategy, is but a recommendation. It entails the willing suspension of disbelief as well as the willing suspension of judgment, the bracketing proposed decades ago by Paul Ricoeur, the twentieth-century French philosopher whose theory of the interpretation of texts was widely appreciated by biblical scholars and theologians. Try it, Uhlenbruch in effect says, and see where it gets you. Do not read the Bible as science fiction to negate the authority of the Bible. Do it to reveal just how weird the biblical world, the world the Bible presents as ruled by YHWH, is. You might be surprised at what an effective indictment such a reading is of our current assumed and accepted real-world realities.

Do it precisely because you are suspicious of the Bible as history and reliable theology. You might be surprised at how current the issues, responses, and imaginings are.

Do it to consider the similarities between science fiction and the biblical texts—when, for example, they both tackle the same big Issues (redemption, apocalypse) or when (what we call) the supernaturalism of the Bible appears in a science fiction story as (what we now call) the paranormal and that feels *right* in both instances. Appreciate the imaginative impulses of both (McGrath 2016b, 86).

Do it because you may discover that "the manipulations necessary to open up the Bible in contemporary culture by employing [such] narrative strategies and disruptive/creative mind-sets" actually allow you, the reader to (re)claim agency as a reader (Uhlenbruch 2016, 8). Claiming your agency as a reader and reading the Bible as meaningful for *your* life is a time honored, particularly but not exclusively, Protestant project.

Science fiction can help to open the Bible to today's skeptics. Science fiction reboots, in the manner of *The Twilight Zone* 2019, help us see that the issues treated in the original (the original *Twilight Zone*, the Bible) are still alive today and not some relics of a long-ago, irrelevant past, even if they have been misconstrued as such. As McGrath (2016b, 84) states, "Bringing the two together is a reminder that both are imaginative products, which only tell us about the universe inasmuch as human art, born out of human insight, provides genuine clues about reality." McGrath continues: "And when two sets of literature turn humanity's gaze in the same direction, provokes reflection on our deepest questions, and evokes the same kind of emotional responses both positive and negative, can there be any doubt that these genres, which might seem to be polar opposites, are in fact two sides of the same coin?" (91).

That is it in a nutshell. Set aside suspicion, whether of the Bible or the supposedly jejune genre of science fiction. Let each speak. Let each speak to the other. They are both quirky, sometimes off-putting, and alien playgrounds in which creativity romps … and inspires, enlightens, and reveals. Science fiction and the Bible are not out to get each other. They are here to help us to see the universe in all its mysterious, frightening, maddening, and awesome refractions. They are here as "a safe place, an underground meeting place," a twilight zone.

Works Cited

Aichele, George. 2011. *Simulating Jesus: Reality Effects in the Gospels*. London: Equinox.

Aichele, George, and Tina Pippin. 1992. "Introduction: Why the Fantastic?" *Semeia* 60:1–5.

Ariel21692. 2020. Review of *Twilight Zone* (2019). *Metacritic*. https://tinyurl.com/SBLPress6708k1.

d'Assario, Daniel. 2019. "TV Review: 'The Twilight Zone.'" *Variety*. 27 March.

Gafney, Wilda C. 2017. *Womanist Midrash: A Reintroduction to the Women of the Torah and the Throne*. Louisville: Westminster John Knox.

Gilbert, Sophie. 2019. "What the *Twilight Zone* Reboot Is Missing." *The Atlantic*. 3 April.

Kermode, Frank. 1998. "The Midrash Mishmash." *The New York Review of Books*. 23 April.

Manlove, Colin. 1992. "The Bible in Fantasy." *Semeia* 60:91–110.

McGrath, James F. 2016a. *Theology and Science Fiction*. Eugene, OR: Cascade.

———. 2016b. "What Has Coruscant to Do with Jerusalem? A Response and Reflections at the Crossroads of Hebrew Bible and Science Fiction." *JHS* 16:79–92. http://dx.doi.org/10.5508/jhs.2016.v16.a9.

Neusner, Jacob. 2005. *Questions and Answers: Intellectual Foundations of Judaism*. Peabody, MA: Hendrickson.

———. 2014. *What Is Midrash?* Eugene, OR: Wipf & Stock.

Poniewozik, James. 2019. "A 'Twilight Zone' Trying to Find Its Dimension." *New York Times*. 31 March.

Suvin, Darko. 1972. "On the Poetics of the Science Fiction Genre." *College English* 34:372–82.

Tallerico, Brian. 2019. "Jordan Peele's Reboot of the Twilight Zone Lives Up to the Original." *Demanders*. 28 March.

The Twilight Zone. 1959–. Created by Rod Serling. CBS.

———. 2019. Developed by Jordon Peele. CBS.

Uhlenbruch, Frauke. 2015. *The Nowhere Bible: Utopia, Dystopia, Science Fiction*. Studies in the Bible and Its Reception 4. Berlin: de Gruyter.

———. 2016. "Introduction." *JHS* 16:2–10. http://dx.doi.org/10.5508/jhs.2016.v16.a9.

Wilson, Ian D. 2016. "Faster Than a Speeding Bullet, More Powerful Than a Locomotive, Able to Rule by Sense of Smell! Superhuman Kingship in the Prophetic Books." *JHS* 16:30–44. http://dx.doi.org/10.5508/jhs.2016.v16.a9.

Contributors

Rhonda Burnette-Bletsch, Professor of Biblical Studies and Theology Department Chair, Eastern University

Frank Bosman, Researcher, Tilburg School of Catholic Theology, Tilburg University

Krista N. Dalton, Assistant Professor, Kenyon College

Tom de Bruin, Member of Sheffield Institute for Interdisciplinary Biblical Studies

James F. McGrath, Clarence L. Goodwin Chair in New Testament Language and Literature, Butler University

Kelly J. Murphy, Professor, Central Michigan University

Jason A. Staples, Assistant Teaching Professor, NC State University

Steven J. Schweitzer, Academic Dean and Professor, Bethany Theological Seminary

Nicole L. Tilford, Independent Scholar, Atlanta, Georgia

Christine Wenderoth, Professor Emerita, Lutheran School of Theology at Chicago

Jackie Wyse-Rhodes, Associate Professor of Hebrew Bible, Anabaptist Mennonite Biblical Seminary

Index of Ancient Sources

Hebrew Bible/Old Testament

Genesis	18, 38–39, 43, 88–89, 93–94, 103, 121, 124, 147
1	6, 17–19, 123, 130, 136, 190
2	16, 18–19, 122, 133, 136, 193
2–3	16, 93, 134
3	6, 16–17, 122, 176
4	103–4
6	35, 59–60
6–9	7, 58, 134
7	60
8	60, 135
9	35, 135
10	35–36, 147, 155
10–11	36
11	7, 35–36, 87–88, 148
12	88
12–50	91–92, 131
13	88, 122–23
15	60, 90, 148
16	6, 8, 87, 89, 90–91, 96
18	91, 123
20	88
21	8, 87, 89–91, 123
25	88, 91
30	85, 88–89
32	89, 97
33	89
35	86, 89
37	89
46	89
49	86

Exodus	
1	89
2	90, 98
3	90
12	21
26	18
33	91
Leviticus	
12	20
18	157
19	199
20	199
Numbers	
6	97
13	124, 245–48
21	123
25	59
Deuteronomy	
4	123
12	104
23	59
Judges	
8	123
19	98
1 Samuel	124
28	199
2 Samuel	124
2	97
5	104

2 Samuel (cont.)

6	104	43			98
7	60	45			105, 149
		48			149
		51			122, 124
1 Kings	124	52			105
6–8	104	58			105
11	90, 157	60			105
19	123	63			106
		65			105
2 Kings	124, 148	66			105–6
17	148				
20	148–49	Jeremiah			
23	157	23			124
25	149	27			149
		28			149
Ezra		29			149
1–6	149	31			124
9	59	33			60
		50			150
Nehemiah		50–51			149
13	150	51			150
Job	123	Ezekiel			105, 200
38	123	10–11			104
38–42	123	28			122
		31			122
Psalms	104	37			124, 188
48	104	38–39			106
137	149	40–48			106
		43			104
Proverbs		44			104
22	97	48			104
Isaiah	105	Daniel	10, 150, 187, 193, 208, 222, 226
2	125	2			150
5	122	3			150
9	124	4			151
11	124	5			151
13	150	7			209
14	150	7–12			212
24	105	10			208
33	105	10–12			208
34	21	11			208, 212
39	148–49	12			212
40	124	14			151

INDEX OF ANCIENT SOURCES

Amos	
2	124
9	124
Zechariah	105
8	105
12	105
12–39	106
14	105–6

Ancient Near Eastern Texts

Atrahasis	58
Code of Hammurabi	88, 146
Gilgamesh	21, 58
Huluppu-Tree	21
Ziusudra	58

Deuterocanonical Books

Sirach	19
Wisdom of Solomon	
10	60
1 Maccabees	
1	212
2 Maccabees	
7	212

Dead Sea Scrolls

New Jerusalem Text	
2Q24	105
4Q554–555	105
5Q15	105
11Q18	105
4Q510	21
4Q511	21
Temple Scroll	
11Q19–20	105

Ancient Jewish Writings

1 Enoch	125, 134, 208
6–11	59
17	125
18	125
21	125
24	125
26	125
31–32	125
89	209
2 Baruch	208
56	59
Josephus, *Antiquitates judaicae*	
1	36, 60
Jubilees	
5	59
33	86

New Testament

Matthew	
21	180
27	177
Mark	
12	188
Luke	
1	97
2	169
21	177
24	189
John	98, 180

Acts
23 — 188

Romans
7 — 192

1 Corinthians
13 — 98
15 — 189

Ephesians
5 — 96

1 Timothy
2 — 95

Hebrews
— 188

1 Peter
3 — 96
5 — 151

1 John
1 — 96
2 — 211
4 — 211

2 John
1 — 211

Revelation — 10, 105, 121, 125, 180, 209, 214, 217, 222, 226
1 — 208–9
2 — 177
6 — 214–15
7–12 — 208
12 — 160
12–18 — 162
13 — 209, 211
14 — 151
15 — 155
16 — 226
17 — 151, 155, 157
18 — 155
19–20 — 106
21 — 105–6, 180
21–22 — 106
22 — 177

Rabbinic Works

Alphabet of Ben Sira — 21, 29
23 — 19–20

b. Eruvin
100 — 21

b. Hagigah
12 — 16

b. Sanhedrin
38 — 16

b. Shabbat
15 — 21

Genesis Rabbah
8 — 18
18 — 18
22 — 18

Numbers Rabbah
16 — 20

Greco-Roman Works

Euripides, *Iphigenia in Aulis* — 93, 224

Herodotus, *Historia*
1 — 147

Homer, *The Iliad* — 224

Plato, *Symposium* — 18
189–193 — 18

Kabbalistic Works

Zohar
1 — 21

3 21

Early Christian Writings

Augustine, *City of God* 152

Index of Modern Scholars

Abbott, Carl	107	Bynum, Caroline Walker	188
Abrams, Nathan	154	Callahan, Allen Dwight	37
Achtemeier, Paul J.	123	Callahan, Daniel	69
Aichele, George	5, 239, 244	Campbell, Joseph	170
Airey, Jennifer L.	214–15	Canavan, Gerry	80, 131, 226
Akbari, Suzanne Conklin	152	Cheyne, Ria	49
Albeck, Chanoch	18	Claassens, Juliana	91
Aldiss, Brian W.	22	Clarke, Elizabeth	94
Almond, Philip C.	201	Coen, Deborah	176
Altman, Mark A.	43	Collins, John J.	208
Amihay, Aryeh	59	Cowan, Douglas A.	196
Apel, Dora	27	Crome, Andrew	5, 73
Arnold, Bill T.	148	d'Assario, Daniel	241
Atwood, Margaret	85, 131, 139	Dan, Joseph	21
Bachmann, Holger	156	Davis Bledsoe, Amanda M.	151
Baker, Kelly J.	226	Delany, Samuel R.	47
Baly, Denis	123	Dendle, Peter	226
Barrett, Duncan	189	DiTommaso, Lorenzo	213, 219
Barrett, Michèle	189	Dowdall, Lisa	219
Bassham, Gregory	113	Duncan, Roby	47
Bellour, Raymond	162	Eco, Umberto	49
Bernardi, Daniel	43	Ehrman, Bart D.	188, 194
Bishop, Kyle W.	220, 222	Eliade, Mircea	19
Blount, Brian K.	211–12	Embry, Brad	35
Bohak, Gideon	21	Fecht, Sarah	63
Booker, M. Keith	42, 45–46, 48, 52	Fenollós, Juan-Luis Montero	37
Bosman, Frank	169, 171, 175, 178–79	Feuerstein, Günther	107
Bouson, J. Brooks	134–35	Filtness, Emma	46
Brinkman, J. A.	146	Finkel, Irving L.	147, 151
Brown, Jayna	47	Fontana, Paul	112
Brown, Samuel Morris	200	Fretheim, Terence E.	122
Brown, Sherronda J.	230	Gafney, Wilda C.	88, 243
Burnette-Bletsch, Rhonda	92	Garber, David G., Jr.	5
Butler, Judith	91	Gennip, Anton van	170, 173
Butler, Octavia	26–27	George, Andrew	146

INDEX OF MODERN SCHOLARS

Gernsback, Hugo	1–2	Kissling, Peter	177
Gilbert, Sophie	241	Koester, Craig R.	106, 125
Ginsberg, Harold Louis	168	Koosed, Jennifer	136
Gold, John R.	107	Kracauer, Siegfried	161
Gottwald, Norman	87	Kroon, Richard W.	43
Graybill, Rhiannon	86	Kugel, James L.	37
Gregg, Peter B.	68, 75	LaHaye, Tim	152
Grewell, Greg	29	Lampe, Peter	195
Grigg, Richard	5, 168, 189	Lang, Fritz	162
Grimbeek, Marinette	134, 136	Larsen, Stephen	170
Gross, Edward	43	Latham, Rob	2
Guffey, Elisabeth	180	Laufer, Catherine	175
Gunn, James	107	Lavender, Isiah, III	47, 49–50, 52
Gunning, Tom	158, 161–62	Le Guin, Ursula K.	4, 25
Haney, William S.	45	Lee, Aquila	168
Hanifin, Laura	219	Lefkovitz, Lori Hope	194
Harari, Yuval	20	Lehtipuu, Outi	194
Haraway, Donna	29–30	Leick, Gwendolyn	146
Hayles, Katherine	23	Leijnenhorst, Cees	176
Haynes, Stephen R.	40	Lemay, Kate	180
Heard, Christopher	87, 90	Levene, Dan	21
Heinlein, Robert	2	Levenson, Jon D.	188
Hellekson, Karen	180	Levi, Primo	21
Higgins, David M.	47	Lietaert Peerbolte, Bert Jan	213
Hillel, Daniel	123	Magerstädt, Sylvie	201
Hillel, Vered	59	Malley, Shawn	161
Hislop, Alexander	152	Malmgren, Carl	48–49, 51–52
Holbrook, Kate	200	Malone, Peter	167–68, 175
Hrotic, Steven	189	Manlove, Colin	245
Hubble, Nick	2, 46	Mann, George	69
Hunt, Dave	152	McDonald, Paul F.	196
Hunter, James Michael	200	McDonald, Peter	179
Hurley, Jessica	217, 219	McGrath, James F.	5–6, 37, 194, 239, 242, 248, 250
Jacobs, Mignon R.	89		
Jarick, John	188	McKee, Gabriel	5–6, 169
Jemisin, N. K.	30–31, 217, 219	Micali, Simona	189
Jenkins, Jerry B.	152	Michaels, Walter Benn	45
Jones, Paul	180	Miller, Fred	192
Jowett, Lorna	200	Minden, Michael	156
Kadari, Tamar	92	Mirsky, Mark J.	19–20
Kauwe, Vanessa de	70, 72	Mohr, Dunja	50, 52
Kee, Chera	220, 222, 226	Moloney, Francis J.	151
Kelly, Nicholas M.	45–46	Moltmann, Jürgen	168
Kermode, Frank	242	Moss, Candida	201
Kirby, David A.	74, 76	Mousoutzanis, Aris	2

Müller, Jürgen	158, 161–62	Schwartz, Susan L.	168
Murdock, Maureen	170	Schweitzer, Steven	105, 107
Murphy, George	168	Seed, David	2
Murphy, Kelly J.	189, 220, 223, 226	Segal, Robert	170
Nakamura, Lisa	112	Seymour, Michael	147, 151
Nama, Adilifu	118	Sheinfeld, Shayna	213–14,15
Ndalianis, Angela	169	Simkins, Jennifer	5
Neese, Kevin C.	5–6	Simopoulos, Nicole M.	87
Neusner, Jacob	242	Smith, Nicholas D.	192
Newsom, Carol	123, 125	Spitzer, Toba	90
Nichols, Ryan	192	Stallings, L. H.	47, 51
Norman, Joseph	46	Stern, David	19, 20
Northup, Lesley	170	Stokes, Mason	27
O'Neill, Louise	93	Stone, Ken	134, 142
Okoye, James C.	88, 91	Stone, Michael E.	59
Orr, Gili	19	Stratton, Jon	226
Owen, David	179	Sullivan, Shannon Patrick	73, 77
Pabst, Irene	88	Suvin, Darko	2–3, 107, 246
Paffenroth, Kim	222	Tallerico, Brian	240
Papandrea, James	168, 175	Taylor, Marion Ann	87
Pippin, Tina	5, 239	Theodor, Julius	18
Pitman, Walter	58	Thomas, Anne-Marie	42, 45–46, 48, 52
Pittman, John P.	49	Tilford, Nicole L.	60
Pleins, J. David	58–59	Trible, Phyllis	89
Poniewozik, James	240–41	Uhlenbruch, Frauke	244–45, 247, 249–50
Porter, Stanley	168	Urbach, Ephraim E.	20
Porush, David	46	Urbanski, Heather	199
Prevas, Christine	231	Vidal, Senén	190, 193
Radner, Karen	146–47	Vilozny, Naama	21
Raglan, Fitzroy R. S.	170	Vox, Lisa	214
Rank, Otto	170	Walker, Seth	96
Ransom, Amy J.	217–18	Walsh, Richard	136, 138
Rhodes, Sonny	128	Ware, Vron	27
Rinzler, J. W.	196	Weems, Renita J.	87–88
Roberts, Adam	1	Weir, Heather E.	87
Robinson, Bernard	91	Wetmore, Kevin J.	200
Robinson, Kim Stanley	80	Williams, Delores S.	24, 88, 90
Rosen, Elizabeth K.	213–14, 217, 219–20	Williamson, Hugh G. M.	150
Rutledge, Gregory E.	49–50	Wilson, Ian D.	220, 227–30, 249
Ryan, William	58	Wolfe, Gary K.	2
Sabo, Peter J.	86	Yarbro Collins, Adela	208
Samanani, Farhan	72, 79	Ziolkowski, Jan	176
Sargent, Lyman Tower	107		
Scheil, Andrew	147, 151–55		
Schmitz, Philip C.	124		

INDEX OF SCIENCE FICTION WORKS

Novels and Short Stories

Adams, Douglas
  The Ultimate Hitchhiker's Guide to the Galaxy   64, 81, 232

Arthur, Robert
  "Evolution's End"   24, 31

Asimov, Isaac
  Foundation   153, 163
  Foundation and Empire   153, 163
  "The Last Question"   24, 31
  Robots and Empire   127, 140
  Second Foundation   153

Atwood, Margaret   2
  The Handmaid's Tale   2, 8, 85–86, 92–93, 94–99
  Oryx and Crake   2, 9, 130, 131–34, 140, 232
  MaddAddam   9, 130–31, 139–40, 232
  MaddAddam trilogy. See *Oryx and Crake*, *MaddAddam*, *The Year of the Flood*
  The Testaments   99
  The Year of the Flood   9, 130–31, 134–39, 140, 232

Balmer, Edwin, and Philip Wylie
  After the Worlds Collide   67, 81
  When Worlds Collide   61–63, 65, 81

Bancroft, Josiah
  Arm of the Sphinx   41, 53
  The Fall of Babel   41, 53
  The Hod King   41, 53
  Senlin Ascends   37–38, 41, 53

Baxter, Stephen
  Ark   61, 63, 67, 81
  Flood   61, 81

Benét, Stephen Vincent
  "By the Waters of Babylon"   155, 163

Bennett, Christopher L.
  Tower of Babel   42, 53

Binder, Eando
  Adam Link, Robot   31
  "I Robot"   23, 31

Bradbury, Ray
  Fahrenheit 451   109, 117
  "The Other Foot"   64, 81
  "Way in the Middle of the Air"   64, 81

Brooks, Max
  World War Z   232

Burroughs, Edgar Rice
  "Under the Moon of Mars"   155, 163

Butler, Octavia
  Adulthood Rites   6–7, 26–29, 31, 93, 130, 140
  Dawn   6–7, 26–29, 31, 93, 130, 140
  Imago   6–7, 26–29, 31, 93, 130, 140
  Kindred   92, 99

Butler, Octavia (*cont.*)
   Lilith's Brood (Xenogenesis trilogy).
      See *Adulthood Rites, Dawn, Imago*
   Parable of the Sower 126–27, 140, 203, 232
   Parable of the Talents   127, 140, 203
   "Speech Sounds"   43–44, 52–53

Card, Orson Scott
   Speaker for the Dead   190, 203
   Xenocide   190, 203

Carey, M. R.
   The Boy On the Bridge   230–32
   The Girl with All the Gifts   10, 224–32
   "Iphigenia in Aulis"   224–32

Catran, Ken
   Deepwater Black   61, 81

Chiang, Ted
   "Hell Is the Absence of God"   203
   "Story of Your Life"   44, 54
   "Tower of Babylon"   37–38, 40–42, 52–53

Clarke, Arthur C.
   Childhood's End   190, 203
   "The Nine Billion Names of God" 213, 232
   The Songs of Distant Earth   61, 65, 81

Collins, Suzanne
   Catching Fire   109, 117, 163
   The Hunger Games   109, 117, 152–53, 162–63
   Mockingjay   109, 117, 163

Cook, Glen
   The Heirs of Babylon   155, 163

Cordwainer, Smith [Paul Linebarger]
   "A Planet Named Shayol"   203

Cousin de Grainville, Jean-Baptiste-François-Xavier
   The Last Man   213–14, 232

Cronin, Justin
   The City of Mirrors   233
   The Passage   232
   The Twelve   232

Dayle, Harry
   Noah's Ark: Survivors   61–62, 81

Delany, Samuel R.
   Babel-17   7, 44, 47–53

Elwood, Roger
   The Wandering   53

Farmer, Philip José
   The Dark Design   193, 202
   The Fabulous Riverboat   193, 202
   Gods of Riverworld   193, 202
   The Magic Labyrinth   193, 202
   To Your Scattered Bodies Go   193, 202

Forster, E. M.
   "The Machine Stops"   233

Frank, Pat
   Alas, Babylon   155, 163

Gibson, William
   Neuromancer   202

Heinlein, Robert
   The Number of the Beast   213, 233
   Stranger in a Strange Land   203

Herbert, Frank
   Children of Dune   168, 183
   Dune   153, 163, 168, 183, 243
   Dune Messiah   168, 183

Hogan, James P.
   Voyage from Yesteryear   61, 81

INDEX OF SCIENCE FICTION WORKS

Huxley, Aldous
   Brave New World   109, 117

James, P. D.
   The Children of Men   233

Jemisin, N. K.
   The Fifth Season   218–19, 233
   The Obelisk Gate   218, 233
   The Stone Sky   218, 233

L'Isle-Adam, Auguste Villiers de
   The Future Eve   23, 31

Le Guin, Ursula K.   4
   The Dispossessed   130, 140
   The Left Hand of Darkness   130, 140
   Rocannon's World   130, 140

Leisner, William
   "A Less Perfect Union"   43, 54

Lessing, Doris
   The Sentimental Agents in the Voylen Empire   44

Levine, David
   "Babel Probe"   41, 55

Lewis, C. S.
   The Chronicles of Narnia   24, 31
   That Hideous Strength   54, 153–54, 162, 164

Liu, Cixin
   The Three Body Problem   2

Lovecraft, H. P.
   "At the Mountains of Madness"   154, 164
   "The Shadow over Innsmouth"   155, 164

MacDonald, George
   Lilith   24–25, 31

Machado, Carmen Maria
   "The Hungry Earth"   216–17, 220, 233

Marion, Isaac
   Warm Bodies   226

Martin, Laura
   The Ark Plan   61, 81
   Code Name Flood   81

Matheson, Richard
   I Am Legend   217–18, 220, 233

McCarthy, Cormac
   The Road   127, 140, 154, 164

Miéville, China
   Embassytown   44, 56

Miller, Walter M.
   A Canticle for Leibowitz   2

Morgan, Richard K.
   Altered Carbon   190, 203

Moore, C. L.
   "Fruit of Knowledge"   25–26, 31

Morrow, James
   "Bible Stories for Adults, No. 20: The Tower"   38–40, 54

Okorafor, Nnedi
   Who Fears Death   30, 32

O'Neill, Louise
   Only Ever Yours   93

Orwell, George
   1984   44, 54, 94, 109, 117

Pratchett, Terry
   The Dark Side of the Sun   54

Ramos, Joanne
   The Farm   93, 99

Rey, Lester del
   "Into Thy Hands"   24, 31

Sawyer, Robert J.
   The Terminal Experiment   202

Serviss, Garrett Putman
   "Second Deluge"   62–64, 81

Shelley, Mary
   Frankenstein   22, 24, 31
   The Last Man   214–15, 233

Simmons, Dan
   Endymion   202
   The Fall of Hyperion   202
   Hyperion   202
   The Rise of Endymion   202

Solomon, Rivers
   An Unkindness of Ghosts   30, 32

Stephenson, Neal
   Snow Crash   44–46, 52, 54

Tepper, Sheri S.
   The Gate to Women's Country   93, 99

Vance, Jack
   The Languages of Pao   44, 56

Vinge, Vernor
   "Long Shot"   61, 65, 81

Wagner, John
   Judge Dredd   165

Walker, Karen Thompson
   The Age of Miracles   65, 81, 126, 130, 140

Wells, H. G.
   The Island of Dr. Moreau   155, 165
   The Time Machine   108, 118, 155, 165
   The Shape of Things to Come   108, 118
   The War of the Worlds   215–16, 233

Wendig, Chuck
   The Wanderers   222–23, 233

Whitehead, Colson
   The Underground Railroad   30, 32

Williams, Charles
   Descent into Hell   24, 31

Williamson, Jack
   "Born of the Sun"   81
   "The Fortress of Utopia"   65–67, 81

Wright, John C.
   Nowither   54
   Somewhither   54

Young, Robert F.
   "Project Hi-Rise"   41, 54

Comics

iZombie   226

Judge Dredd   153

Justice League of America
   "Tower of Babel 1: Survival of the Fittest"   43, 54
   "Tower of Babel 2: Seven Little Indians"   43, 54
   "Tower of Babel 3: Protected by the Cold"   43, 54
   "Tower of Babel 4: Harsh"   43, 54

Promethea   233

"Snowpiercer"   233

Speed Spaulding   82

Superman
  "Superman"   62, 82, 168, 183

"The Trumpets They Played!"   233

The Walking Dead   233

Film, Radio, and Television

28 Days Later   155, 162

The 100   61, 63, 82, 234

2001: A Space Odyssey   154, 162

Alien   153–54, 163

Altered Carbon   2, 190–91, 193, 202

Arrival   44, 54

Avatar   129, 140

Babylon 5   53

Babylon 5: Thirdspace   163

Batman Beyond
  "Babel"   43, 53

Battle for Terra   61, 67, 82, 129, 140

Battlestar Galactica   10, 62, 82, 128, 141, 190, 198–200, 202
  "Saga of a Star World"   62–63, 83
  "War on the Gods"   200

Battlestar Galactica (reboot)   5, 10, 62, 64, 83, 127–28, 141, 190, 198–200, 202, 234
  "Black Market"   83
  "Epiphanies"   116–17
  "Miniseries"   127, 141

"No Exit"   199
"Resurrection Ship: Part 2"   67, 83

The Black Hole   203

Black Mirror   240
  "Be Right Back"   201
  "San Junipero"   202

Blade Runner   23, 42, 53, 108, 117, 153, 163

Blade Runner 2049   109, 117

The Book of Eli   233

Buck Rogers in the Twenty-Fifth Century   109, 117

Caprica   198–200, 201

Children of Men   226, 233

The Chronicles of Riddick   153, 164

The Day the Earth Stood Still   169, 183

Deep Blue Sea   154, 163

Deep Impact   169, 183

Defiance   234

Devs   201

Doctor Who   5, 7, 68–80, 153, 196–97, 202
  "The Ark in Space"   61, 73–77, 82
  "The Beast Below"   77–80, 83
  "The Bomb"   68–73, 83
  "Dark Water/Death in Heaven"   197
  "The End of the World"   131, 141, 234
  "Enlightenment"   197
  "The Five Doctors"   197
  "Inferno"   164

INDEX OF SCIENCE FICTION WORKS

Doctor Who (cont.)
    "The Long Game"   165
    "The Plague"   68–73, 83
    "The Return"   68–73, 83
    "The Satan Pit"   235
    "The Steel Sky"   68–73, 83

Downsizing   61, 82

Dredd   153, 163

Event Horizon   203

The Fifth Horseman   234

Firefly   109, 117, 128, 141, 152, 162–63
    "Out of Gas"   128, 141

Frankenstein   42, 53

Freejack   42, 53, 163

Galactica 1980   83, 190, 198–200, 203

Ghostbusters   42, 53

Gravity   126, 140

The Handmaid's Tale (movie)   85, 99

The Handmaid's Tale (series)   85–86, 92–93, 94–99

The Hitchhiker's Guide to the Galaxy   37, 53, 64, 81, 234
    "Episode 1.6"   83
    "Fit the Sixth"   81

I Am Legend   155, 164, 217, 222, 233

I, Robot   42, 53, 164

The Incredibles   168, 183

The Island   203

Jurassic Park   154

John Carter   155, 164

Judge Dredd   153, 164

Knowing   190, 203

The Last Man on Earth   217, 234

The Leftovers   234

Logan's Run   109, 117

Loki
    "Lamentis"   67, 83, 234

The Matrix trilogy   see *The Matrix*, *The Matrix Reloaded*, *The Matrix Revolutions*

The Matrix   8, 103, 110–17, 153, 164, 168–69, 183

The Matrix Reloaded   8, 103, 110–17, 168–69, 183

The Matrix Resurrections   110

The Matrix Revolutions   8, 103, 110–17, 168–69, 183

Melancholia   126, 140

Metropolis   9, 23, 37–38, 54, 108, 117, 155, 156–62, 164

Moonraker   62, 82

Night Gallery   240

Night of the Living Dead   220–23, 234

The Omega Man   217, 234

INDEX OF SCIENCE FICTION WORKS 269

Pandorum   61, 67, 82

The Passage   235

Planet of the Apes   130, 140, 154, 162, 164, 234

Prometheus   154, 162, 164

Raised by Wolves   62, 83

Resident Evil   154, 164

"Restoration"   191, 202

The Road   126, 154, 165

Salvation   63, 83

Santa Clarita Diet   226, 235

Seeking a Friend for the End of the World   67, 82, 126, 140, 234

Serenity   109, 117, 152, 154, 162, 164

The Sixth Day   190, 203

Sky Captain and the World of Tomorrow   61, 82

Snowpiercer (film)   234

Snowpiercer (series)   61, 83, 235

So Weird
    "Babel"   44, 53

Space 1999
    "Mission of the Darians"   65, 67, 83

Stargate: Atlantis
    "The Ark"   63, 82

Stargate: SG-1
    "Lifeboat"   62, 83
    "Scorched Earth"   64–65, 83, 129, 141

Star Lost   67, 83

Star Trek (franchise)   2, 5, 37, 42, 126, 129, 131, 153, 195–96, 243

Star Trek: Deep Space Nine   52
    "Babel"   42–43, 53

Star Trek: Enterprise
    "The Aenar"   42–43, 53
    "Babel One"   42–43, 53, 163
    "United"   42–43, 54

Star Trek: The Next Generation   202
    "The Inner Light"   64–65, 83
    "Relics"   192
    "Second Chances"   192

Star Trek: The Original Series   202, 241
    "The Apple"   126, 141
    "For the World Is Hollow and I Have Touched the Sky"   83
    "Journey to Babel"   42–43, 53, 164
    "The Way to Eden"   126, 141

Star Trek: Voyager   128, 141, 202
    "Mortal Coil"   196

Star Trek II: The Wrath of Khan   129, 140

Star Trek III: The Search for Spock   129, 141, 196

Star Wars (franchise)   9, 112, 152–53, 162, 164, 168, 195–96, 239, 243

Star Wars: The Clone Wars   202
    "Destiny"   195

Star Wars: Episode III—Revenge of the Sith   195, 202

Star Wars: Episode IV—A New Hope 112, 117, 168, 183, 202

Star Wars: Episode V—The Empire Strikes Back   112, 117, 168, 183, 202

Star Wars: Episode VI—Return of the Jedi   112, 118, 168, 183, 202

Star Wars: Episode VIII—The Last Jedi   109

Starship Troopers   153, 164

Supernatural
    "99 Problems"   155, 163

Sweet Tooth   235

The Terminator   164, 168, 183, 234

Terminator 2: Judgment Day   169, 183

Terminator 3: Rise of the Machines   169, 184

Things to Come   108, 118

Titan A.E.   61, 65, 82

Twilight Zone   240–43, 248, 250, 250
    "A Nice Place To Visit"   203
    "Nightmare at 20,000 Feet"   241
    "Probe 7, Over and Out"   24
    "Two"   24

The Twilight Zone (reboot)   240–43, 248–49, 250, 252
    "All Men"   241
    "Nightmare at 30,000 Feet"   242
    "Point of Origin"   241
    "Rewind"   241

"The Traveler"   241

Upload   190, 202

WALL-E   61, 82

The Walking Dead   223, 235
    "What Lies Ahead"   235

The War of the Worlds   234

Warehouse 13
    "13.1"   44, 52

Westworld   193, 203, 235

When Worlds Collide   82

White Zombie   220–21, 234

The X-Files   240
    "Babylon"   163

Electronic Games

Child of Light   10, 175–77, 179, 182–83

Doom   53

Fallout 3   10, 179–82, 183

Half-Life   167, 171–72, 175, 183

Half-Life 2   171–72, 175, 183

Half-Life 2: Episode One   171–72, 175, 183

Half-Life 2: Episode Two   171–72, 175, 183

Halo   153–54, 163

Resident Evil   154, 164

Singularity 173–74, 177–79, 182–83

Star Trek Online 42, 54

www.ingramcontent.com/pod-product-compliance
Lightning Source LLC
Chambersburg PA
CBHW021658230426
43668CB00008B/659